My Gender Workbook

how to become a real man, a real woman, the real you, or something else entirely

Kate Bornstein

with illustrations by Diane DiMassa

Routledge   New York and London

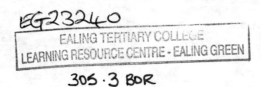
Published in 1998 by
Routledge
29 West 35th Street
New York, NY 10001

Published in Great Britain by
Routledge
11 New Fetter Lane
London EC4P 4EE

Copyright © 1998 by Routledge
Text Design: David Thorne

Printed in the United States on acid-free paper.

0-415-91672-0 (cloth) 0-415-91673-9 (paper)

My Name Is _____

and this is MY Gender Workbook.

photo: Dona Ann McAdams

I'm dedicating this workbook to two transgender pioneers: Sandy Stone and Marsha Botzer. They've been friends, mentors, sisters, moms, daughters, and co-conspirators with me and with hundreds of others. Sandy and Marsha did the hard work years ago, while the rest of us were still shivering in the dark wondering what the heck was wrong with us. They continue to do more hard work today, and I'm so grateful to have each of them in my life. Thanks, my darlings.

Here's What's In Your Workbook. Look!

My favorite thing is to go where I've never been.

—*Diane Arbus*

Of course I realized there was a measure of danger. Obviously I faced the possibility of not returning when first I considered going. Once faced and settled there really wasn't any good reason to refer to it.

—*Amelia Earhart*

There must be quite a few things a hot bath won't cure, but I don't know many of them.

—*Sylvia Plath*

As far as I'm concerned, being any gender is a drag.

—*Patti Smith*

Welcome to Your Gender Workbook

From the moment we take our first breath (and sometimes even before that, what with sonic imaging technology), the cry "It's a boy" or "It's a girl" ushers us into this world. As we grow into adulthood, everything about us grows and matures as *we* grow and mature. Everything except gender, that is. We're supposed to believe that our gender stays exactly the same as the day we were born. Our genders never shift, we're told. The genders we're assigned at birth lock us onto a course through which we'll be expected to become whole, well-rounded, creative, loving people—*but only as men or as women.* From where I stand, that's like taking a field of racehorses, hobbling the front legs of half of them and the rear legs of the other half, and expecting them to run a decent race: it doesn't work. Gender, this thing we're all seemingly born with, is a major restraint to self-expression.

That doesn't make sense to me. Why should we be born with such a hobble? Does that make sense to you? Well, this is a workbook about questioning things like that, so let's get right to work and start questioning things, shall we?

Discovering Your Gender Aptitude

Would you like to know more about your own gender and how it's been affecting your life? Just how freewheeling and open are you when it comes to the subjects of gender and sexuality? Do you have much flexibility when it comes to grasping the mechanics of *changing* genders? How about the people who are questioning their own genders these days? Are they a little crazy for doing that? Here's a series of questions that will give you a good idea of exactly where you stand when it comes to gender.

This isn't a quiz or an exam to see how good you are at this. There are no right or wrong answers. Just take your time and check off the answers that *most nearly match* the way you feel about each question. When you're done, you'll know your GA—your Gender Aptitude—and from there, we'll go on a little journey together through previously unexplored and under-explored areas of gender, identity, sexuality, and power. Now, doesn't that sound exciting? I should think so! All right, let's begin.

⑥ Your Gender Aptitude, Section I: Assumptions

Which of the following most accurately describes you?

___ A. I'm a real man.
___ B. I'm a real woman.
___ C. I'm not a real man or a real woman, but I'd like to be.
___ D. None of the above. I'm something else entirely.

Give yourself 5 points if you checked A, 3 points if your checked B, 1 point for C, and no points for D.

Write your score for this section here.

⑥ So...Are You a Real Man? A Real Woman?

I'm not attempting to look like a man, but there are a whole lot of the straight folks who mistake me for one. It's real hard being a butch little kid, and being beat by boys who thought I was a boy wearing girls clothes. Sometimes it's hard being a grown up and being told you're going to the wrong washroom, or get called sir by a whole lot of folks. When I was 9 months pregnant, and in maternity clothes, I was still called sir. I sure don't feel like a man.

—Tammy Potter

At first glance, that seems to be a simple pair of questions. Most people when asked those questions would smile and say, "Of course I'm a real man," or "Of course I'm a real woman." It's not something most of us question. The difficult part comes when we're asked to remember the times we've been made to feel we're not quite as manly or as womanly as we could be or should be. Maybe it was the day we found ourselves deeply afraid or weeping uncontrollably, and we (or someone else) questioned how much of a man we really are. Maybe we've not been able to get pregnant, or maybe we haven't wanted to, and we (or someone else) questioned how much of a woman we really are. There are so many qualifications for those categories, aren't there? We make jokes like "Real men don't eat quiche," or admonitions like "A real woman would be married by now." Not that anyone has ever written *all* these qualifications down, mind you. People have tried, but there's been too much disagreement about what constitutes a "real man," and what constitutes a "real woman" for there to be one acceptable document containing the absolute definitions of either of those categories of identity. So by trial and error we learn the reality of our real manhood and real womanhood. We build our own definitions for these, and we're very pleased to know people who agree with our definitions. When enough people agree with us, we begin to assume it's *natural.*

Well, here's a question: If gender is so natural, then why hasn't it been written down and codified? Most everything else that's considered "natural" has been codified. Why isn't there some agreed-upon manual we could hand our children and say, "Here, honey. This is what a real man is. Learn this well." Why do we mystify these categories to such a degree that we assume "everyone knows" what real men and real women are?

Let's keep looking at your Gender Aptitude when it comes to the subject of these categories called "real men" and "real women."

⊚ Your Gender Aptitude, Section II: Perceptions

1. ***Do you stand up to pee?***
A. Yup, most of the time.
B. No, never.
C. Well, I've tried it a few times.
D. It all depends on the effect I want to create.

2. ***Have you ever worn the clothes of "the opposite sex?"***
A. Hey, give me a break. No way!
B. Yes, but when *I* wear them, they're for the *right* sex.
C. What sex in the world would be opposite of *me?*
D. Several of the above.

3. ***Do you shave?***
A. Yup. Except when I'm growing my beard or mustache.
B. Depends. I go back and forth on the hairy armpit thing.
C. Where?
D. Yes, but not myself.

4. ***When you go into a department store to buy yourself clothing, do you shop mostly in a department labeled for your assigned gender?***
A. Well, duh! Where else?
B. No, because sometimes the other departments have stuff that fits me better.
C. Yes, because it's very important to me to do that.

D. Offer to sell tickets to gawking passers-by?

3. *Has it ever happened that you've been in a group of people who are similarly gendered to you, and you find yourself behaving in a way that's gender inappropriate?*

A. No.

B. No, I'm very careful about that.

C. Yes.

D. Yes, it happens all the time.

4. *You receive an invitation to a concert. The top of the invitation reads, "All Genders Welcome." Do you . . .*

A. Wonder why they phrased it like that.

B. Get nervous about who or what might show up.

C. Feel defensive.

D. Feel included.

5. *Have you ever been mistaken for being a member of a gender other than that which you think you're presenting?*

A. No.

B. Yes.

C. Yes, but not as frequently as before.

D. I intentionally try to confuse people.

6. *Have you ever agonized over your appearance to the point of canceling a social obligation because*

you feel you don't look right or won't fit in?

A. No.

B. Yes, I've agonized, but I haven't canceled.

C. It doesn't have to be some social obligation; sometimes it's just easier not to leave the house.

D. Yes.

7. *Have you ever been discriminated against, harassed, or attacked because of your gender presentation*

A. No.

B. No, I've been careful.

C. Yes, and it happens to women every hour of the day.

D. Yes.

8. *Is acceptance by or membership in some men's or women's organization important to you?*

A. Not really.

B. Yes.

C. Yes, but I don't hold out much hope for that.

D. No, we're starting our own.

9. *Which of the following most nearly matches your definition for the word transgender?*

A. It's some disorder that results in men cutting off their penises.

B. Being born in the wrong body, or having the wrong sex for your gender.

C. Changing from one gender to another, or just looking like you've done that.

D. Transgressing gender, breaking the rules of gender in any way at all.

10. *Which of these phrases describes you most accurately when it comes to rules about personal behavior and identity?*

A. I pretty much make up the rules to suit my needs, and I follow those rules as long as I'm getting something out of it.

B. I think many social and cultural rules governing individual behavior and identity are necessary.

C. I'm trying to figure out which rules to follow and which rules to ignore.

D. Rules? Honey, the Identity Police have arrested me so many times, I've got a cell with my name on it.

Give yourself 5 points for each A answer, 3 points for every B, 1 point for a C, and no points for any D answers.

Write your score for this section here.

⊚ Why It's Me Who Gets to Ask These Questions

I don't know who discovered water, but I'm pretty sure it wasn't a fish.
—*posted on the Internet*

This is a book about gender, because gender is what I know inside and out. It's what I've been questioning and researching all my life because that seems to be the journey I was given to make this time around. I'm what's called a transsexual person. That means I was assigned one gender at birth, and I now live my life as something else. I was born male and raised as a boy. I went through both boyhood and adult manhood, went through a gender change, and "became a woman." A few years later, I stopped being a woman and settled into being neither. I wrote a book about gender-as-neither, and I travelled with several plays and performance pieces about gender-as-neither. On the personal side of things, my lesbian lover of over three years decided to become a man. We lived together for a few more years as a heterosexual couple, then we stopped being lovers. He found his gay male side, and I found my slave grrrl side. What a whacky world, huh? I can't think of a day in my life when I haven't thought about gender. I think what I've found is a pretty interesting hole in the theory that there's actually such a thing as a real man or a real woman. And that's what this workbook's about and why I got to write it.

But enough about me, let's get back to you.

⊚ And Just Who Do You Think You Are, Anyway?

You're *not* the same person you were ten minutes ago.

None of us is.

Each of us makes dozens if not hundreds of minor decisions in the space of ten minutes. And unless we're truly hermits, each of us is subject to influences by and connections with the world around us that change the course of our lives. No, they're not dramatic changes, but they are changes nonetheless.

Maybe someone smiled at you on the street this morning and made you feel good. Maybe you heard something on the news just now that made you wonder how much say you have in our government. Perhaps it was a phone call from a long-lost friend. It could have been a bit of email, or some passage or question in this book, or a piece of poetry, or just a bird landing on your windowsill that made you change your mind about the state of your life. Interactions of most every type have a tendency to change us; that's what growth is all about. We're so used to these mini-changes that we give them no thought, but the fact is we're not the same people we used to be.

―――

I've gone through some pretty dramatic changes. I've changed my gender, several times in fact. But I think the question we should be asking ourselves is: "Why is that so dramatic?" I'm not saying it's not dramatic. I think it is. I'm just asking what is it that the culture taught me to make me think that changing gender is dramatic?

―――

We change our attitudes, our careers, our relationships. Even our age changes minute by minute. We change our politics, our moods, and our sexual preferences. We change our outlook, we change our minds, we change our sympathies. Yet when someone changes hir gender, we put hir on some television talk show. Well, here's what I think: I think we all of us *do* change our genders. All the time. Maybe it's not as dramatic as some tabloid headline screaming "She Was A He!" But we do, each of us, change our genders. In response to each interaction we have with a new or different person, we subtly shift the *kind* of man or woman, boy or girl, or whatever gender we're being at the moment. We're usually not the same *kind* of man or woman with our lover as we are with our boss or a parent. When we're introduced for the first time to someone we find attractive, we shift into being a different *kind* of man or woman than we are with our childhood friends. We all change our genders. I'm just saying it's time we knew exactly what we are doing and why. So, let's get on with the next section of our Gender Aptitude questionnaire and see just how flexible your gender might be. Hang on, we're going to dig a bit deeper now.

◎ Your Gender Aptitude, Section IV: Flexibility

1. ***When the kind of person to whom you are normally attracted begins to flirt heavily with you, you***
A. Envision the great sex you're going to have later tonight.
B. Try to get to know this person a bit better.
C. Panic because it's been so long and you wonder if you know how to do it right any more.
D. Flirt right back, matching move for move.

2. ***When the kind of person that normally turns you off begins to flirt heavily with you, you***
A. Hit the person.
B. Leave.
C. Tell them, "Honey, you flirt with this hand."
D. See if there's anything about it you can enjoy as long as it's only flirting.

3. ***When was the last time you were aware of something about your gender that was holding you back in the world?***

A. I can't recall a time like that.
B. Do you want that in minutes or seconds?
C. Do you mean the times I did something about it, or the times it overwhelmed me?
D. It was just before I changed my gender the last time.

4. ***How many genders do you really think there are?***
A. Two.
B. Well, there are two sexes. Is that what you mean?
C. I'm going to guess there are lots of genders and two sexes.
D. When do you want me to stop counting?

5. ***Do you feel it's possible for someone to change hir gender?***
A. No. And what does "hir" mean, Flake-o?
B. I think people can try, but no. Not really, no.
C. Yes, with proper supervision, surgery, and hormones. I think so.
D. How many times?

6. ***What do you believe the***

essential sign of gender to be?

A. The presence or absence of a penis.

B. A combination of genitalia, secondary sex characteristics, hormones, and chromosomes.

C. It's an energy thing. People have male or female energy.

D. What*ever*.

7. *If someone tells you they're neither a man nor a woman, and you find out they mean it, you think to yourself*

A. This person is either kidding or is really, really sick.

B. The poor, brave dear!

C. Whoa! What a trip!

D. I found another one at last!

8. *If you meet someone who you think is one gender, but you find out they used to be another gender, you think to yourself*

A. Is this some costume party?

B. The poor, brave dear!

C. Wow, and I didn't even know!

D. Yeah, yeah. But can you do a good Elvis?

9. *If you see someone on the street whose gender is unclear to you, do you*

A. Dismiss that person as a freak?

B. Try to figure out if it's a man or a woman?

C. Mentally give them a makeover so they can pass better as one or the other?

D. Notice they're staring at you, trying to figure out what *you* are?

10. *Is the male/female dichotomy something natural?*

A. Well, duh. Of course.

B. It's probably a combination of nature and nurture.

C. Probably, but there are a lot of exceptions walking around!

D. There's a male/female dichotomy? On what planet?

Give yourself 5 points for each A answer, 3 points for every B, 1 point for a C, and no points for any D answers.

Write your score for this section here.

◎ A Word about Comfort

I want to say this pretty early on in the book: some of this exploration of gender might make you uncomfortable. That's what I heard from early readers. I'm sorry. I really am. It's an uncomfortable subject, I know. I've tried to be as compassionate as I can be about the discomfort this book is going to cause some people, but as hard as I try to make you comfortable, the real comforting is going to have to come from inside yourself. It's taken me a long time to learn that one.

I had very little compassion for the part of myself that couldn't live up to being either a real man or a real woman, and also little reason to be *willing* to be compassionate with myself. When I finally started to come to grips with this gender stuff of mine, I ran into the odd position of discovering people who were much more willing than I to simply let me experience my gender quandary.

A Catholic priest taught me the value of compassion for myself. I was in Alcoholics Anonymous at the time, still a guy and still afraid of dealing with my transgender stuff. I went on a men's retreat to a Catholic monastery. We did all the standard retreat-type workshops and meetings, but the last thing we each had to do was sit down with a priest and go over our "personal issues." The priest assigned to me was an older man; I'm guessing he was in his seventies, a real nice father-type guy. He asked me what the "big issue" in my life was, and I figured oh fuck it, I'd tell him. So for about a half an hour, I spilled out my transgender story. At the end of my tale, this priest looked at me—maybe his eyebrows were a little further up on his forehead—and he said "Well, I'm certainly not qualified or experienced enough to give you any specific advice about a sex change, but I can tell you this: your comfort level is somewhere down around your ankles, and you need to do something about that." He went on to tell me that I should do at least three things a day to make myself more comfortable, and then he said, "Al, you need to learn to treat yourself like you would treat an honored guest in your house." That was about twelve years ago, and it's still some of the best advice I've ever received. Whenever I'm beating myself up about gender stuff or anything else, I can usually get back to the point of treating myself like an honored guest.

EXERCISE: Has there ever been a time in your life that you haven't been treated like a real man or a real woman? If so, did you give yourself any negative messages about that? If you did, write them down here.

I don't know about you, but I grew up with the idea that you simply do not write in books. Well, I wrote this book to be written in, okay? And don't worry . . . there are no right or wrong answers to any of these questions and exercises, okay?

> Now, what if a dear friend of yours were to come to your house. Ze sits down and tells you that ze is exploring hir gender identity with the idea of maybe changing genders, but ze tells you ze has reservations about doing it. Ze lists out all the reasons in the box you just filled in above. How would you counsel your dear friend?

Was there any difference between the way you counsel yourself and the way you would counsel your dear friend? Think you could treat yourself the way you treat a friend?

> EXERCISE: Do three simple things for yourself today to make yourself more comfortable. Anything at all that makes you comfortable, and doesn't place a lot of stress or guilt on yourself for doing it. Repeat this exercise daily for at least a week. At the end of the week, write down any changes you notice in the way that you feel about yourself.

If we don't show ourselves the same amount of compassion we show others, we'll eventually come to resent the compassion we have for others. I think there's little enough compassion in the world right now, so we need to grow our own to compensate for that.

All right, I'll be checking on your comfort level from time to time. But now that you've got the idea, let's get into some deeper questions so we might better assess your Gender Aptitude.

◎ Your Gender Aptitude, Section V: Love and Sex

1. *Do you have a "type" of person you regularly fall for?*
   A. Definitely, yes.
   B. I try to keep my mind open about this sort of thing, but I usually fall for one type.
   C. I seem to fall for lots of "types" of people, but usually they're all the same gender.
   D. What? You want to know if I fall for typists? What a silly question. I fall for people I can connect with and who connect with me.

2. *If you fell in love with a heterosexual woman, you would be*
   A. Pleased as punch.
   B. Really confused.
   C. Nervous as hell.
   D. Curious, curious, curious.

3. *If you fell in love with a heterosexual man, you would be*
   A. Reassuring yourself that the old Greeks had friendships like that.
   B. Pleased as punch.
   C. Nervous as hell.
   D. Curious, curious, curious.

4. *If you fell in love with a lesbian woman, you would be*
   A. Apprehensive, but titillated.
   B. Nervous as hell.
   C. Pleased as punch.
   D. Curious, curious, curious.

5. *If you fell in love with a gay man, you would be*
   A. Reassuring yourself that the old Greeks had friendships like that.
   B. Resigned to your fate.
   C. Pleased as punch.
   D. Curious, curious, curious.

6. *If you fell in love with a woman who used to be a man, you would be*
   A. Concerned how well she would pass in public.
   B. Wondering why you couldn't have met her *before* her change.
   C. Nervous as hell.
   D. Curious, curious, curious.

7. *If you fell in love with a man who used to be a woman, you would be*
   A. Convinced that he's really a woman and you're not really a faggot.
   B. Really confused.
   C. Nervous as hell.
   D. Curious, curious, curious.

8. *Who's ultimately responsible for birth control?*
   A. She is.
   B. He is.

C. I am.

D. Honey, I haven't had to worry about that one for *years!*

9. *I like it...*

A. On the bottom.

B. On the top.

C. In the middle.

D. Yes I do!

10. *Who's ultimately responsible for keeping sex safe during this time of the AIDS epidemic?*

A. I am.

B. I am.

C. I am.

D. All of the above.

Give yourself 5 points for each A answer, 3 points for every B, 1 point for a C, and no points for any D answers.

Write your score for this section here.

⑥ No Gender, No Cry

Warning Label: This workbook gets into the subject and area of something we can call for lack of a better (or any) term "no gender." That's how I see myself: I live pretty much without a gender, which paradoxically means I can do many genders.

Signs of impending no-genderedness might include but are not limited to vertigo, light-headedness, confusion, revulsion, whimsy, gut-wrenching angst, giggles, nausea, or all or none of the above.

Disclaimer: This workbook is not intended as a cure for the above symptoms, or for any other symptoms for that matter. Should these or any other symptoms persist, CALL A DOCTOR! Or call a friend.

Ha ha ha! Just kidding. No-gender is an interesting place for me to live. I made this point in my first book, *Gender Outlaw,* and received quite a bit of correspondence that boiled down to, "Okay Kate, you say you live without a gender. How exactly do you do that?" Well, there's a real easy answer to that one. Honest, it's simple. This is the key to the whole workbook. Really. Ready?

The way you live without gender is you look for where gender is, and then you go someplace else.

If you've got that, you don't need to read any further. Give me a call, and let's go out for tea or something. If, however, it's not that easy to spot where gender is or if once you've spotted it, it's difficult to find a place where gender isn't, then maybe reading and doing the exercises in this book would be a good idea. Let's see how you fare on the final criteria of your gender aptitude: issues of no gender whatsoever.

◎ Your Gender Aptitude, Section VI: No Gender

1. *Which one of the following statements most nearly matches your idea of gender?*
   A. Gender simply is. If you don't like yours, get over it.
   B. I've been working on my own gender for a long time, and I'm getting to the point where I may actually have made it my own.
   C. I think there's a lot about gender that we don't know about yet, and I wonder why that might be.
   D. Gender is what happens to me when I get dressed in the morning.

2. *Which one of the following statements most nearly matches your feelings about gender?*
   A. My *what* about gender?
   B. I guess my feelings range anywhere from anger and frustration to happiness and exhilaration.
   C. Gender confuses me. I don't know why it is the way it is.
   D. I feel . . . I feel . . . I feel a song coming on!

3. *Has there been any time when you've felt you have no gender?*
   A. No, I'm never really aware of my gender anyway.
   B. No, I'm very aware of my gender nearly all the time.
   C. Maybe sometimes when I'm alone or I'm in some situation where gender doesn't matter.
   D. Lots of genders, no genders. What's the difference?

4. *Have you ever questioned the nature of gender itself?*
   A. No, it's not polite to question Mother Nature.
   B. I question the nature of my own gender, but gender itself? No.
   C. I question gender, but I get the spooky feeling I'm not supposed to do that.
   D. The nature of gender? Isn't that an oxymoron?

5. *If there were no more gender, do you think there'd be any more desire?*
   A. Well of course not! That's why it's impossible to reach a point of no gender.
   B. That's a good question. I'll have to ask my group.
   C. My head says no, but my heart says yes.
   D. Oh dear. You really think a little thing like no gender is

going to get in the way of *my* sex life?

6. ***If you woke up one morning and discovered you were neither a man nor a woman, you would***

A. Kill yourself, or stay in hiding the rest of your life.

B. Discuss this new development with your group.

C. Read the rest of this book as fast as you could.

D. Yawn and get dressed.

7. ***Do you think there's some sort of connection between your gender and your spirituality?***

A. My gender and my *what?*

B. Well yes, it's all about *yin* and *yang* and the inherent duality and non-duality of the universe, isn't it?

C. Perhaps gender is part of our spiritual challenge.

D. My *what* and my spirituality?

8. ***Have you ever killed off part of yourself you didn't like?***

A. There's really nothing about myself I don't like.

B. I've *let go* of parts of myself I haven't liked, yes.

C. Sometimes. Are you saying that applies to gender?

D. Oh baby, wanna see where I stashed the bodies?

9. ***Why are you reading this book?***

A. I certainly didn't *choose* to read it, that's for sure.

B. I think it's important to try to understand what it is that other people experience.

C. It's been dawning on me that maybe these might sort of be, well, my issues too.

D. Because *nearly* everything else about gender has been positively *dreary,* darling.

10. ***If you thought this book was leading you into some sort of radical gender change, you would***

A. Stop reading and throw the book away.

B. Finish reading the book, then sell it at the used book store.

C. Put the book up on the shelf and read it a whole lot later.

D. Hahahahahaha. Kate would never lead anyone into that unless they wanted to be led there!

Give yourself 5 points for each A answer, 3 points for every B, 1 point for a C, and no points for any D answers.

Write your score for this section here.

◎ Okay, Boys and Girls! On the Count of Three, Change Your Gender! One... Two...

No, no. The goal of this workbook is *not* for you, dear reader, to completely change your gender from male to female or from female to male. I'm not asking you even to ponder the idea of doing that unless that's something you've had in the back of your mind to do anyway. This is not a book for and about transsexuals only. I'm not going to ask you to join some massive underground movement. I'm not recruiting rebels to "The Cause." I'm not going to exhort you to stop being a man or a woman. Why should I do that if that's what you enjoy being? This is simply a book about gender, and who hasn't got one of those? Transsexual or not, you've got a gender, don't you? Well, have you looked at it recently? I mean really really looked at it? Well, take a deep breath, because here we go.

◎ This Is Your Gender Aptitude!

Congratulations! You've finished your gender aptitude questions! Now, go back and collect up all your subtotalled scores for each section. Write the total of your score for all six sections here:

You have a range of possible scores from zero to 255, and if you haven't guessed it by now, when it comes to your Gender Aptitude (GA), smaller is better. But don't fret, please. It's just an aptitude, and like any other part of human potential, with a little or a lot of work you can always improve. Let's see what the numbers translate into.

If your GA was: **Then your Gender Aptitude Level is:**

0-60

Gender Freak
Whoa! This stuff must seem like kid's play for you. Either that or water in the desert, huh? Have fun reading the book any ol' way you want to. It's going to make you feel a lot less alone in the world. Call me and let me know if I got this stuff right, will you?

| 61-100 |

Gender Outlaw
You've been working not only on your own gender, but the subject of gender itself for quite some time, huh? I'm willing to bet things are still a bit scary and a bit serious for you in your life. If I were you, I'd read this book with the intent to get the most fun out of it. Have a ball!

| 101-175 |

Gender Novice
Gee, it's like you have one hand in respectability and the other hand someplace where both of you like it. You're not always taken for "normal," are you? In fact, you probably get an infrequent but regular bout of the gender willies from time to time, don't you? Fret not. You've got a very rewarding journey ahead of you. All it's going take is some practice. Read on, read on. Make sure you do all the exercises, okay?

| 176-235 |

Well Gendered
Hiya, Mister Man! Hello, Ms. Lady! I'm guessing you're not reading this book to learn anything about yourself, am I right? Maybe you're reading it as a class requirement, or maybe a friend or family member wanted you to read it. Well, I think that's very commendable. Keep on reading, and do what's comfortable for you to do. I promise I'll be gentle.

| 236-255 |

You're Captain James T. Kirk!
Omigod, I've always wanted to meet you! Can I have your autograph, please? Ah, Captain, you finally get to truly go where no man has gone before.

There. Now you know more about yourself and your relationship to gender than most people in the history of the world. Isn't that neat?

No, there's no further significance to your Gender Aptitude than that. Yes, it's accurate, but no, it's no big deal. Let's keep going.

⊚ Butterflies Are Not Always Free

A couple of people have written me asking why I don't just write down everything I've learned about gender. Sort of do the "Everything You Wanted to Know about Gender but Were Afraid to Ask" approach, with all the answers. Well, a while back someone told me something interesting about butterflies. I don't know if it's true or not, but I like the concept, so I'm going to believe it.

It seems that butterflies have a rough time of their transition from caterpillars. These li'l caterpillars weave weave weave and end up with a cocoon all around them, in which they're able to physically transform into a butterfly. Now that's a lot of work all by itself, but the interesting part comes next: they have to get out of the cocoon. The butterfly in the cocoon has to *really* struggle to get out of that thing. Now, let's say you're walking through a field, and you see this cocoon. It's pretty obvious there's a butterfly in there, struggling to get out. Humanitarian that you are, you bend down and very gently open the cocoon to free the butterfly. Good deed? Nope. It seems that Nature in hir wisdom has decided that the butterfly *needs* the struggle: the struggle itself triggers some sort of chemical process in the butterfly that allows it to live once it's out. If you free a struggling butterfly from its cocoon, you're signing its death warrant.

That's why this is a workbook. You can study gender until the cows come home. You can read all the books, interview all the transgendered people, you can take courses in this stuff. But unless you actually do the work on a personal basis, you're not going to understand the life of it. If you truly want to see what it might be like to live without a gender, or to change your gender, or to even *understand* the gender you've perhaps got and really like, then there's only one way for it: you need to do the work.

Illustrator Diane DiMassa and I have tried to make doing the work a bit more fun, and that's the best we can do. The rest is up to you.

⊚ Some Notes on Style

Language is a tailor's shop where nothing fits.
—*Rumi*

There's a cultural phenomenon that's come and gone throughout many civilizations, and it's just beginning to surface big time again in ours. Today, some people call it *genderfuck*. It's the intentional crossing, mixing, and blending of gender-specific signals all at once. You may have seen some examples of this yourself. You may *do* it yourself. It's the riotgrrrl in

Not a Phallacy

Armatrading. Bowie. Lennox. Prince. Androgyny. Balance. Equilibrium on a continuum of sexuality and sexual being. Not the same as being sexual. It is being a person: neither man nor woman. Relating to other people as persons: neither men nor womyn. A coming together from apposite poles. A centre-ring. Not a 50s butch caricature of a man. Nor a 70s Stonewall transvestite. An 80s child maturing in the 90s. A nonsexual being; not an asexual one. A truly imperfect ambisexual political person. Free from the bondage of stereotype: unwrapped, unboxed. Subversive. Often undesirable. Rights of admission never reserved. But very very costly. No phallus required.

—Charlotte Noonan

her short skirt, combat boots, and crewcut. It's the eyelined and lipsticked gothic boy in black velvet, deep burgundy satin, and frothy white lace. Passing is the opposite of genderfuck. Passing is getting as many signals as possible all lined up. You've seen this one too. Maybe this is closer to what you do. It's the girl who looks like she walked out of a J. Crew catalogue. It's Seinfeld and his wannabes. No doubts about their genders.

Well, the style of this book might be called *theoryfuck*. I'm hoping the mix of styles I've used to get this theory across highlights the constructed nature of the theory, because I really don't believe there's any single correct theory. In terms of theories about gender, I'm more convinced about what gender isn't rather than what gender is. I'm hoping that makes it easier for you to create your *own* theory out of what you might find interesting in here.

⑥ They Shoot Horses, Don't They?

Humanity has always been fascinated with the process of transformation. As children, we play with clay or Silly Putty and we transform it continually from one shape to another. We wonder at caterpillars that become butterflies, we write stories about ugly ducklings that become swans. As scientists, we attempt to transform docile matter into unlimited energy. Our literature and our philosophy, our science and our folklore, our religions and our politics all boil down to some kind of transformation. Through transformation, we perceive we're alive and growing. The opposite is also true: when transformation stagnates or is blocked, we approach death of one sort or another. And this has placed transformation at the nexus of spirituality and higher learning as a marker of either our spiritual progress or our wisdom.

Why, do you suppose, some cultural phenomena are permitted to be dynamic and mutable, and so transformative, while other cultural phenomena, including gender, are considered to be static?

Do you think there exists the possibility of a transformative nature in gender? And if so, how can we tap into that?

I think there *is* a transformative nature to gender, but I think it's blocked in most cultures and stagnates in two ways:

1. The questioning of gender itself is essentially made taboo.

2. Any information concerning the possibility of gender as anything but natural and essential has been essentially forbidden to public discourse.

What we're doing in this workbook is:

1. Questioning gender from as many angles as we can.

2. Providing the public discourse with the possibility of subjective proof that gender is neither natural nor essential, but rather the performance of self-expression within any dynamic relationship.

ⓖ Gender as a Game of Truth or Dare

We can't perform something well, much less transform it unless we know what it is to begin with. That goes for our identities as a whole, which would include our gender identities. Without having questioned, discovered or defined for ourselves the complexity of who we really are, we're left in the uncomfortable position of having to fake it from time to time, until we can learn more about ourselves and how we wish to express ourselves. During the time of "faking it," however, we are in effect presenting a false identity to the world.

And that seems to be universally the least forgivable crime: we're not who we seem to be. People will forgive us quite a bit, but that one takes a lot of work. If we don't know who we are, if there's some aspect of ourselves we've not explored fully, then that's the aspect we lie about, cover up our ignorance about, and apologize for. That area of unknown self is the one that's going to rear up and bite us hard when we least expect it. That's the one we're going to get caught up in.

I have been alternately pissed off and delighted by the gender dichotomy in our society. Even as a preteen sending away for magazines, instead of checking Ms, Miss, Mrs or Mr, I'd scribble them out furiously!

I watched my grandmother grow a beard and develop a basso voice while gramps shrank and became weak and vulnerable and decidedly more alto as the years went on. Did this mean they were undergoing gender transformation? I didn't think of it that way. They were just getting old. In fact, I had an idea that old people and babies knew that gender was largely a performance. As a teenager, I hated the terms "masculine" and "feminine" because I felt that they were sexist and irrelevant.

On the other hand, I like femming it up and "being a girl." On the other other hand (Oh, god, what is that creature? It has three hands!!!) I like to be "Earl the Girl," a 5-o'clock shadow kinda teenage trouble-maker who looks much better in a baseball cap than I do! Maybe it's San Francisco's influence.

—Lexie Underwood

I was told that I looked like a boy, I walked like a boy, I acted and spoke and moved like a boy, I threw a ball like a boy but I was never called a boy, unless it was a mistake made by a witless stranger, at which time I was expected to correct him at once. Then, it seems, I was to feel embarrassed and vaguely sinful, all for some unknown purpose, mostly because we were Catholic and it felt good.

The torment of a tom-boy is this then, to be told these countless times to act like a lady, walk more like a lady, yet having legs that do not seem to bend quite like a lady's leg should and hair that would not lie or curl quite like a lady's hair would, and did this mean I had to quit hockey and forget how to throw a ball? All this disturbed me greatly and did not begin to make sense until many years later.

—Ivan E. Coyote

Until we've fully explored all our identities, until we've explored our genders and made some choices about them based on informed consent, we're presenting consciously or unconsciously a more or less false picture of ourselves to the world.

I'm going to continue to throw those terms around in this book: "real man" and "real woman." They're at once vital concepts and meaningless, useless terms. They're vital concepts because nearly everyone believes there *is* such a thing as a real man or a real woman. Many people think they themselves are one or the other, or awfully close. They're meaningless, useless terms because of the nearly universal disagreement about what those terms actually *mean*. Step across a generation line, and you'll get a shade of different meaning for "real man" or "real woman." Step across subcultures and those terms could shift radically in definition. Let's test that one out, shall we?

EXERCISE:

1. Ask two of your friends what they think a real man is. Then ask them what they think a real woman is. Make notes of their answers, paying close attention to the words they use to describe real men and real women.

2. If your parents are alive and you're in touch with them, ask them the same questions. If not, ask someone close to you who's a member of their generation. Make notes of their answers, paying close attention to the words they use to describe real men and real women.

3. If you have children, ask them the same question. If you don't have children, ask someone who's close to you who would be of that generation. Make notes of their answers, paying close attention to the words they use to describe real men and real women.

> 4. Ask two people of a different race than you those questions. Make notes of their answers, paying close attention to the words they use to describe real men and real women.
>
> 5. Ask two people of a different culture than you those questions. Make notes of their answers, paying close attention to the words they use to describe real men and real women.
>
> 6. (optional) If you have access to a computer and the Internet, go online and open a channel called something like #realmenwomen. Ask each person who pops in your two questions, and keep a log of your session.

Did you get more than one answer to each question?

What does that say about the terms "real man" and "real woman?"

———

Some people think what I'm saying is that there are no men and no women. That's not what I believe, and it's certainly not what I observe. I do believe there are men and women. These are very real categories. I just think that these two categories alone are inadequate to describe the current multifaceted, elusively defined condition of humanity.

———

I was afraid that I could never be a convincing woman, no matter what I did to my body. So I kept running away from myself and my destiny. Then I decided to do some re-thinking. I asked myself, "What is a woman?" Someone who is small and slender? Someone who is soft and pretty? Someone who has little body and facial hair? Someone with breasts and a vagina? Someone with more estrogens than androgens? Someone with XX chromosomes?

I found that it was almost impossible to come up with a definition of a woman that wouldn't exclude a lot of women. I decided that being a woman (or a man for that matter) is a lot like being an Aryan superman—a myth. Gender is a continuum with very few people at either extremes, and everybody else in the middle. At some point you just have enough characteristics of one or the other where society sees you as being of a particular gender. What do you think?

—Pat Nivins

◎ The Author's Agenda

I've been researching gender using whatever tools I have had at the time for nearly all my life. I've yet to find an answer to even the simplest questions: What's a real man? What's a real woman? Why do we have to be one or the other? But I've learned a great deal from *asking* those questions. So while I can't give you any answers regarding gender, I do want to give you *something*. Since I probably don't know you, it makes it difficult to shop for you. But I found a snippet of verse by the Sufi poet, Rumi. It's answered all my shopping dilemmas!

You can't imagine how I've looked
for something for you. Nothing seemed appropriate.
You don't take gold down into a goldmine,
or a drop of water to the Sea of Oman!
Everything I thought of was like bringing cumin seed
to Kirmanshah where cumin comes from.
You have all seeds in your barn. You even have my love
and my soul, so I can't bring those.
I've brought you a mirror. Look at yourself,
and remember me.

So now I give mirrors to people. And that's what I'd like this book to be for you: a mirror. Forget me . . . just look at yourself. After all, you're not the same person you were when you started to read this book, are you?

Solving the Gender Puzzle

So, what is gender anyway? It's not such a difficult puzzle after all.

The Not-So-Difficult Puzzle After All

ACROSS:

2. a fanatical cult, demanding blind obedience to mostly unwritten, unagreed-upon rules, regulations, and qualifications.

5. any standard (usually, but not necessarily biological) by which we can easily and without much thought conveniently divide the human race into two neat parcels. (e.g., sociological, genital, chromosomal, psychological, hormonal, et cetera, *ad nauseum*)

6. an oppressive class system of two and only two classes, usually held in place by the assumption that the class system is "natural," in which system one class has nearly total economic and political power over the other.

7. a means of cultural traction, an identity or persona by which to identify oneself to another or maintain some position within a relationship or culture.

DOWN:

1. currently a system of dividing people into one of two impossible-to-live-up-to standards: male or female.

3. a means by which we can express our sexual desire.

4. a means by which we can attract others, to whom we are attracted.

(Answers on page 33)

Now that wasn't very hard, was it? Of course not. Where gender begins to get difficult is when we mix sex into the equation.

⊚ Everything You Need to Know about Sex Versus Gender. Honest!

She has sex, but no particular gender.
—*Marlene Dietrich on Greta Garbo*

Gender and sex are two distinct phenomena working in any given culture as well as in and on our minds. Gender and sex obviously influence who we are and how we relate to others. The weird thing is that the concepts referred to by *both* words tend to get jammed into "sex," as in
"What sex do you think that person across the street is?"
or
"I think we all need to take responsibility for safer sex in this day and age."
The concept of gender is muddled enough without our confusing it with something entirely different like biology. Sure, some people differentiate sex and gender by saying things like "My sex is male, but my gender is woman."
But why not say "I'm a woman with a penis!"
For so long, we've bought into a biological imperative that has labeled genitalia as "male" or "female"; what's more, we've dignified that imperative by giving it its own word: *sex!* Anyway, who says penises are male and vulvas are female? "Sex" as a designation of gender says it. Sex-as-gender says that penises are male, and that vaginas, vulvas, and clitorises are female. I don't get it. I know too many male men with vaginas and too many female women with penises to any longer buy into some wishful thinking on the part of old-guard scientists who'd like to have things all nice and orderly in some predictable binary. For a long time, we've tried to explain two different, admittedly related concepts, with one word: sex. We need to pull them apart if we're going to make any sense of it.
Gender is real easy to sum up in one word: categorization. Anything that categorizes people is gender, whether it's appearance or mannerisms, biology or psychology, hormones, roles, genitals, whatever: if we're trying to categorize or separate people out, it's gender. So where does that leave sex? Sex is fucking: any way, shape, or form, alone or with another or others. Once we've got *that* distinction, things start to clear up. Let's do a little chart thing here to sort it all out.

⊚ A Little Sex/Gender Chart

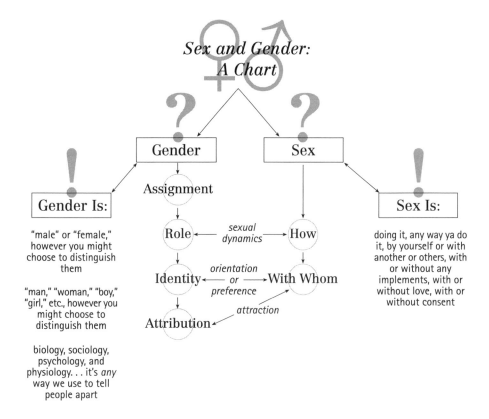

Sex and Gender: A Chart

Gender

Sex

Assignment

Gender Is:

"male" or "female,"
however you might
choose to distinguish
them

"man," "woman," "boy,"
"girl," etc., however you
might choose to
distinguish them

biology, sociology,
psychology, and
physiology. . . it's *any*
way we use to tell
people apart

Role ← *sexual dynamics* → How

Identity ← *or* → With Whom
orientation *preference*

Attribution ← *attraction*

Sex Is:

doing it, any way ya do
it, by yourself or with
another or others, with
or without any
implements, with or
without love, with or
without consent

Components of Sex and Gender

These things are *really* tangled up! Let's take this chart apart, starting with
SEX. The world becomes a lot brighter when we say that sex is simply the
act, that it does *not* mean the designation of category. Taken in this light,
sex has only a few aspects, mainly: how you'd like to do it, and whom (if
anyone) you'd like to do it *with*.

*Naming sex as the act and only the act robs essentialist thinkers of their biological
imperative, which is usually based on some arcane combination of genitals,
chromosomes, hormones, and reproductive ability. Who says that biology has the last
word in determining someone's identity anyway?*

It's one thing to say that someone has a vulva, vagina, clitoris, breasts, ovaries, etc., etc. It's quite another thing to assume that person is either female, feminine, or a woman.

Gender, unlike the straightforward word sex, has several aspects:

@ **Gender Assignment** answers the question, "What do the authorities say I am?" In most cultures, it's the M or F designation. What the doctor says you are at birth, usually determined by the presence (male) or absence (female) of a penis. Most cultures assign some permanent, immutable gender at birth. A few cultures allow people to change their gender assignment later in life; some cultures even build in a possible switch in gender assignment. Gender assignment is something that's done *to* each one of us, long before we have the ability to have any say in the matter.

@ **Gender Role** answers the question, "What does the culture think I should do with my life?" It's the sum total of qualities, mannerisms, duties, and cultural expectations accorded a specific gender.

@ **Gender Identity** answers the question, "Am I a man or a woman or something else entirely?" Most people don't think about this one very much. They let gender assignment nonconsensually stand in for gender identity. But identity *is* personal; it's what we feel our gender to be at any given moment. Sure, this feeling might be influenced by biological factors that have a cultural tag sticking out of each one of them. The feeling of being some gender might also have to do with a sexual fantasy, or a preference for some role. There are as many good reasons for having or choosing a gendered identity as there are people.

@ **Gender Attribution** is what we all do when we first meet someone: we decide whether they're a man or a woman, or something indeterminable. We attribute a gender to someone based on an intricate system of cues, varying from culture to culture. The cues can range from physical appearance and mannerisms to context, and the use of power.

Where It Gets Messed Up

So far, so good. Seems simple. Here's where the tangles lie:

@ In the majority of cultures in the world, the socially acceptable easy way to define one's sexual preference or orientation (who we want to be sexual with) depends on the *gender identity* of our sexual partners. To make things worse, the gender identity we're attracted to must also be phrased in terms of men and women. We're attracted to men or women or both; that's the sum total of our desire. So, sex (the act) becomes hopelessly linked to gender (the category).

⊚ And what about sexual attraction? That's linked to gender attribution. First we attribute a gender, then we decide if we want to be attracted to that person; but the first filter is almost always "Is that person the right gender for me, sexually and romantically?"

⊚ Finally, what we enjoy actually *doing* sexually, the sex act itself, often involves a specific sort of genital play, and as genitals have been gendered in this culture, so sex has become gendered.

Instead of the nice, easy gender puzzle we had before, once you add sex into the gender mix, we end up with a puzzle that looks more like this:

⊚ The More Difficult Puzzle

E	H	N	E	E	U	Q	G	A	R	D	S	R	G	B	S	A
H	L	I	I	T	L	V	F	R	R	E	O	I	U	H	T	Y
R	E	A	M	M	Q	D	Y	U	X	L	R	T	E	T	O	A
L	Y	S	M	M	I	K	Z	D	E	L	C	M	R	B	H	T
L	E	O	H	D	U	I	M	Y	T	H	A	A	T	P	O	T
Q	A	S	B	E	O	D	E	B	F	L	C	R	R	A	M	R
J	H	U	B	M	X	O	Y	H	E	T	A	C	I	N	O	I
J	E	Z	X	I	O	G	G	K	I	N	L	P	O	S	S	B
G	V	P	W	E	A	T	Q	O	S	G	Z	C	T	E	E	U
C	P	P	P	G	S	N	N	V	B	V	N	R	G	X	X	T
E	O	R	E	L	G	O	E	F	N	A	P	L	R	U	U	I
T	E	V	R	E	D	S	R	M	E	V	D	Q	R	A	A	O
H	O	R	N	E	T	Q	I	E	O	M	E	K	R	L	L	N
L	R	D	S	I	J	L	A	T	T	A	M	L	E	B	R
G	E	I	T	W	J	P	E	K	T	E	T	L	M	Y	H	H
R	R	E	L	A	U	X	E	S	I	B	H	O	E	E	A	S
E	W	R	E	D	N	E	G	S	N	A	R	T	B	E	F	G

Can you find the gender and sex-related words in this puzzle? (It can be done, but wasn't the first puzzle a lot easier? And I only used a *few* of the words we can mix up in our lives!)

For a list of the words hidden in this puzzle, turn to page 33 of this chapter.

A woman wearing a man's suit, *and getting away with it*, in this [corporate] environment is subversive. Don't get me wrong, I do not try to pass as a man. I am a woman in the uniform of a corporate businessman. I don't walk those halls without gender, I do it without a *specific* gender . . . or perhaps with multiple gender. I believe that the dissonance of my female body in that masculine garb causes other folks to recognize the shades of, and yes, to question gender. In those double takes, I see confusion and fear and sometimes a small smile. Sometimes I also see anger. I think all of those are necessary for humans to evolve. The fact that we are so rarely confronted with issues of gender—that we simply accept it as either/or—means that we haven't really had the opportunity to reflect upon it. What makes gender? Who decides? What does it mean to be male? Female? What does it mean to be something other?

I don't have answers, don't expect to ever figure gender out, really, but I do know that being challenged is prerequisite to thinking, and thinking is prerequisite to growing.

—Teresa Stores

The Easy Way Out Is Neither Easy Nor a Way Out

No wonder people want to use the term "sex" for both the identity (gender) and the act (sex). The two have become interdependent. In terms of our sexual desire and our gender identities, we've opted for the easy way out, the "everybody knows it's this way" solution. "Everyone knows that the way I define my desire is by the gender of my partner."

Personally, I can't buy that. If the world's great thinkers have taught us anything, it's that we rarely achieve personal fulfillment by mindlessly wandering through life, taking the path of least resistance and little or no responsibility for our actions. We need to question our assumptions, and that includes our assumptions about sex and gender, if we're going to understand those aspects of ourselves and others.

⊚ Gender: The Shell Game

I've been living on the border of the two-gender system for the past couple of years. Sometimes I manage to escape the system entirely. I claim no socially sanctioned gender, and I'm trying to retrace the steps it took for me to arrive at this point. I think it comes down to an understanding of gender as simply one aspect of identity. Gender is a kind of identity, that's all.

The question "How do you live without a gender," broadens into "How do you live without an identity?" I think we create our identities, or actively fortify the identities we seem to be born with, in the same manner and with a similar purpose that a crab excretes the substance that eventually hardens into a shell, its armor. It's *safe* having an identity, it's secure. It's safe having a gender. But there's a price for safety and security within some hard shell. We can't grow any more. Our identities become so hard and so restrictive that we can no longer stretch and explore, we can't find new ways of experiencing the world, new ways to delight ourselves, new ways to please others. We're frozen in that shell. And the only thing to do is to come out of that shell, leave it behind us, and begin the whole process over again.

◎ Connecting with Your Inner Gender

Hahahahahaha! No way. I'd never inflict anything called an inner gender on anyone. But the fact is if we want to connect with gender, then we need to connect with it on a deeply personal level. Connecting with gender on a purely social or intellectual or even political level isn't going to bring about a personal understanding of the subject.

We can read about gender and identity all our lives. We can study gender and identity, put them under a microscope, talk with people about them, and see endless movies about this stuff, and we won't really know any more about them than we did when we started. We'll be more curious, uh huh. We'll be a lot more apprehensive about the traps we've read about, perhaps. But we won't really know anything. Not until we experience gender—consciously—ourselves.

It's when we begin to poke around in the piles of accumulated emotions, mannerisms, attitudes, and values, when we really let ourselves look at what we've gotten ourselves into; that's when we can begin to get some clarity on gender. That's when we can construct a gender identity for ourselves that best lets us express our needs and wants in this world.

[T]he fear is worst before the fact. Until the first time someone burst out laughing at me, I didn't know how I'd survive the humiliation. Until the first time I had to refuse in public to fulfill my gender duties, I didn't know how I'd ever face my friends again. Until the first time I was beaten up, I didn't know how I would survive the trauma. But now I know what it feels like to be laughed at. It is frustrating, but not frightening. Now I know that I can stand up and refuse to play gender games in public, even if I turn beet red as I do so. Now I know that even broken bones don't hurt forever.

Fear? There is always fear. Anything new is frightening. The only way to get over a fear is to shut your eyes and ignore the pit in your stomach. The second time you do it the pit will be smaller and one day you will have trouble remembering that what you are doing used to be hard.

—Laura Franks, Moscow, Russia

I was on a radio talk show out of southern Florida once. The (white, heterosexual male) host literally wouldn't let me say on the air I'm not a man or a woman. He accused me of living in some fantasy world. ::shrugging:: What can I say? To some degree he was right. But what good is a fantasy if there's never any hope that you can one day live it out?

* ::laughing:: Oh right! That's a convention I'm going to be using in this workbook from time to time. Words set off by a pair of double colons will follow the cyberspace convention of indicating an action being done by the speaker, or in this case an action being done by me the writer. ::waving happily:: means I'm waving up at you from the page here.*

⑥ The Ten-Minute Gender Outlaw Excercise

Here's a simple, basic exercise to begin poking around in gender. It's one you can do once a day. It doesn't have to take a long time. Take one or more of these three questions a day, and write down a series of answers.

What is a Man?
What is a Woman?
Why do we have to be one or the other?

The trick is that the answers have to be phrased in questions. ::grin:: Yeah, I know . . . kinda like the television game-show *Jeopardy* that way, but it works. It keeps the questions open, which is where I think they belong. It doesn't matter what *track* those further questions take, just as long as more questions come out of it, until the question itself is enough for you and you don't need to write anymore.

So, one day it might look like this:

> *What is a man?*
> *What's a woman, for that matter?*
> *What's a boy?*
> *Was I ever a boy?*
> *What was it like to be treated like a boy?*
> *Did I like it?*
> *What did I like about it?*
> *How do I like to be treated today?*
> *Does that make me a boy, still?*

or the next day, it might look like this:

> What is a woman?
> Why am I even bothering to ask that?
> Doesn't everyone know what a woman is?
> Who the hell is everyone anyway?
> What business of theirs is it to tell me what a woman is?

and another day, it might look like this:

Why do we have to be one or the other?
What other choices are there?

Or you may go on for pages and pages. The point is to get to a question you want to think about some more, one that really tickles your brain—something you can ponder on for the balance of the day. Once you get to *that* question, you stop. That's all there is to it. Try it every day at first. It's a good discipline for learning to explore one of the most basic facets of our cultural identities. Once you've gotten into the routine of asking these questions, you can taper down to once every couple of days, to once a week, to once a month, as the questions begin to linger. But for now, make it a point to ask yourself one of these questions every day for one month, and to answer it *only* with other questions. Mark it on your calendar. Start today, okay?

> I know that I will externally and internally always be a "woman," even though I'm not sure what a woman is or what a man is anymore. I'm just glad for the fact that many of us have both characteristics.
>
> —Mara Oong

Answers to "The Not-so-Difficult Puzzle," pg. 25
1. gender 2. gender 3. gender 4. gender 5. gender 6. gender 7. gender

**Gender- and sex-related words hidden
in "The More Difficult Puzzle," pg. 29**

attraction	heshe
attribution	heterosexual
bad	him
bisexual	homosexual
bottom	it
boy	lesbian
butch	love
desire	male
dragqueen	pansexual
female	riotgrrrl
femme	role
gay	sex
gender	shemale
girl	tomboy
good	top
grrrl	transgender
he	transvestite
her	

Who's on Top?

(and why are we on the bottom?) (and is that really such a bad place to be?)

⑥ Safety First

If real men and real women are in fact social constructs, that means they're constructed of *something*. I've been looking more and more closely at gender, and I think I've got a better idea of its components, beyond the basics discussed in the last chapter. But this is tricky stuff, and we need to proceed safely.

One of the first tenets of safety is awareness. Ask anyone who works with hir hands: you need to know where you are, where your tools are, what they're capable of doing, how they're capable of hurting you if they're misused. So the first step in safety around gender play would be to look at what gender is, what it's made up of, what tools we use to perform man, woman, or whatever it is we're performing. If we *haven't* looked very closely at whatever comprises our gender, we may change something about ourselves that we truly value.

> Right now, I think I am [living a life without gender]. People don't want to consider me a woman, and I don't want to be a man, so I walk in the middle not because I wish to, but because I am forced.
>
> —Nyssa

⑥ How Do We Look at Gender?

Since gender itself can't be seen, we tend to rely on models and metaphors. There are quite a few models these days for gender, none of which I've found adequate to describe the deathgrip gender-as-system has on us both personally and culturally.

⑥ There's the old *binary* model: these are two completely opposite creatures, and only two, who have nothing to do with each other. It doesn't

I spent so many years wondering and feeling lost and scared. I thought I was the only one who was a transsexual lesbian. I am a 24 year old half-Japanese, half-caucasian male who has been living wondering if I was the only one who felt this way.

I don't know what a man is or what a woman is . . . all I know is that I feel like the yin and yang. Where the mind, soul, and flesh is the black circle, the white circle and the flesh is the outer circle of what we are not who we are. There is a life in this circle of three that is both man and woman and sometimes neither.

—S. L. Morita

work. That particular metaphor leaves me and a whole lot of people out of the picture. Maybe you, too?

◎ There's a *yin/yang* model that looks like this: black and white, being opposites, form a circle with each other, and each half contains a portion of the other. That might be a real good metaphor for principles like "active" and "passive," but we still don't know what comprises "black" and what comprises "white" when it comes to *gender*.

◎ The idea of a *continuum* is currently coming into vogue among those who study gender, as well as with some transgender activists. This is a better metaphor, allowing as it does for a wide range of genders along a pole, with *man/male* on one end, and *woman/female* on the other. I don't like it for two reasons: the man/male part, and the woman/ female part. Seriously, why hold those two as fixed points by which we define ourselves, when we can't for sure say what the two fixed points are made up of?

◎ Several Native-American nations have described gender as a *circle,* and anyone can be anywhere on the circle of gender expression. That's about the closest I can agree with. It does away with any idea of a binary, but I still don't find it satisfying, because again there is no clearly defined marker on that circle against which I can measure myself.

These days, people are coming up with new, truly creative systems to describe or delineate gender. One such schematic can be found in the book *The Apartheid of Sex,* by Martine Rothblatt. Ze's come up with a fascinating and seductive way to determine gender, using a metaphor of colors. Rothblatt isolates what ze refers to as three basic elements of sexual identity (hir words), and assigns each of them a basic color. Hir three basic elements are: ". . . activeness (or aggression), passiveness (or nurturing), and eroticism (or sex drive)." The idea is that as each of the basic elements shift in proportion to the others, then the resulting color combination will change,

How about seeing gender as a Mobius strip? That's the "one-sided" piece of paper that has two sides. You make one by taking a strip of paper, putting one twist in it, and then making it into a circle. If you start to draw a line along it, you eventually end up right where you started!

—Terry Mason

providing a unique representation of that gender. A truly innovative theory. My opinion is that while Rothblatt's color wheel may in fact be an excellent way to construct our genders in a world that accepts hir three criteria as essential to gender (and why not? they are very loving criteria), we need something that illustrates the destructive construct of gender within the dominant culture (which seems to have more criteria than Rothblatt's three areas) more clearly, if for no other reason than that we might begin to dismantle it. *Then* we can look at the possibility of mindfully constructing a very beautiful gender system, using Rothblatt's model.

The gender-as-color model, while possibly something to aim for in the future, is missing an intermediary model, as it does not reflect the current world that's driven by binary thinking. Rothblatt's gentle vision does not express that which we need to first overcome: a world driven by greed, acquisition, and the very human need to belong to some exclusive (and excluding) group. I wanted to come up with a visual representation of gender *the way it is* in the world today, something beyond man/woman in a world that says there's no such thing as "beyond."

◎ Gender Is a Pacifier! Nah. Close, but No Cigar

I don't know if man or woman have ever been adequate ways to categorize people in such a way as to offer individuals the respect we each deserve. Certainly, the bipolar designation invisibilizes many unique qualities that people possess as individuals.

The bipolar gender system serves as a kind of safe harbor for most of us, and I'm definitely including myself in that, even though I don't personally identify as either a man or a woman, because I walk though this world *appearing* to be a woman for the most part. I *pass* as a woman. I can do that. And I do it because it allows me to rest for a moment. I use my passing times as moments when I don't have to fight the good fight against gender tyranny. It's a safe harbor from all the jeers and oppression that attend gender transgression. But I'm reminded of the text I read once on a rather smarmy Hallmark-type poster: "Ships are safe in harbor, but that's not what ships are built for."

I must admit that I'm sort of on the outside looking in. Being a white, heterosexual male puts me in a very comfortable position. Well, it used to. I am constantly amazed at the number of times I have been asked if I am gay, a cross-dresser, have ever done drag ... simply because I'm a fan of RuPaul.

My mother still isn't totally convinced that I'm straight. So, let it be known, while white hetero's aren't exactly Gender Outlaws, we do sometimes become Gender Outlaw Sidekicks.

—Travis Prebble

All right, then . . . how can we look at gender?

◎ Gender Is a Circle! No, no . . . It's a Square! No, no . . .

I like pretzels.

◎ That's It! Gender Is a Pretzel!

No, no . . . gender isn't a pretzel.

◎ It's Not?

Well, maybe gender *is* a pretzel, but that's not the model I want to use. I *really* like pretzels. I eat boxes of them, the real salty hard sourdough variety from Pennsylvania, if you ever wanna send me some. And I was eating pretzels one day, and I was reading the back of the box, and lo and behold, there was the US Food and Drug Administration's Basic Food Group Pyramid. It was a true *eureka* moment, let me tell you. Here's what their food group pyramid looks like:

See? The really good stuff is at the bottom: grains, complex (interesting word) carbohydrates, stuff we're supposed to eat a lot of, stuff that's good for us. Fruits and veggies come next on the pyramid; they're very important. So are dairy and meats, but less so. And at the very tippy-top, there are fats, oils, and sugars. Bad bad bad . . . a little goes a lonnnnnng way, and they're not all that good for you, right? Well, my *eureka* moment with that box of pretzels was simply that gender is like that pyramid.

Works like this. We're accustomed to defining gender by some sort of biological component, be that hormones or chromosomes or genitalia or reproductive ability. We've defined gender by biology. Okay, that's old. It's too simple for today's complex world. Some "forward thinkers" have said, ahhhhhh, but that's *sex*, and sex is biology, but gender is psychology. That sort of thinking still posits something (sex) that's biologically essential.

Right idea, wrong solution. Let's get off that merry-go-round once and for all.

———
This would be a very good time to do your Ten-Minute Gender Outlaw Exercise. Good for what ails ya.
———

Some theorists are now saying that sociological factors have a lot to do with gender, and I think this is closer to the mark. If gender is a social construct, which includes respectful nods to biology, physiology, and psychology, then let's develop a model of gender that *demonstrates* that system.

The hallmark of today's *two*-gender system is that the preferred gender, the privileged gender, the gender that goes home with all the cookies, is labeled male. In sociological terms, though, we need to be more specific. The easy thing would be to say "It's all men." But it's not, not if this pyramid image reproduces the way gender structures hierarchies in the world today.

Examining the food-group pyramid we've got this wide base at the bottom: grains and carbohydrates. We're supposed to eat a lot of these things, they form the basis of our healthy diet. They're good for us. Working up the food group pyramid, we require fewer and fewer of these foods in our diet, until we get to the very top: sugars and oils. Don't eat too much, they're not all that good for you. Okay, I'm going to do some metaphor stretching. What if the pyramid represented humanity as it's living in our Western or Western-influenced cultures today, and the height of the pyramid was a function of power? The higher up on this pyramid you are, the more power you have to do whatever it is you want to do, and the more access you have to things like wealth, care, protection from harm and wrongdoing. And what if the very topmost point on the pyramid represented some perfect identity, some perfect gender, that we've all been taught to be, be like, or be liked by. All of a sudden, this pyramid idea of gender makes sense, and we have the representation of a graduated gender system that reflects power and privilege as it exists in the world. If the breadth of the pyramid reflects quantity of people, the model also interestingly enough seems to reflect relative numbers of people *belonging* to the different levels of this graduated gender system. The higher up we go on the pyramid, the fewer people there are belonging to that preferred gender. The higher up we go, those fewer people have more and more power.

———
Please keep in mind: I don't think this is how gender can be. I just think that this pretty accurately describes gender the way it is.
———

⑥ **The Case for a Perfect Gender**

i am a queer woman of color. by the very nature of the term i break all gender constraints, because what we imagine to be gendered is never a woman of color. by the very virtue of being colored i break every rule that white feminists have created regarding gender, by being queer i break every rule that communities of color have created for a woman. so by the virtue of my being, of my existence, i am breaking every rule and convention of gender.

living without gender? hmmmm . . . well, i guess i'd like to one day, but it's really hard when everyone in the whole fucking world reminds you of it constantly and consistently, like even [your] questionnaire. it is impossible for a queer woman of color to live without gender in the same way as it is impossible for us to live outside of race. hope this adds some color to the approach.

—c. b.

This phenomenon of graduated perfection in gender is easy to spot; it gets back to the troublesome concept of "real men" and "real women." In terms of gender, there will be in any group of men some who are going to be more "real" as men than others. Similarly, in any group of women, some are going to be more "real" as women than others.

For example, when I was growing up, I was a boy. In any mixed crowd of girls and boys, I was one of the guys. But, and this is very important, when I was with a group of boys only, I wasn't a boy—I was a Jew. Because of our age, none of us were "men." We were all boys. Is "boy" another gender? I think so. And among those boys, was I less male simply because of my ethnicity, my religion? Yup, I was less male.

I would even go so far as to say Jewish men are a different gender than Christian men, and that's the way I see it, but *it's not a bad thing*! It's just a fact. It's how Jews are perceived within the larger culture, and so it has some cultural weight. No doubt, some people are going to think I'm saying that Jewish men are *lesser men* than Anglo-Americans. No, no, no. That's an old anti-Semitic argument that survives to this day, but it's not how I see it—and it's certainly not limited to Jewish men. Moving up or down on this pyramid representation of the gender system is a function of *power,* not a function of humanity. What I'm saying is that there's a *difference*; and that by some standard, not mine, Jews are *judged* by those differences to be *less*, as are Asians, African-Americans, Hispanics . . . the list goes on and on, and even includes *most* Anglos (when you get into areas of age, class, education, appearance, social polish, etc., etc., etc.).

I'm not saying that each of these categories necessarily considers *themselves* to be less. I'm taking the point of view from the top of the pyramid, right? From that point of view there's an attitude of perfection, and everyone else is less, or Other. Everyone else is less perfectly gendered. What I'm thinking is that different kinds of men might as well be tagged as different *genders*, different ways of expressing oneself within some sort of male range, none of which measures up to the cultural ideal: the perfect gender. Wanting to be *considered* a "real man" by impossible standards keeps most men in the position of *supporting* the impossible standards.

Since the perfect gender does seem to be defined in terms of the culturally accepted male range, then is there a "perfect woman" in this system? If so, it's not by any standard set by women themselves, as most cultures currently accept male-defined qualifications for women.

Your Gender Is HOW Long?

What makes me curious is why anyone *cares* what a real man is or isn't. Why is that so important? What is it about the classification "man," or the category "woman" for that matter, that makes us so enraged (and we *do* get enraged) when someone accuses us of not being a "real" one or the other? *Those* are some valuable questions to ask, and once they're finally raised, we can begin to topple the system that's been keeping us bound up in living most of our lives running around in some hamster wheel, failing to measure up.

Truthfully I would say that the only time I HAVE lived without gender is before the concept of it was absorbed into my own psyche. Given the verbal and non-verbal "talk" that is given by adults I would say this was probably before the age of one.

Gender to me is neither bad nor good. It is the assuming that just because one wears lip gloss or drives a Mack truck makes them predictable and placeable as higher or lower life forms that bugs the hell out of me.

—Jennifer Weinke

The Top of the Heap

I wanted to nail down this perfect gender, so that I'd know who or what it is I have to watch out for. Contrary to the laws of physics, I started building my gender pyramid at the top. I looked for the folks who have most of the power and wealth, the folks who claim to be the ideal, the *very* few people who can actually hold themselves up as REAL MEN in the world. More than that, I wanted to see if there was anyone who himself was not conflicted by that designation. Some guy who's got all the confidence in the world, and the power to back it up. I put him at the top of the pyramid because there *are* so few of him, and frankly, they're like the oils and sugar: take them in moderation. They have no nutritional value, they're not good for the culture. And we'll get to see exactly what they look like in just a bit. But first, let's see how *you* measure up to the idea of some perfect gender.

> EXERCISE: Draw your idea of a perfectly gendered person (yes, only one) in the left-hand box. Then, draw yourself in the right-hand box.

This isn't a test of your artistic abilities. You're doing it for yourself and it'll be just fine however you do it. I promise.

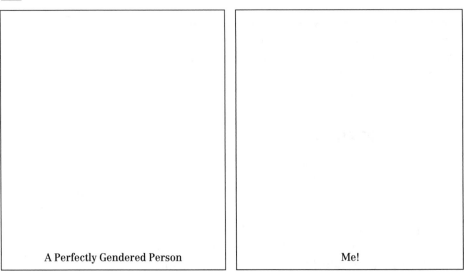

| A Perfectly Gendered Person | Me! |

There! You did it! Okay, now keep this image in mind as we look a little bit deeper into gender perfection. You'll have a few more cracks at this exercise later in the book.

◎ The Gender/Identity/Power System

We're starting to define "gender" as a hierarchical dynamic masquerading behind and playing itself out through each of only two socially privileged monogendered identities. The power of this kind of gender perfection would be in direct proportion to the power granted those who can stake legitimate claims to those identities. The power is derived from the very invisibility of the gender/identity hierarchy. This makes gender, identity, and power each functions of each other, inextricably woven into the web of our culture beneath an attractive tapestry called the bipolar gender system.

::panting::

Thanks. I needed that. My need for the occassional theoryspeak is something akin to my need for the occassional Whopper Junior and fries.

So what does the dude at the top of this pyramid look like? Remember, the height of the pyramid measures the amount of power a person wields in the world, and the breadth of the pyramid measures the number of people who wield that much power. I'm thinking the guy at the top looks like this:

- white
- citizen of the USA
- Protestant-defined Christian
- middle-aged
- middle- to upper-class
- heterosexual
- monogamous, monofidelitous
- able-bodied
- tall, trim, and reasonably muscled
- attractive, according to cultural standards
- right-handed
- well-educated
- well-mannered
- professional or executive level
- politically conservative
- capitalist
- self-defining and self-measuring
- physically healthy, with access to health care
- in possession of all rights available under the law
- free and safe access to all private and public areas as allowed by the law
- property-owning
- binary-oriented
- logical (linear thinking)
- uses power over others
- possessing a well-formed, above-average-length penis, a pair of reasonably matched testicles, and at least an average sperm count
- parent of more of the same

The reason I chose these categories out of the many possible is that each of these factors contributes to the amount of power a person currently wields in the world. If the gender/identity/power pyramid is to work as a metaphor, than each of these factors must truly be a measurement of not only how much power a person wields, but also how much of a real man or a real woman that person might be; how close to being the perfect gender that person is. Assuming the characteristics above are somewhat complete, the gender/identity/power pyramid might look something like the one on the following page.

The Gender/Identity/Power Pryamid

Can you spot someone like yourself in this picture?
Can you spot your neighbor?
Can you spot someone you're afraid of?
Can you spot your friends?
Can you spot someone who's got more than you?
Can you spot someone you'd like to be?
Can you spot someone who you wish would like you?
Can you spot yourself in more than one place?

Each of these components or qualifications can, of course, be further qualified. In any group of people who meet these criteria, there will always be someone who is taller, more educated, has more or "better" sons, and is healthier, etc., etc., etc. . . . so the pyramid reaches its point with *some* hypothetical person at the very top who's "better" (more culturally valuable, has more power) than everyone else. Conversely, as the qualities defining this perfect, unnamed gender identity drop away from an individual, that individual's gender identity shifts itself downward to the bottom of the pyramid where there are more and more people with less and less power.

It stuns me that most everything in the culture forwards this ideal gender identity and its exclusivity. Nearly everything in the culture pushes us to:

- ◉ *be* some perfect gender (impossible for most of us)
- ◉ be *like* that gender (possible for a very few people)
- ◉ or be *liked by* that gender (possible to many, but not all people)

What's more, the further removed we are from the qualities expressed by the top of the pyramid, the less and less our gender is perceived as *real*. For example, if our genitals are in any way anomalous to the prescribed genitals for our gender, that obviously makes us unreal men or women, right? Similarly, if we're in our late teens or early twenties, we're told we're not-quite-men and not-quite-women; we're told we'll grow into that.

No, I'm not going to try to name it beyond referring to it as the Perfect Gender. I'm sure by reason of my own cultural indoctrination that I've left out some of its defining qualities, maybe important ones. But you can give it a name if you want to, all the while listening to the names that others have given it.

◉ The Case for a Perfect Identity?

I'm toying with the idea of putting the gender/identity/power pyramid into three dimensions, calling it simply an identity/power pyramid. It's tempting to call the top of this pyramid, the very tip-top, the Perfect Identity. Looking down from the top, from the viewpoint of this perfectly identified individual, each side of the pyramid can be defined by some aspect of classification *by the standards of the top's own claimed perfection*. That is, how do the folks at the very top see the rest of us, and does the very top of the pyramid reflect a possible common source of oppression for many if not most oppressed groups?

For example, the two-dimensional side we've been looking at is gender. Another side *could* be race. Another side *could* be age, or class, or religious beliefs. There are so many ways to classify people, but the top of this pyramid just might remain the same: the Perfect Identity. At the top we'd have the Perfect Gender *and* the Perfect Race *and* the Perfect Class. So, the culturally agreed-upon standards of perfection just might all converge into one identity that's got the bulk of the power in the world, and *that* identity relies on its granted perfection from each of the classifications that support it.

The posited "perfect identity," this powerful oppressive force made up of the composite perfections of all systems of classifications, has a lot of names today. Feminists call it MAN. Jews have called it GENTILE. African-American activists call it WHITE. Bisexuals, lesbians, and gays call it STRAIGHT. Transgendered folks are beginning to call it GENDERED. In this binary-slanted world, we keep naming our oppressor (some person or group who has more power than us and is using that power to withhold access, resources, or wealth) in terms of some convenient opposite. On the other side of the fence, we have a tendency to call *our* gender or identity the "good" gender or the "good" identity. "Transgendered is better than traditionally gendered because blah blah blah."

We have to knock that off, all of that good-and-bad way of thinking. It's a tactic of the privileged to name others by using themselves as a yardstick. We need to realize that no single attribute gives a person enough power to oppress us. No *single* quality of identity resulting in a privileged status gives a person enough power to keep the rest of us in thrall.

Just something to think about, that's all. Try it out for yourself. See what it's like to devise other faces to this pyramid, call them race, age, class, whatever . . . see if it holds up for you.

But for now, let's get back to gender, shall we?

⑥ The Moment of Truth, The Big Exam: Are <u>You</u> Perfectly Gendered?

Test instructions: This may not be a fun test, unlike the last one. The last little quiz determined your aptitude for playing with gender; it was about your potential. This one is going to take a look at how you stack up in terms of gender perfection right now in your life. This isn't a fair test. I wanna get that out in the open from the start. But it's written in the same way that we're tested every day of our lives in this culture, so if it's not fair, it's an accurate measure of where we stand in the world, and that's the purpose of this test. The good news is that it will be a pretty fair measure of where you stand gender-wise in terms of being a real man or a real woman.

———

If parts of the test make you angry, sad, lonely, or whatever, it might be helpful to make some notes about that: Where exactly did you start feeling like that? What question brought stuff up? Was there ever something in your life experience that brought up the same or similar feelings? Part of the emphasis of this workbook is to find the places that are scary, the places that are shameful. I think that's an important step in making this gender exploration more safe. I promise there's stuff later in the book where we examine exactly what is frightening you, angering you, or shaming you, okay? For now, it's time to be really honest.

———

Just check the answer that's *most* accurate, okay? Okay, here we go.

Part One: Your Birthright

A. Penises

1. Were you born with and do you still have a penis?
- ❒ a. Yes, with a matching set of testicles, thank you
- ❒ b. Yes, but I was also born with a vulva and a vagina
- ❒ c. No *or* No, but I grew one later

    (NOTE: If c, skip to Section B, "Other Genitals.")

2. Is your penis
- ❒ a. Five to eight inches long?
- ❒ b. Longer than eight inches?
- ❒ c. Shorter than five inches?

3. Do you and others think your penis is attractive and well-formed?
- ❒ a. Yes
- ❒ b. Most of the time, yes
- ❒ c. No

B. Other Genitals

4. Were you born with and do you still have a vulva, vagina, and clitoris?
- ❒ a. No
- ❒ b. Yes, but that's not all
- ❒ c. Yes

5. Do you or others think your vulva, vagina, and clitoris are attractive and well-formed?

❏ a. Yes

❏ b. No one's complained yet

❏ c. No

C. The Rest of Your Body

6. *Could your race be described as white or Caucasian?*

❏ a. Yes

❏ b. No, but people think that's what I am

❏ c. No

7. *What's your age?*

❏ a. 35-55 years old

❏ b. 25-34 years old

❏ c. Other

8. *Others would describe you as*

❏ a. Fit and trim

❏ b. In pretty good shape for your age

❏ c. Fat, skinny, or otherwise out of shape

9. *Are you free of any chronic or congenital diseases?*

❏ a. Yes

❏ b. I don't know, *or* I'm not sure

❏ c. No

10. *Do you have, or have you ever had a sexually transmitted disease?*

❏ a. No

❏ b. I don't know, *or* I'm not sure.

❏ c. Yes.

11. *Is there some disease that by reason of family history, you're susceptible to contracting at some point in the future?*

❏ a. No

❏ b. I don't know, *or* I'm not sure

❏ c. Yes

12. *Do you have what might be considered a mental disorder?*

❏ a. No

❏ b. Possibly, I don't know

❏ c. Yes

13. *Are you under professional care for, or currently taking medication for some mental or emotional problem?*

❏ a. No

❏ b. No, but I used to be

❏ c. Yes

14. *Are your hormone levels balanced according to the current medical standards for the gender you were assigned at birth?*

❐ a. Yes

❐ b. I don't know

❐ c. No

15. *Are your "gender" chromosomes either XX if you were assigned*
    female at birth, or XY if you were assigned male?

    ❐ a. Yes

    ❐ b. I don't know

    ❐ c. No

16. *Is your body capable of reproduction, according to the gender you*
    were assigned at birth? (high healthy sperm count or good quantity of
    healthy eggs)

    ❐ a. Yes

    ❐ b. I don't know or I'm not sure

    ❐ c. No

17. *Is your corpus collosum the proper shape for the gender you were*
    assigned at birth? (tubular for male, bulbous for female)

    ❐ a. Yes

    ❐ b. I haven't the foggiest idea. What's a *corpus collosum*?

    ❐ c. No

18. *You are:*

    ❐ a. Right-handed

    ❐ b. Ambidextrous

    ❐ c. Left-handed

19. *Would you be considered "differently abled" than many people, either*
    by reason of your senses or the shape or configuration of your body?

    ❐ a. No

    ❐ b. Yes, but people might not know at first

    ❐ c. Yes

D. Interactions

20. *Do others sometimes take you for a gender other than that which you*
    were assigned at birth?

    ❐ a. No, never

    ❐ b. Sometimes, but not frequently

    ❐ c. Yes, frequently

21. *Do others sometimes take you for a gender other than that which you*
    wish to present?

    ❐ a. No, never

    ❐ b. Sometimes, but not frequently

    ❐ c. Yes, frequently

22. *You are considered by others to be*

❏ a. Handsome

❏ b. Beautiful

❏ c. Plain, average, or unattractive

23. *Others would describe you as*

❏ a. Having an ideal height

❏ b. Having an average height

❏ c. Too short or too tall

24. *Do you dress with some awareness for your safety?*

❏ a. No

❏ b. Depends on where I'm going

❏ c. Yes

25. *Do you dress with some awareness of compensating for some flaw in your appearance?*

❏ a. No, never

❏ b. Sometimes

❏ c. Yes, frequently

26. *Do you generally feel safe walking alone on the streets of a city?*

❏ a. Yes

❏ b. It depends on the neighborhood and time of day

❏ c. No

27. *Your class status could best be described as*

❏ a. Middle or upper class

❏ b. Working class

❏ c. Other

28. *Do you agree with the gender you were legally assigned at birth?*

❏ a. Yes

❏ b. Sometimes

❏ c. No

29. *Have you ever been hospitalized against your will for some mental disorder?*

❏ a. No

❏ b. I almost was, *or* I should have been but I wasn't

❏ c. Yes

30. *Have you ever been arrested or convicted?*

❏ a. No

❏ b. I almost was, *or* I should have been but I wasn't

❏ c. Yes

31. *Have you broken some law for which you could now be arrested or convicted?*

❏ a. No

❐ b. There's no way I could be caught, *or* the statute of limitations is up

❐ c. Yes

32. Is there some situation you know of where your fundamental human rights are not protected by the law?

❐ a. No

❐ b. Maybe, I don't know

❐ c. Yes

33. Were your birth parents legally married to each other at the time you were conceived?

❐ a. Yes

❐ b. I don't know

❐ c. No

34. You were raised by

❐ a. Both your birth parents

❐ b. One of your birth parents

❐ c. Others

35. In what religious belief were you raised?

❐ a. Protestant-defined Christian

❐ b. Other Christian

❐ c. Other

36. You or others would describe your political views most nearly as

❐ a. Conservative

❐ b. Liberal

❐ c. Radical

Part Two: Getting As Close As You Can

A. Membership

37. Are you a member of, or do you support some civil rights organization or movement?

❐ a. No

❐ b. Not actively, but I believe in their rights

❐ c. Yes

38. Have you ever converted to a Protestant-defined Christianity?

❐ a. No, that's where I started

❐ b. Yes

❐ c. No

39. Are you now or have you ever been a member of what might be called a cult?

❐ a. No

❐ b. No, but I've thought about joining one.

❐ c. Yes

40. *Are you currently active in any religious group or organization, other than Protestant-defined Christianity?*

❐ a. No

❐ b. Occasionally

❐ c. Yes

41. *Have you ever had and worked hard to get rid of some regional accent or dialect?*

❐ a. I never had one to start with

❐ b. Yes, I had one but not any longer

❐ c. Yes, I had one and I still do

42. *Do you make conscious decisions to dress correctly (and differently) for different parts of your life, rather than for the fun of it?*

❐ a. Yes, but it requires very little thought

❐ b. Yes, I've got wardrobes worked out for different things I do

❐ c. I can do that, but mostly I dress for the fun of it

43. *Do you sometimes either wish for or actively seek membership in some group that's defined by some identity you're not usually acknowledged as having?*

❐ a. No, I belong to the groups I need to belong to

❐ b. Yes

❐ c. There *are* groups like that, but I don't want to belong to them

44. *Do you pass up buying or wearing something you might like because others you want to be liked by might not approve?*

❐ a. I would pass things up, but not because of any individual's disapproval, rather because it simply wouldn't be proper

❐ b. Yes, frequently

❐ c. Not really

B. Relationships

45. *Are you a birth parent of one or more sons?*

❐ a. Yes

❐ b. No, but I'm adoptive, foster, or stepparent to a son or sons

❐ c. No

46. *Are there people toward whom you definitely feel superior?*

❐ a. Yes

❐ b. Only the bad ones

❐ c. No

47. *If you chose to marry your lover, could you do so legally?*

❐ a. Yes

❏ b. Depends on which lover

❏ c. No

48. *For who and what you are, do others consider you generally to be "within your place or station" in the culture?*

❏ a. Yes

❏ b. I try

❏ c. No

49. *Are there some people you don't wish to associate with, primarily because of how it might make you look?*

❏ a. Yes, and I don't associate with them

❏ b. Yes, but I associate with them anyway

❏ c. No

50. *Do you feel less important than members of some groups of people?*

❏ a. No

❏ b. Yes, but rarely

❏ c. Yes

51. *Others would describe your sexuality as*

❏ a. Heterosexual

❏ b. Lesbian or Gay

❏ c. Bisexual, Pansexual, Omnisexual, Sex Worker, S/M player or other

52. *Others would describe the general nature of your relationship(s) as*

❏ a. Monogamous, faithful

❏ b. Monogamous, unfaithful

❏ c. Non-monogamous, polyamorous, or other

C. Ideas

53. *Which of these statements about power most nearly matches your own point of view?*

❏ a. Power should be wielded solely by the responsible

❏ b. Power, in the wrong hands, is dangerous

❏ c. Power should be shared on a consensual basis

54. *Which of these statements would you* most *agree with?*

❏ a. There are two kinds of people in the world: those who agree with that statement, and those who don't

❏ b. There are two kinds of people in the world: and depending on the day of the week, I'm one or the other

❏ c. There are as many kinds of people in the world as there are people

55. *With which of these statements can you most fully agree?*

❏ a. I have an essential identity by which I can easily measure the identities of others

❏ b. I measure myself against the essential identities of others

❏ c. My identity is not essential to me

Part Three: Sense of Self

56. *Do you find yourself interrupting others' conversation for one of these reasons?*

   ❏ a. I only interrupt another when the other person isn't making sense or is saying something less important than what I have to say

   ❏ b. Whenever I do, I feel I'm being impolite or pushy

   ❏ c. I try not to interrupt another unless interrupting is part of the social or cultural convention for that group

57. *When you find a seat in a movie theater, are you concerned that you might be blocking someone else's view of the screen? (perhaps a child's or someone else shorter than you?)*

   ❏ a. No, the theater is a public space

   ❏ b. I never really thought about that

   ❏ c. Yes, and I sit somewhere else if I can

58. *When someone sits in front of you in a movie theater and blocks your view even though there are plenty of other seats available, you*

   ❏ a. Take it personally, and get upset

   ❏ b. Get annoyed and don't say anything

   ❏ c. Ask them to move or slide down and if they don't, then you move

59. *When there's a long line to get into some event, you*

   ❏ a. Figure out the best way to get to the front of the line ahead of the others and do it

   ❏ b. Get annoyed because the people in front of you shouldn't be in front of you

   ❏ c. Wait your turn in line

60. *When a clerk or agent overlooks the person in front of you in line and serves you first, you*

   ❏ a. Proceed with your transaction, gratefully

   ❏ b. Feel guilty and proceed with your transaction

   ❏ c. Allow the person who was in front of you to be served first

61. *When you're introduced on a first-name basis to someone for the first time, you*

   ❏ a. Shorten their first name to a nickname, and use that

   ❏ b. Use their name the way you were introduced

   ❏ c. Get around to asking the person how they like to be addressed

62. *Is there some particular group of people that you don't belong to, about whom you enjoy telling jokes or listening to jokes about them? (e.g., blondes, Pollacks, men, Irish, etc.)*
    ❐ a. Yes
    ❐ b. I listen and sometimes I laugh, but I rarely if ever tell those jokes
    ❐ c. No

63. *Is there some group of people you believe are better suited to do work you find unpleasant to do yourself?*
    ❐ a. Yes
    ❐ b. Yes, but I do the work anyway
    ❐ c. No

64. *When someone who you think does not have a similar identity to you tries to claim the identity you have, you would probably*
    ❐ a. Simply refuse their claim
    ❐ b. Try to find out why they think they have that claim
    ❐ c. Try to find out why they think they have that claim, and why you thought they shouldn't

65. *Do you think you take up too much physical space in the way you sit, walk, stand, or speak?*
    ❐ a. I never really thought about that, *or* People have told me that, but I don't understand it
    ❐ b. Sometimes I consciously or unconsciously take up less space
    ❐ c. I try to take up as much space as I need, not more, not less

66. *Do you believe there is some group of people who deserve their bad fortune and/or mistreatment?*
    ❐ a. Yes
    ❐ b. Yes, but I'm trying to see their side of things
    ❐ c. No

67. *When someone from an under-represented group to which you don't belong accuses you of discrimination, you usually*
    ❐ a. Feel you're a victim of reverse discrimination
    ❐ b. Feel sorry for them
    ❐ c. Listen to them, and if they're right you work to avoid repeating that kind of behavior

68. *Without having met someone personally, are there ways you know you're better than someone, just by the way they look or dress or behave?*
    ❐ a. Yes
    ❐ b. Yes, and I try to act compassionately
    ❐ c. No

69. *Is there something you own that makes you feel better or more important than someone else?*
    ❏ a. Yes
    ❏ b. Yes, but I don't let that affect how I deal with that person
    ❏ c. No

70. *If you were told you weren't allowed in some space set aside for an under-represented group to which you don't belong, you would most likely*
    ❏ a. Ignore that and go in anyway
    ❏ b. Feel hurt or angry, and complain to others about it
    ❏ c. Work to understand the need for their exclusion of you, and honor that

71. *If you were to hear that some group is complaining that they aren't properly represented in some field or organization in which you are represented, you would probably*
    ❏ a. Dismiss the claim on the grounds that they're not working hard enough to be included or tell them you will take their best interests into account anyway.
    ❏ b. Agree with them that they should do something to become represented *and/or* tell them to form their own group
    ❏ c. Work with them to ensure equal representation within your group

72. *Do you commonly refer to some other people in terms of their not being something you are? (e.g., nonwhites, lower classes, transgendered, non-transgendered, or disabled)*
    ❏ a. Yes
    ❏ b. Yes, but when I do, I don't mean that I'm better
    ❏ c. No

73. *Are there any questions on medical, membership, or government forms or applications that leave you out?*
    ❏ a. No
    ❏ b. No, but I can see where there are some questions that might leave out others
    ❏ c. Yes

74. *If you hear that some group is trying to get a new word or words into the language by which they might identify themselves, you might*
    ❏ a. Feel they're being nit-picky and then refuse to use the new word
    ❏ b. Use that word to their face, and the old words for everyone else
    ❏ c. Adopt the word and use it

75. *If you hear that some under-represented group to which you don't belong is legislating for laws that would name them specifically in laws that already exist, you would most likely*

❏ a. Fight them on the grounds that they want special rights

❏ b. Assure them that the law could be interpreted to include them

❏ c. Do what you can to support them

76. *Did you grow up believing that you were entitled to a certain good standard of living, or that a good standard of living was within your grasp if only you worked for it?*

❏ a. Yes, and it's true

❏ b. Yes, but I think the world has changed since then

❏ c. No

77. *Do you sometimes find you mistake a person for another person because it's difficult to tell those kinds of people apart? (e.g., another race, age, body type, person in a wheelchair, etc.)*

❏ a. Yes

❏ b. Yes, but I really don't meet enough of those kind of people to tell the difference

❏ c. Not usually, but if I do, I work to find out where I'm not looking

78. *When you meet someone on the phone, in a letter, or online, do you assume they're the same race or class or age or other aspect of identity as you?*

❏ a. Yes

❏ b. Yes, and I'm embarrassed if I find out it's otherwise

❏ c. No

79. *Do you regularly credit, by name, the ideas, beliefs, or opinions of others?*

❏ a. No, there's really no need to

❏ b. Sometimes, but I believe we all have or can have the same ideas anyway

❏ c. Yes, whenever I can

80. *Do you sometimes adopt the dress or mannerisms or craft of an under-represented group to which you do not belong without acknowledging its origin?*

❏ a. Yes, because I don't believe anyone has any special rights to those sort of things

❏ b. Yes, but I think that's part of our melting-pot culture

❏ c. I try not to

Part Four: Bonus Points

(check all that apply to you)

❏ 81. Blond

❏ 82. Blue eyes

☐ 83. Manager or executive

☐ 84. Annual income over $35K

☐ 85. Annual income over $50K

☐ 86. Annual income over $100K

☐ 87. Own a car

☐ 88. Own your own business

☐ 89. Proud of your parents

☐ 90. Parents are proud of you

☐ 91. Proud of your children

☐ 92. Children are proud of you

☐ 93. Have your own Net account

☐ 94. Have Net access without a commercial service

☐ 95. Have all your hair and don't color it

☐ 96. Don't need glasses or contact lenses

☐ 97. Play some sport (men only)

☐ 98. Have received some honor or medal as an adult

☐ 99. Have an excellent credit rating

☐ 100. Never questioned your own gender before reading this book

◉ Okay! Let's Score!

Congratulations on the work you did in answering these questions. Assuming you were really honest, you'll be able to see how closely you match up to the Perfect Gender.

Penises

◉ In this world, the Perfect Gender is first defined by a penis and matching testicles. In fact, if you didn't check 1A on this section, you simply are not in the running. So, here's how you can score this section:

1.a. 250 points

1.b. 5 points

1.c. 0 points

◉ For the remainder of this section, give yourself

10 points for every A answer

5 points for every B answer

2 points for every C answer

◉ Maximum points this section: 270

Total Points This Section _____

Other Genitals

⊚ Genitalia other than penises simply don't give you much of a leg up on the ladder to Perfect Genderhood. Sorry, that's just the way it is.

⊚ For this section, give yourself

2 points for every A answer

5 points for every B answer

10 points for every C answer

⊚ Maximum points this section: 20

Total Points This Section _____

The Rest of Your Body

⊚ Your race, age, state of health, and how you measure up to the posited gender norm, are each important factors in determining just how perfectly gendered you are you are.

⊚ For this section, give yourself

10 points for every A answer

5 points for every B answer

2 points for every C answer

⊚ Maximum points this section: 140

Total Points This Section _____

Interactions

⊚ How we're perceived, and what freedom we have to move around in the world also contribute highly to the perfection of our genders.

⊚ For this section, give yourself

10 points for every A answer

5 points for every B answer

2 points for every C answer

⊚ Maximum points this section: 170

Total Points This Section _____

Membership

⊚ While formal or informal membership in some organization isn't as important as your body or your birthright, it does give some indication of how well you pass in the world, so it's worth some points.

⊚ For this section, give yourself

5 points for every A answer

2 points for every B answer

1 points for every C answer

◎ Maximum points this section: 40

Total Points This Section _____

Relationships

◎ How we structure our relationships is a factor in how we're perceived, and so you're going to get more points for this section.

◎ For this section, give yourself

7 points for every A answer

4 points for every B answer

2 points for every C answer

◎ Maximum points this section: 56

Total Points This Section _____

Ideas

◎ The directions in which we think will eventually lead to how we live our lives, and to what degree or aspect of perfection we wish to attain.

◎ For this section, give yourself

20 points for every A answer

10 points for every B answer

5 points for every C answer

◎ Maximum points this section: 60

Total Points This Section _____

Sense of Self

◎ An important indicator of those with a Perfect or near-Perfect Gender is a sense of entitlement. Race, age, physiology, education, and many other factors may contribute to this sense. If we feel *entitled,* that's a pretty good indicator we're nearly Perfect in some regard.

◎ For this section, give yourself

15 points for every A answer

10 points for every B answer

5 points for every C answer

◎ Maximum points this section: 300

Total Points This Section _____

Bonus Points

⊚ This is all whim. Or it's not. This section is totally unfair. Give yourself 10 points for every category you were able to check off. In fact, if you can think of some *more* reasons that you might be better, more perfect, more privileged, or in any way more powerful or higher up than other people, go ahead and give yourself 10 points for every reason you can come up with. If you can't think of any other ways you might be better or better off than others, go ask some friends of yours. Remember, it's 10 points for each way you come up with! Cool, huh?

⊚ Maximum points this section: 200 or 300 or *more*!

Total Points This Section _____

TOTAL SCORE _____

⊚ Ratings

1500 + Cool, doode! You are PERFECT! Well, almost. Since you took this test, you must have some doubts, so you're ALMOST perfect. Very cool, though. Very. A question, though: Why in the *world* are you reading this book???

1200-1499 You're definitely up there in the top, say third, of the gender pyramid. Almost everyone loves you and wants to be near you. Well, everyone who *counts,* that is. You can easily pass for being a real man or a real woman. Odds are you probably don't get all the respect you want, right? And sometimes you feel guilty for the respect you *do* get. Here's the deal: you'll never make it to the top, and you've got a lot of privilege to scrape off if you ever hope to make it to the bottom. It's up to you.

1050-1199 You're considered very important in the circles in which you travel. While others might question your occasional eccentricity, it's doubtful they would question your gender identity as a real man or a real woman. If the world was a banquet, you'd be the meat and potatoes. You're working hard at being accepted, and it probably shows. If you play your cards right, you can probably move up a notch or two on the social ladder, which in turn would help you move up your job ladder.

750-1049 You know your place and pretty much stick to it. People tend to appreciate you like they'd appreciate a loyal dog, right? Don't count on others being too surprised when you start playing with your gender. Don't count on too much support, either. The good news is that without much work, you could very easily nose-dive into real outlaw status.

550-749 Um, you don't get invited to a lot of ritzy places, do you? Look, if you're going to be Perfect, you've got a lot of work to do. Probably too much work to bother with, you're so far away from Perfect. On the plus side of things, there's that old line from the Kris Kristofferson song made popular by Janis Joplin: "Freedom's just another word for nothing left to lose." You're pretty close to that, aren't you?

0-549 Heh, heh. You're weird. You *know* you are, so why'd you take the test? Oh, I know: you take pride in what the culture persists in calling your flaws and imperfections, no? My kind of outlaw!

Okay, so the scores are totally arbitrary. Right. So's the rest of the culture. So are the ideas of real men and real women. So's gender in general. So there.

◎ It's Just a Metaphor

The moon is female.
The sun is male.
Ah, darlings,
we must be the *stars*!

—Emily Lloyd

The benefit of any agreed-upon metaphor is that it gives people a framework around which to develop theories and question concepts. A good metaphor for a good metaphor might be a coatrack on which we get to hang our favorite ideas. The *danger* of an agreed-upon metaphor, including this pyramid model of the gender/identity/power system, is that it might inhibit the development of newer, more inclusive metaphors.

So while I think there are a lot of ways you *could* break the remainder of the pyramid into little components (like the top half of the pyramid is all the people with penises, and the top part of *that* is all the people who are white *and* have penises), I don't think that's the point. The point is that as soon as we fall away to any degree from the established, privileged norms, we start to become a less-than-perfect gender; our anxiety to attain that perfection and its attendant power increases as we continue to find ourselves short in any of its defining categories.

⊚ Is It Possible to Shift Power or Identity without Shifting Gender?

Our genders are comprised of identifiable qualities that shift in importance and intrinsic power depending on the values we and others place upon those factors. That being the case, we need to come to terms with the fact that the identities by which we name ourselves are also susceptible to constant shifting. We think we're one thing, then we move to another town and we're seen as something else entirely. Or maybe we find a lover, only to discover that our identity has shifted from single to coupled. Or maybe a loved one gets very sick, and our primary identity shifts from lover to caretaker.

Just look at all the things we've been in our lives: child, adolescent, employee, student, healthy, sick . . . the list goes on and on, and with each shift in even an identity we'd normally take for granted, our genders shift imperceptibly. Over a lifetime, those changes can add up, and we suddenly find ourselves in the position of being someone we never intended to be.

Some of my own former identities include boy, young man, guy, middle-aged man, marketing director, Scientologist, husband, sailor. I'm making a list of all the things I used to be. I'm combing those identities for things I liked, and I'm trying them back on for size. How about you? If you're questioning your gender, or even if you'd simply like to know more about the gender you've got right now and are quite happy with, mightn't it be a good idea to examine what you've *been,* so that you can pick and choose some qualities you threw out with the bathwater once you left that identity behind?

> "My Androgynous Summer" was the summer two years ago when I transitioned. I wasn't ready to go full out, so I just let the wind take me where ever. I took the nickname Kat and made an effort not to give store clerks any clues when they used gender references. Part of what made it work was simply not caring—and a certain part of me which enjoyed watching people trip over their pronouns and contradict one another.
>
> But I think a person has to be ready to live without an identity for a while. People can't relate to you like that, and you become an object or oddity to be looked at.
>
> —Katherine Turner

EXERCISE: Make a list of the different things you've been, *and no longer consider yourself to be.* Alongside each former identity, list out some things you liked about it, and some things you didn't like at all.

◎ Would You Sell Your Genitals for a Million Dollars?

Still attached to your genitals despite all this great theory? Fond of those puppies? Let's have a look at why that might be the case.

I'm not knocking a fondness of one's own genitals, or a fondness for anyone else's for that matter. I'm simply wondering why we have insisted for so long that biology and physiology comprise the entirety of gender? Why, even now, when gender can be a wide-open field, do we dignify biology and raise it above any other criteria by referring to biological gender as "sex?" Why did we stop there and rest for so long before we're finally questioning that?

> If I had been born female physiologically I would be happy in that identity and would probably have never had all the stress that goes with gender conflict. If I could stand at the threshold of conception and direct a sperm bearing an X-chromosome toward the ovum, I would. But I was born stressed instead. That's what chose me.
>
> —Mona

I think the answers to those questions have a lot to do with knowing how dangerous (to ourselves and to the culture we've created) it would be to question gender. I think it's also partly because we haven't wanted to admit how truly fragmented we've become as a species, how disconnected and different we've become from one another. By positing some large class to which most of us belong (MALE or FEMALE, MAN or WOMAN, GIRL or BOY), most of us can belong to one or another. So, we have the *illusion* of membership despite the fragility of the defining lines of the group to which we belong, despite the conflicting definitions: at least it's *something*. It's safe. And if we make something more or less concrete, like genitals, the sole qualifier for some identity, it's predictable that most of us will fall into *some* identity category to which we *belong*.

And what is it we're claiming to belong *to* by reason of these genitals of ours? A gender! Why is that so important? And what happens when we question or play with that identity?

Let's Take a Look beneath Your Genitals

People talk about gender-bending these days. It rolls trippingly off the tongue in casual conversation; it's no longer confined to the talk shows or tabloids. But gender-bending isn't simply a matter of genitals, and gender itself isn't the only identity one can bend. Gender-bending is only one way to bend identity; it's currently an extreme way, but it's not the only way.

Gender, like sexuality, just happens to be an identity that nearly everyone in most cultures is forbidden to play with; and with the recent developments in medical technology over the past fifty or so years, genital manipulation has come to be considered an extreme way of bending gender; but it's not the only way, not by a long shot.

Genitalia as Membership Card

In our age of identity politics, it takes a lot of courage to bend or question *any* identity. Those acts nearly always result in our being cast out from some group. If we understand identity as the sole qualification for membership in a group, then the equation goes like this: I am an identity, so I belong to a group of people who have only the same identity.

> If I identified as a lesbian, I was welcome [in a Lesbian Avengers meeting]. When I sometimes jokingly identified as just your average straight white guy with a cunt, heads started to turn and folks started to get anxious. I had not changed, but my cultural identity had, simply by saying aloud the words "I am . . . " Instant sex-change. Gender not only as performance, but as performativity.
>
> —Riki Wilchins

A group member who abandons the group-sanctioned identity for any reason can raise questions within the group about the *value* of their chosen identity; and that can result in the group labeling the playful or questioning one as outcast.

It's all a matter of degree.

A Simple Scale of Cultural Rejection

- If we *question* gender, we might be considered eccentric.
- If we play with our gender presentation, we might provoke hostility.
- If we cross the sacred line of the biological imperative and alter ::gasp:: our genitals, we are in effect banished from the culture, unless we hide very well indeed.

How does this scale relate to the broader concept of identity? Very nearly one to one.

- If we simply *question* a basic identity, we might be considered eccentric.
- If we play with our presentation of some basic identity, we might provoke hostility.
- If we cross the sacred line of the bottom-line qualifier for some basic identity, we are in effect banished from the culture, unless we hide very well indeed.

EXERCISE: Take this book and read a section or two on public transportation, or in some public place. No, I don't think it would be a good idea to read aloud, but do be very obvious about *what* you're reading. Let lots of people see the title of the book. Note their responses to you.

It's Lonely at the Bottom (and it's still worth it!)

I live in Moscow. Gender roles are more distinct here than in most parts of the United States. In the metro, for example, men are supposed to let women out first, if possible. Women, for their part, are supposed to be as close to the door as possible, so the men don't have to stand back and wait for them to get out once the train pulls in to the station.

I am currently semi-passable in my cross gender. Some days I'll find my path to the door blocked by a wall of women. Other days a path will open through a sea of men and I find myself being swept forward to the door. And some days, for whatever reason, both things happen at the same time.

On the days when I am pushed the right way, I am happy. On the days when I am pushed the wrong way, I am frustrated. On the days when I am pushed in both directions at once, I feel like I am breaking the rules.

—Laura Franks

Outcast, Unclean, Outlaw . . . all terms for one identity not too many people want, especially if there's no nearby group of similar outcasts in which we might claim membership. For me, it boils down to loneliness, and that gets back to an even more basic drive: connection with others. Doing any kind of gender play can result in some degree of outcast status. It can result in a pretty horrible loneliness, and part of preparing for playing with or even simply questioning gender is to prepare oneself to deal with that loneliness.

No, I don't know how to prepare anyone to deal with loneliness. The best I can do right now is let you know it's going to happen. I think dealing with loneliness, coming to terms with it, and ultimately embracing alone-ness is a journey we all need to make on our own.

I'm learning the old difference between lonely and alone.

Lonely, for me, means I want to belong to some crowd, and I don't belong. *Alone,* on the other hand, is the same sense of apartness, but without the overwhelming desire to *belong.*

Feeling lonely is a signpost to myself that I'm coming unstuck, usually unwillingly, from some fixed or unnatural identity.

Feeling alone is a signpost to myself that I'm coming to a point of self-acceptance and integrity.

Alone is the way I try to experience life. But there's always a tug: I've always wanted to be included. I've always been tempted to settle myself into one identity and say to the group, "Hey! Now I'm one of you, now can I spend time with you?" I like companionship. I like hanging out with folks. I just don't want to lock myself into an identity in order to do it, and what I've done is move on when I no longer have any room to shift and grow.

How about you?

EXERCISE: What was the last group or relationship you were a member of and no longer belong to? Write down the reasons you left or were asked to leave.

Do any of those reasons have anything to do with a shift in your identity, gender or otherwise? How do you feel about yourself now that you're no longer a member of that group or relationship?

Gender Is Pure and Simple When You're Pure and Simple, but Who Ever Really Is?

Playing with *any* identity can be scary, but our fear seems proportional to how valuable the identity is to our existence. Pure identities (or identities that pass as pure) are valuable things. They're valuable to those who have them, because there's a sense that *someplace* will always be *home,* a space with others who claim similar pure identities. And our pure identities are valuable to others. We become easier to deal with. Other people know who we are. So we begin to lean into an identity, we support our lives on some identity, and when we or someone else starts to mess with it, then all of a sudden we've got something, this identity, to lose, and we get very protective not only of our own identity, but of the purity of that identity as a membership requirement for others. This might be how identity politics does itself in. We need to get past this.

You mention [in *Gender Outlaw*] that we, as [transgender] "fools" must not belong to any group permanently. I'm wondering if this is a lesson you learned in your own life, one you learned through reading of Native American Shamanic paths, or what. In my life, though I only recently owned up to my own TG nature, I've never really fit in any one place for very long, and I seem to move from place to place, group to group on a semi-regular basis. I gotta tell ya, it makes for some hard times, to suddenly feel outside the group that only yesterday seemed to want your presence so badly. It leaves me feeling hollow and empty and lost.

—Taaleb, otherwise known as Katherine

I wonder if it's possible to live without an identity; because that's the direction in which I seem to be moving. I want to keep peeling these identities back from myself, one by one; and I'd like to spend my time with people who, if they aren't doing that themselves, will at least be happy that I'm doing it. Taking liberties with identity wreaks havoc with identity politics. It raises questions about the value of identity itself.

So Okay, Would You Sell Your Identity for a Million Dollars?

What value do you place on the factors that make up your identity? Would you sell part of your identity for, say, a cool hundred thousand?

What's your identity worth to you?

I wonder about all our identities, all the ways we say to ourselves "This is me, not you." They're so valuable to us, these markers, that despite knowing their shortcomings, we cling to them like children to a raft in the middle of a stormy lake. We need some sort of security, don't we? And gender is one identity, by reason of the agreed-upon bipolar system, to which we find it extremely easy to cling. Well, cling we do. But is that necessarily a good thing?

Insecurity, commonly regarded as a weakness in normal people, is the basic tool of the actor's trade.
—*Miranda Richardson*

In this next exercise, let's find out in more detail what you *like* about the various components of your gender identity. That way, going into some changes that might allow you to better express yourself, you'll be aware of what you might lose, what you don't *have* to lose, and what you may have to give up.

1. How does being a member of your race enhance or detract from what you consider to be your gender?

2. In terms of your gender, what do you enjoy about being a member of the ethnic group you are?

3. How does being as old or as young as you are affect how you enjoy or dislike your gender?

4. Are there any rights, privileges, or maybe any freedom you get from being a gendered member of the class you belong to?

5. Being the gender you are presenting, does the kind of work you do give you anything particular that enhances that gender presentation, either materially or socially?

6. Is there something that gives you pride in your gender that you get from being as educated (or not) as you are?

7. Do your religious, philosophical, or spiritual beliefs make it good to be the gender you are?

8. Are your genitals a source of pleasure for you just the way they are? How?

9. Is there something about your body type, shape, abilities, or disabilities that you really like?

10. Is there some sort of security or safety you get out of defining yourself in terms of the gender or genders you are romantically attracted to?

11. What benefits might you get by naming yourself something based on what you like to do sexually?

12. What does simply being the gender you were assigned at birth give you?

13. Is there something you enjoy about being defined by or defining yourself by something you used to be? (e.g., an ex-nun, a former woman, a widow)

14. How do your politics or your political beliefs make being the gender you are pleasing to you?

15. For someone of your gender, is how much economic power you do or don't wield particularly pleasing or disappointing to you?

16. What is it you might not want to give up that you get from defining yourself by your physical health, or lack thereof?

17. What do you (or have you) like(d) about being known as Other?

18. What sort of comfort or security do you get from defining yourself by your relationship to someone else (familial or otherwise)?

19. Is there anything about being defined by others as something you don't consider yourself to be, that you would miss if people no longer did that?

20. What perks do you get from being on the outside of some group or identity that won't have you as a member?

21. Is there something about your particular astrological sign or some other identity-system category you fit in that reenforces the way you see your gender?

22. What gendered benefits do you derive by reason of your membership in some club, group, party, or organization?

23. In addition to those listed above, what benefits or perks do you get from other identities or self-descriptives you use for yourself?

24. In addition to those listed above, what privileges or comforts do you enjoy by reason of any other identities or descriptives that others define you by?

In Terms of Gender, Upwardly Mobile Is a Contradiction

People continue daily to buck different parts of the gender/identity/power system, with varying degrees of success. There's a genuine need to claim more rights and access, a very genuine need to free ourselves from what we perceive is holding us back, limiting our self-expression, or locking us out of a circle of people who have more privileges at the expense of many others. Unfortunately, I think, this need is translated into a move *upward* on the gender/identity/power pyramid, as if being squeezed into some teeny tiny pure and simple and perfect identity with no hope of change would be a fun thing. Rather than move upward in hopes of achieving one's fair share of the power and access, why not simply dismantle the pyramid itself?

It all starts with questioning gender. Just like you do in your daily Ten-Minute Gender Outlaw Exercise. You've been doing that, haven't you? Hmmmm?

Be All That You Can Be!

Essentially the theory part of this workbook is over and done with. The rest of the book is going to get a lot more personal and practical. We're going to work our way down the gender/identity/power pyramid with the purpose of freeing ourselves from a system that restricts and forbids our individualities. The exercises will be less and less about what you already are, and more and more about whatever you could be.

If you *do* want to go on reading and working, then it's only fair to warn you that I think you're going to step over a line here. I think that if you don't already consider yourself transgendered, then it's possible that you are or will be considered that by other people. I'll be talking about a "journey" through gender, because from this point on in the workbook that's what you're going to be doing: you'll be getting ready to take your own gender journey.

Easy, easy. No one's expecting you double your wardrobe, or to make an appointment with some surgeon. Gender journeys come in all shapes and sizes. More on that later in the book. For now, just consider this gender journey to be something that explores the outer limits of being a man or a woman, okay?

The sadness comes from my complete and utter distaste for the type of femininity that was shoved down my throat (thank goddess I didn't swallow) growing up in Memphis, Tennessee . . . but to be a well-dressed femme to a suave butch is STILL genderfucking, at least, and a far cry from the type of gender brainwashing I underwent eleven years ago at Miss Hutchison's School for Young Ladies.

I may be female, I may even be a bit femme at times, but I am NOT "feminine" or a "lady." I may not have undergone physical surgery, but I have most definitely undergone a gender transformation . . . from a feminine young-lady-southern-belle-wannabe to an autonomous, self-defined human being.

—Nancy Marcus

Katie's Opinion on Exactly Who Might Be Transgendered

Some folks think that in order to qualify for bottom-of-the-gender-pyramid status you'd need to do something drastic with your body; others

I feel sorry for people who invest huge amounts of time energy and pride in insisting that there are limited ways in which one can be either femme or butch, because I feel that ultimately all identities are fragile, highly subjective, and subject to interpretation.

I know people who feel *so* proprietary about these identities. I wonder why they bother. Transgression is inevitable.

—Shannon Coulter

think you'd need to wear clothing of another gender; some people think you would have had to have felt "wrongly gendered" for most of your life. Not me. While I'm quite happy with my own surgically altered and hormonally enhanced li'l bod, I think you're transgendered, a gender outlaw if you will, for two reasons.

You're Transgendered If . . .

1. You're not perfectly gendered according to the pyramid model, and in this culture that's a crime against gender.
2. You're gaining an entirely different perspective on gender from the one that's been force-fed us all for an awfully long time.

What, Me Transgendered?

I think anyone who wants to question or study gender is transgressing gender. I think anyone who has either the desire or the courage to admit their transgressions against gender is transgendered. Beyond those qualifications, I think *how* transgendered we are is only a matter of degree.

Let's put that to a little test.

EXERCISE: The following is a list of some behaviors. Check "T" for the ones that would mark someone as transgendered, and "G" for the ones that would mark someone as gendered. (Yes, you can check both boxes if both apply.) You may need to read some of these pretty carefully.

T   G
❑   ❑   surgically altering one's genitals to approximate another kind of genitalia
❑   ❑   surgically altering one's body (other than genitalia) to approximate something considered more pleasing
❑   ❑   surgically altering one's body (including genitalia) to approximate something considered more pleasing
❑   ❑   wearing the outer clothing of another gender out on the street
❑   ❑   wearing the outer clothing of another gender for a costume party

---

T   G

☐   ☐   wearing the underclothing of another gender, beneath one's own gendered clothing

☐   ☐   taking a job not traditionally associated with one's assigned gender

☐   ☐   changing one's name to a name associated with another gender

☐   ☐   having a birth name usually associated with another gender

☐   ☐   making no change in one's body, but claiming to be another gender

☐   ☐   claiming no gender at all

☐   ☐   having questions about ones own gender identity

☐   ☐   having questions about the nature of gender

☐   ☐   consciously or unconsciously adopting the trappings of a gender *other* than the one assigned at birth

☐   ☐   consciously or unconsciously adopting the trappings of the gender one *was* assigned at birth

☐   ☐   reading this book for the purpose of discovering the nature of one's own gender identity

☐   ☐   reading this book for the purpose of discovering the nature of gender identity in general

☐   ☐   being taken as a man in public, while being a woman who feels like a woman

☐   ☐   being taken as a man in public, while being a woman who feels like a man

☐   ☐   being taken as a woman in public, while being a man who feels like a man

☐   ☐   being taken as a woman in public, while being a man who feels like a woman

☐   ☐   being taken in public as a feminine man, while feeling like a masculine man and having been assigned female at birth

☐   ☐   being taken in public as a feminine man, while feeling like a masculine man and having been assigned male at birth

☐   ☐   being taken in public as a masculine man, while feeling like a masculine man and having been assigned female at birth

☐   ☐   being taken in public as a masculine man, while feeling like a feminine man and having been assigned male at birth

☐   ☐   being taken in public as a feminine man, while trying to appear as a masculine man and having been assigned male at birth

T G

❏ ❏ being taken in public as a masculine woman, while trying to appear as a feminine woman and having been assigned female at birth

❏ ❏ being taken in public as a feminine man, while trying to appear as a feminine woman and having been assigned male at birth

❏ ❏ being taken in public as a masculine woman, while trying to appear as a masculine man and having been assigned female at birth

EXERCISE: Using the language of the list above, describe yourself here. What is unique about the inconsistencies in you? What combination of qualities makes your gendered identity unlike anyone else's? Where don't you match up to that perfect gender? Describe yourself. You can be as flamboyant or as scholarly as you like. After all, you get to decide what's appropriate for you, right?

⑥ Wait, What Perks Come with This Outlaw Game?

I finally went through my closet and drawers the other day and got rid of all my girl clothes. Everything went—my jeans that never fit right, girl underwear I hadn't worn in years, and femmy-looking overalls and shorts. Felt great! Felt liberating! Now I have room for all the men's clothing I have been accumulating . . .

—jayneway

Good question. Most of the perks *I've* gotten out of playing with gender wouldn't be highly valued by any materialistic culture. I've less access to "good" jobs, I face more danger on the streets, and the writing I do has not been embraced by millions of people just dying to pay me for saying this stuff.

But let's get serious. Are those the kind of rewards we can honestly expect? Can we expect to break the laws or violate the taboos of a culture, and then be *rewarded* by the culture in the same coin the culture uses to pacify those who don't disturb the status quo? I don't think it works like that.

We do get punished by the culture whose laws we break, whose taboos say "Don't study this forbidden knowledge, and certainly don't *use* it!" Depending on the extent to which we use or communicate that forbidden knowledge, we're denied equal rights, equal pay, equal access. We're not permitted to educate or maintain custody of our children. After all, we're no longer seen as "real men" or "real women," if in fact we ever were.

But we're making space for ourselves in this world through the very acts of questioning and ultimately toppling the gender/identity/power system; and the kind of space we make for ourselves can be as fabulous as we'd like it to be! We've got nothing holding us down to any kind of monogender-specific appropriate behavior so what we've got is a freedom of expression beyond the scope permitted to members of any bi-gendered culture in the history of the planet. We get to decide what's appropriate for ourselves. We get to sample life from any angle that strikes our fancy. We get to laugh an awful lot, and what's more we get to say whatever comes into our heads and hearts without fearing some loss of identity status. And honey? Honey, that is SO MUCH FUN!

So what do you think . . .

Darling, I dress like Joanna Lumley in *Absolutely Fabulous,* even in the shower. My legs are too good to cover up. I shave them under a microscope. I look magnificent till I see myself in a mirror in the shopping mall. They always have to sweep up a lot of glass after I've been through.

I also try to call everybody "darling" in that wonderful bitchy way—you know, *darling*, darling. Most of my friends were born female (as far as I know) and they do this too. I think we all find it a turn-on. We certainly all find each other a turn-on. I am not a drag queen and don't look like one but they do.

—Alberta Winkler

⊚ Is that something you'd like?
⊚ How valuable is personal freedom of expression?

> EXERCISE: Go do something silly. Go on. Do something that might be considered gender neutral or genderless. Right now. Go do something that makes you feel like a little kid. When you get back from doing that, write down what you did.

Good, now . . . how valuable is the freedom to speak your mind?

EXERCISE: Think about a time you told someone else what was really on your mind. Granted, the way you said it might not have been the most compassionate or loving way, but the *way* we say things is something we can practice and improve. Overcoming the fear of abandonment that often attends honest self-expression is the first step. So go ahead . . . when was the last time you really expressed your true feelings to someone else? Okay, now . . . think about these questions.

⊚ How did it make you feel to have expressed yourself? (not *how* you expressed yourself, just the fact of having done it)
⊚ How did it make the other person feel about you? (what you said, not how you said it)
⊚ If you're still in touch with that person, do you feel more confident about being able to express more of yourself with hir?

Learning to express different aspects of ourselves, including previously unexplored shades of our identities that have become gendered by cultural standards, is very much like that: we eventually wind up with some courage and self-respect. Those kind of perks are worth facing our doubts, fears, and demons. Do you agree?

If all this gender play can be so much fun, then why haven't a whole lot of us done this a whole lot earlier? Well, many of us have, but aside from the fact that most bi-gendered cultures tend to severely punish gender transgression, there's another factor at work here, and that's simply fear.

⊚ The Gender We Love to Fear Is No Gender

The basic fear, the one I think it all boils down to, is the fear of death . . . of something or someone dying, disappearing, going away. If we're the ones doing the changing, it's a fear of our own death, the death of some way of being in the world that we're used to or comfortable with. If someone else is doing the changing, then it's a fear of *their* death, a fear of the death of the relationship we had with them.

The fear of death is so basic because it's probably the fear we love the most. Why else would we hold on to it as tightly as we do?

"Fear of Death" when considered in the context of a gender shift may sound extreme, but let's work backward for a moment, back to the subject of transformation. Many philosophical or spiritual systems allow for transformation as an inevitable by-product of death. Whether it's transformation of the body into dust, or the spirit into another life, there's transformation—inevitably ushered in by a real or symbolic death. If we then seek to transform ourselves, be it our gender or any other form of identity, we're really talking about killing off part of our lives.

And if we're killing off part of our lives, then who's left?

What is the "who" of us that gets to keep on living and growing?

I'm thinking this line of questioning is going to reveal the transformative nature of transgressing gender.

If we're looking at gender as more than physiology or even psychology, then the possibility increases of crossing over into something entirely beyond our current ability to name a point of arrival. The possibility increases of opening some Pandora's box in terms of our own identities. The simple act of questioning gender can jeopardize not only gender, but all its links to race, age, class, and the litany of factors that comprise our identities. Question gender, and we question so much more. Here are some interesting questions that might be helpful to ask before beginning some sort of gender journey.

⑥ Are You Ready to Become What You Fear?

1. Is there something you would *not* want to become? Something that's offensive or frightening to you? If so, what?

2. Are there aspects of your life that you have been cultivating in order to avoid becoming what you don't want to become? If so, what would those cultivated aspects be?

3. Are there parts of your life or personality which are right now *close* to being what you don't want to be? If so, describe them.

4. Is there some aspect of your personality that you use to hold another (less appealing to you) aspect in check? If so, write about that.

◎ Hey, I Wouldn't Ask You To Do Anything I Haven't Done

Since going through my gender change, I've become quite a few things I hadn't planned on becoming: a lesbian, a straight woman, a not-man-not-woman, a sadomasochist, and a pansexual all-of-the-above. Additionally, I've become a phone sex hostess, an author, and a performance artist. I've dropped out of my middle-class life and values, become economically challenged, and because of the estrogen-based hormone regimen I'm on, I've lost a good deal of my body strength, not to mention the possibility of having become more susceptible to this arcane form of leukemia I've recently been diagnosed with. I didn't *plan* on becoming any of these things; they all more or less happened when I started my gender transitions rolling. On the plus side, once I began making changes and fell out of that close-to-the-top section of the pyramid, I became free to explore the rest of it, free to explore more facets of all the lives I'm capable of leading.

And it hasn't stopped yet. Now, I'm looking at some other, more frightening things to become: I'm looking at all the man-stuff I've got inside me as a result of both nature and nurture, and I'm saying to myself, what's all *this* about? I don't want to live a life whose impetus is dictated by fear of what I am, what I might become, or what I might be seen as. I want to see for myself everything I am, everything I can be, so I can be conscious in choosing an identity in which to nest . . . if such an identity exists for me or for any of us! I have a feeling that the direction to move in is the one marked "This delights me," and that's what's happening to me more and more these days: I am delighted.

Are you with me? Once we get through the hard part, there's a lot to enjoy. And you'll have as much company as you'd like. There are quite a few people in the world right now celebrating some pretty innovative self-defined gender identities. Would you care to meet more than a hundred of them right now?

◎ 101 Gender Outlaws Answer the Question, "Who Am I?"

I put the word out on the Internet that I'd like people to define themselves in twenty-five words or less. Several couldn't resist going on for more than twenty-five words, but I liked what they wrote so much I put them in here anyway.

So, responding to the questions "Who Are You, What Are you," I'm proud to present 101 amazing answers from 101 amazing people.

1. A woman who had a spontaneous pre-natal sex re-assignment.
2. As an intersexed person born with XY chromosomes and testes, but a female gender identity and appearance, I confirm that nature intended for there to not always be an identity between sex and gender.
3. An anachronous simulsanguesexual literary faerie (gyrl).
4. I'm a good little boy, but I'm a BAD little girl!
5. *the VERY short version:* transgendered redneck
   the pretty short version: transgressively gendered butch/FTM and halfheartedly-recovering redneck.
   the not-that-short version: queer female-to-butch/male transgenderist, sex radical, tree-hugger, anarchist, parent, activist, writer/performance artist & halfheartedly-recovering redneck.
6. Basically, I'm a 34 year old bisexual femme guy. I regularly wear necklaces, pins and earrings, I dress in bright flamboyant colors, and in social settings it is quite obvious that I'm more at ease talking with women than with men. In short, I am fairly feminine in behavior and sensibility. I'm not transsexual, and I doubt I would be considered transgendered, however, as this culture defines such terms I happen to be more feminine than masculine in my tastes and behaviors.
7. always queer, finally dyke, a run-of-the-mill hermaphrodite mom.
8. a born again woman.
9. A God+Godess, part of everything, owned by nothing.
10. I think . . . I am a female fag, who is a drag Queen, who is a mother, has a soon to be transman lover and may very well be a tranny hisself. I hate labels it's all so complicated, but I think it fits the bill today. Change is good right?
11. Badass motorcycle boot-wearing expensive lingerie consuming femme biker switch warrior. 'Nuff said? ::grin::
12. Kitt, aka AlexFox, Alaskan Fox, Mom-Dad, P.(arental) U.(nit), Sweetie, She was pretty as a woman, but omigawd he's even handsomer as a man!
13. The fabulous Boy-Girl-posthuman-It-Thing JordyJones. Artist Writer and Whore. Multi-tasking media-darling, polymorphous pervert and irreverent illiterator.
14. a transgendered tomgirl making hir (It's time we had our own pronouns) way in to the world.
15. i am . . . boy-girl-faggy butch with an avid appreciation for femmes & het sex.
16. What am I? It depends.
   When I speak of Brandon Teena, a transsexual man who was raped and then murdered because he dared identify as a man while possessing a vagina, I am a transsexual man.
   When I speak of a transsexual woman who is being excluded because of her past, I am a transsexual woman.

When I speak of a pre-op transsexual who is being hurtfully categorized by the shape of the tissue between his or her legs, I am a pre-op transsexual.

When I speak of a post-operative transsexual who is being denigrated as the destroyer of his own body's integrity, I am a post-op transsexual.

When I speak of those who dare not reveal the pleasure they derive from wearing clothing reserved exclusively for use of the opposite sex, I am a transvestite.

When I speak of those who are regarded as degenerate because they find certain items particularly stimulating of pleasurable fantasy, I am a fetishist.

When I speak of those who enjoy games of erotic power exchange, I am a sadomasochist.

When I speak of those who prefer the same sex to the opposite for intimacy, I am a homosexual.

When I speak of those who open their arms to intimacy without restriction based on sexual polarity, I am a bisexual.

When I speak of any woman who is being hurt because she dares to challenge or seek respect, I am a sister.

When I speak of any man who is being hurt because he dares to prefer sensitivity to durability, I am a brother.

When I speak of any person who is being hurt because they do not identify as either man or woman, I do not identify.

I am all of these things. In being so, I make a difference where and whenever difference is being used to make hurt.

17. Twin-spirited extraterrestrial with a primal urge to get fucked by something that fits.

18. I am . . .
    1. An embryo in the prime of life
    2. A cross between Calamity Jane and Lucy Ricardo
    3. The Donna Reed of S/M.

19. Nattily attired 40-going-on-11 first alto female-to-male transsexual . . . subject to change without notice.

20. Riki Anne Wilchins author of *Read My Lips* is lesbian or bisexual, transexual or transgender, man or woman living in Greenwich Village or New York City. Her hobbies include the Transexual Menace, the Lesbian Avengers, attacking false binaries or any *other* political system which oppresses her or just really pisses her off. She is Executive Director of Gender PAC.

21. As far as a phrase to describe myself, I often give people some variation of: "Radical feminist transgender political lesbian."

    I know that at least you understand the original meaning of the phrase "political lesbian." I once identified myself as a political lesbian to a drag queen who thought I was gay, and she asked "What's that?" I laughed and said, "I like the clothes!" I prefer an ethnic, but femme look—silk or cotton skirt, cotton top, embroidered vest, silver jewelry. But sometimes when I'm feeling subversive, I'll put on a butch dyke look—blue jeans, trucker's wallet, boots. Of course my black leather motorcycle jacket goes with either look.

Since I'm out to over a dozen people, I don't mind if you use my real name and say I'm from Minneapolis. I've been hiding from my womanliness for too long, and I can't see how transgender people can be accepted unless a few will come forward and refuse to be shamed or humiliated. It is easier in my case, since my breasts are naturally so large when I show people they think I am on hormones already. My hips are wide too. If anyone tries to shove me back in the closet, I plan to ask them to explain why my body looks like it does. I think the Creator made me special for her own reasons.

I have a woman's heart too—I have a hard time turning down someone who needs legal help—learned lots about domestic abuse and domestic abusers that way. Now that I have seen how men use force, threats and violence to dominate women (and each other, including me), I can honestly call myself a radical feminist. I'm educating myself on this fast.

I really am a lawyer (and a civil engineer)—I'm glad I've achieved as much as I have; even with my vulnerable woman's heart, no one can make me feel like a circus freak or perverted misfit.

22. i've been pondering your query about how we define ourselves/know who we are. i would have to say that i become a reflection of whatever dance i find myself doing with whomever i am falling in love with at the moment.

23. On the way to finally being ME.

24. M2F shaman/artist and consecrated Galla of Cybele (my wife) and intersex FA2MA (feminine androgyne to masculine androgyne) leather top and priest/ess of the Dark Goddess (me).

25. FTM transgendered bulldagger, gentleman stone butch dyke with fag tendencies. Or as my girlfriend says, a drag queen trapped in a man trapped in a woman's body.

26. I'm a bi-gendered boychick with balls and boobs. Call me Ken, or call me Barbie—same doll, different packaging; some assembly required; sex, clothing and accessories sold separately; available in fine boy-tiques everywhere.

27. Someone who grew up in the exile of duality, who is now entering the garden where he/she, you/me, are inseparable.

28. Liz and Al Pierce, a professional couple in a small midwestern college town, forced into a closet of sorts by necessity of current circumstance—there are the subtle sign-systems by which we communicate with the handful (literally) of like-minded sexual outlaws who live in the area, but we have found that

what was once (when living in urban areas, such as SF) potent means of communication among ourselves and others on the streets is now diluted into mainstream fashion trends—current accessorizing fetishes used to be a semiotics of sexual proclivity—and people don't even know what they are doing (or SAYING) with their sartorial choices—it's somewhat amusing. All one can be is amused.

Note: a week later, a correction arrived.

I've been thinking about the byte I sent you and it's not quite right—certainly needs to be amended at the end to add that I top my master "as a boy." It's hard for me to define my sexual self outside of my current relationship—it depends upon it—just the way it will shift with the next primary relationship, if there ever is one. What's central is that we PLAY with gender in our relationship: I can be a femme-whore bottom or a faggot top: he is my het-man master, or my slut-girl; or gender is erased, and we are simply engaged, immersed in each other. Now you've got me going on this . . .
liz and al pierce

29. Publisher, author, GenXer and daughter of mothers who believes if you don't make the dust, you eat the dust.

30. I'm Della Grace aka Delboy, Del, He, She, Sir Vesuvio, Transfag, Hermaphrodyke and Queer as Fuck My Arse Photographer. Previously known as a Pussy Licking Sodomite and a Practicing Pervert until I upset my mother.

31. Celibate Buddhist dyke residing in a gay man's body while waiting for Hello Kitty to turn her into a nymphomaniac straight girl.

32. A gorgeous girl in a dress—you do the rest.
    A suit and tie stud make you drop on your knees.

33. I used to be a span
    Bridge between woman, man,
    Now I'm the ferryman,
    Sailing where no bridge can,
    No end to knowing.

34. A pretty typical Orthodox Jewish woman, who just happens to be transexual. Being a Nice Jewish Girl sure beats being a Nice Jewish Guy.

35. Out/M-F/stopped short of the knife/keeping M name to remember history/alone on a limb?/WHERE THE HELL ARE THE REST OF YOU GUYS!!!/estrogened/multidisciplinary performance artist/ . . . human

36. . . . as long as I can still kick ass, it ain't nobody's business if I'm dick or dyke.
    or alternatively,
        . . . I'm an old butch whose jackets may now bunch up around my hips and whose jeans may rub at my thighs, but at least my ties still go around my neck.

37. I am a strongly identified woman in my gender with occasional masturbatory fantasies of being endowed with male genitalia.

38. I'm a butchy-femme, omnisexual, polyamorous, genderbent, kinky, queer—I am most attracted to queer, genderfuck boys : transboys, boychicks, bioboys, makes me no diff.

39. I'm The Dyke of Androgyny . . . i get called sir more than maam, despite the sizable mammary glands protruding from my chest. The hair on my head is the shortest found on my body, a gentle societal mindfuck, if you will.

40. Transsexual dyke, submissive pervert, percussion fetishist, computer geek, and subversive queermonger.

41. Just another brassy womyn who happened to be born with a penis.

42. Two-spirit mixed-blood transgender working-class sober queer boy dyke daddy.

43. OK—who am I? Spencer Bergstedt, Attorney at Law. FTM, rabble-rouser, gentlemanly pain in the ass. What am I? Trans-man Hetero-queer Daddy Top.

44. A granola femme with an SM twist, a dyke drawn primarily to butches & FTMs.

45. call me: fuzzy femme compelled-to-be&tell-my-truth jewitch girlfag dreamer.

46. happy going, fluidly-gendered, pan-sexual eurotrash Canuck switch with a sweet tooth for the taste of untried and new genderomantic flavours and twists.

47. Everlove'nStudMuffinButtBustingGenderTwistingSadomasochisticHype DaddyDyke!

48. Jewish Lesbian/Feminist. Butch in the sheets, but I love fem sheets.

49. Sadistic High Femme Top/Switch/Babygirl beggin' masochist
    And there you have it . . . so to speak.

50. I'm a Poetess-bi-dyke-drag-chick (sometimes-i-crave-dick)—Gasp! Laugh. grrrrl2grrrrl into hip-hop-funk-folk, addicted to phat beats, and heavy, open, dangerous minds.

51. oh shit. butch, female bodied, human persona-ed, male appearing, daddy, momma's boy, mother fucker, cross dressing, gentleman, top, smooth talking, dirty minded, nasty fingered, lover of women . . . is one of the things I am.

52. A big leather dyke on a big fucking bike.

53. Radical redheaded, depends on what day of the week it is, Femme/Mommy/Daddy/ 8 yr. old/ beautific grrl Dyke.

54. Omnisexual, omnigendered pervert fag transman in a biofemale body.

55. Up until 11, I was certain I was a boy, but everything started making gender-sense again in my 30s when I finally threw out all my panties and got boxers. Okay, well, I kept a coupla pairs for REALLY kinky sex.

56. I hate labels for the boxes that tend to accompany them but if I had to choose

it would be transfag/dyke (both having equal weight) with dual citizenship whose passport/visa is in peril at the whim of any Devotee of the One True Path, revocation of which will certainly not prevent me from crossing the border. I consider myself intersexed by choice as well as a queer androgyne.

57. I'd have to describe myself as a femme hybrid—Half Michigan, half raging homo, or in other words, half baked and half-way home, but 100 percent pussy.

58. I'm a devilishly handsome dyke with angel wings who knows how to treat every woman, of any gender, because I *know* they're all different and I like them that way.

    Or how about:

    I'm a spiritual woman with a strong belief in the strength of her own right arm and devastating charm . . . *grin*

    Or maybe:

    Sorry boys, can I help it if redheads prefer gentlewomen?

59. From the outside, people see me as a woman (yay! that's true!) and a femme (bummer! that's not me!). Inside, I'm a radical hungering for justice, bisexual, and relaxed about gender. I see a flash of kinship recognition in the twinkly eyes of all the tender, sweet-spirited people in the world.

60. Mean femme dyke when I'm not being a tender man holding my lady or a mama feeding my babies.

61. A celibate Transgender Lesbian trying to live an honorable and ethical Unitarian Universalist life.

62. I'm someone whose gender would have been considered inverted because I love women, or I would have been assumed to be passing as a man because I wear jeans and flannel shirts, or I would have been accused of rejecting my womanhood because I haven't married or born children, or I would be considered intergendered because I have big tits & big muscles, or I would have been considered mixed spirits because I love to cook and love to play rugby. But in this time and place I'm just called a strong, dykey, woman. You can call me whatever you want!

63. here are 3 [definitions] I occasionally use for myself, even though I'm not satisfied with any of 'em. If you like 'em, use 'em:

    —openly transsexual leather faggot without a cock

    —ftm ts, mtf dq (digital queer)

    —zeroboy in the city of the queen of angels

64. a bigendered, bisexual (or perhaps pangendered and pansexual) switch, a gay/bi FTM drag queen (transfagdrag)!

65. I am: Young, female and feminist, bisexual, homoemotional, trying to change the world and stop it from changing me too much!

66. Supremely arrogant, drop-dead gorgeous, brilliant, sexually compulsive erotic femsub. Modest, too.

67. A spiritual wisechild metagenderly packaged for your convenience.

68. OK, define myself. (fuck, I don't know this is a tough one—I've got so many labels—it depends on the moment.)

69. A motorcycle ridin', pool playin', softball hittin', average kind of dyke who's afraid of ruining her nails!

70. A constant flow: a journey from one way of thinking, to the wide open expression of what it really means to be me. or . . .

      militant-feminist female-2-male butch genderfuk daddy transexual fag or . . .

      I changed my mind. This happens a lot.

      "anomalous" I think that's my gender. If you have space or want to or whatever, you can put 'em both in. Whichever. I like anomalous better though.

71. SM butchdyke, heavy bottom boychick, I like fat girls!

72. Hey, thanks for asking. I was just thinking about my gender the other day after I went shopping for a pair of boys shorts and a strapless bra. My clothing has more gender than I do. So here are a few first minute thoughts on the subject, organized into shorter and short: How do I define my gender? I don't.

      A child once asked me "are you a boy or a girl?" I said, "both." Now, I would say "neither."

73. I am a bisexual androgynous woman rebelling against the male body I was born in and the masculine facade that I have created to fit in to my male dominated society. The same society that insisted I be tough, "manly" and aggressively competitive. The same society that punished me for showing emotion and being more sensitive than the "other boys."

      Ironically, I have succeeded in being the "alpha male of my pack." I am a soldier; an officer and a gentleman, as such, to be respected and obeyed. I am a physician and healer. I am an explorer and athlete and scholar. I am many people who were expected to be male in less enlightened times.

      Now, having finally admitted the truth to myself, I have quit trying to chase my femininity into the dark shadows of my psyche. I am now taking steps to alter my body as I see fit to express the gender I wish to express. I am maintaining the strength and fortitude I developed in my quest to be a "real man" and I am using it to endure the even harder path to expressing myself as a woman.

      Whether I am in high heels or combat boots, running with wolves or contemplating a sunset . . . I am me. I am alive, free and in the pursuit of happiness.

74. Priest in their religion, priestess in ours.

75. Ill-defined, ill-gendered; over/under defined, over/under gendered; beyond definition, beyond gender. Definition fatigued yet gender starved. Barely a woman, but allways a dyke.

76. I am . . . an Aussie FtM TS spin bowler, straight (but likes guys now and then), who hopes to be the first transsexual on his state's *men's* cricket team . . . maybe someday I'll play for the country and beat the Poms (that's Australian for Englishmen) at Lord's (cricket ground) and win the Ashes yet again. :)

    Oh yes, the Ashes are a trophy played for by Australia and England in cricket.

77. Transsexual Woman Estranged Parent Catholic Lesbian Ex-Engineer Waitress with "delusions of 'blandeur'" and a happy love of God and each of Her/His children.

78. I'm a multidimensional butch daddy dyke shaman artist alien who fucks with stereotypes. I believe I could answer that differently each and every day.

79. In me, binary American culture can only see an FTM. My best MTF friend calls me "Wrong Way Walker" :) I'm mixed-gendered, i'm other-gendered, i'm a Third.

80. I'm your average . . . normal . . . person . . . who happens to be a Female to Male Transsexual, (a heterosexual—"with a twist") A "spiced up" version of the average.

90. I'm gay-positive (bent!) straight Jewish formerly working-class white grrl feminist who teaches women's studies and is going to be a new mom to a sweet babe from China!

91. I am a Kate More. I'm not entirely sure what a Kate More is, but I know what one does, it lusts after belonging.

92. A free-roving TwoSpirit with shades of a Shoalin Monk with a little Scottish Highlander thrown in for spice. But failing that, I am Life.

93. If I knew what I was, I would be lot happier at the moment. Lets see, butch enough to drive a motorcycle and repair it, femme enough to pass as a (ex)model, if I cared enough. Butch enough to do martial arts, silly enough to own a couple of frilly tart dresses. I do attract butches and femmes, although I am turned more on by butches at the moment.

94. I am a Gen X, highfemme, non-monogamous, sexworker/teacher/healer/performer, switchable SM dyke.

    That looks so short, but I think of it as the headlines in the newspaper of my life. I don't think I was ever anything else, really. I always felt comfortable in my gender. Sexual expression and behavior is my battlefield.

95. My greatest cruelty is in my kindness. I am a butch queer leather Daddy; a gentlemen sadist. Those who love me refer to me as The Whore Of Babylon.

96. A Lesbian trapped in a man's body.

97. What labels do I wear? Left-handed MTF transsexual lesbian sadomasochist transfag-hag anarchist with a Ph.D.

98. Viragoid TranSexual. Dyke (femme), PolyPerverse Bottom, Harpy, TransHag. Game Designer. Superheroine. Not pretty. Say—how do you feel about sex-maddened Trans Groupies, anyway? Heehee!

99. I was born intersexed but identify as a Pre-operative Transexual Lipstick Lesbian. In laywomyn terms, "I'm just a Flirt in a Skirt with no room in my life for men."

100. My current identity tag is: priapic butch fella and bloodsports triathlete, reclaiming the haircuts of my oppressors—heh!

101. lesbian father-to-be, excited, romantically intoxicated butch fiancee of the lesbian femme-of-my-dreams

Wait! There's a few more!
(well, it's silly to think there are only 101 gender outlaws in the world.)

102. I am a Transperson: Not a Transvestite and not a Crossdresser, but a person who is Two-Spirited. This means that I have two first names, two closets for clothes, two bank accounts, two sets of credit cards, two ways of eating, two ways of speaking and two ways to spend my money. Now if I only had two paychecks . . .

103. "I'm finally me. Completely, totally me."
      There—did it in only six words and a couple of punctuation marks. :-)

104. Veterinarian, cowboy, wrangler wearing, shirt free when able, man who for some time lived as what our society viewed as a woman.

105. Fence-straddling, Bridge-burning, machoflaming bisexual prettyboy faggotdude—a singer of the high and the low

106. Sexy, sensual, good-looking guy who just so happened to be born female but is working to change that!

107. Happily recovering from the dark world of unknown to the world of light. Enjoying the life I knew was always inside, could never hide, & letting others see the "real" me! I smile & laugh so much now, I'm another person! I hope to see the day when others are able to shine in their light!

_____

Okay, if you've just finished reading the 101 Gender Outlaws section, why don't you take a little break right now. Go on, go for a walk. Take a nap. Come back when you're fresh and ready to go, okay? Because next, we're going to talk about sex, and you probably want to be rested for that, right?

_____

How're you doing? Okay? Anything you've thought about that you'd like to remember later? Go ahead—you can write down some notes for yourself here. Just some stuff to jog your memeory later, okay? (Or you can use this page to work out all the math problems.)

Fuck Your Gender!

Love, Sex, Desire, and Gender

Tell me who you love and I'll tell you who you are.
—*Creole Proverb*

Gender over the past couple of millennia has been twisted into a lop-sided power arena as represented by the gender/identity/power pyramid. Within that framework, gender is virtually useless beyond perpetuating its own system. However, there *are* uses for gender that make the obsessive dismantling of gender a reckless thing to do. Simply put, gender gets used for the purposes of attracting our desires, and that's just not a bad thing. Sometimes, however, while we're in some place of no gender, we end up attracting someone or something we hadn't intended to attract.

I'm OutlawGal in this snippet of online conversation.

Then Simo asks me, "so, what do you sleep with" Leading me to try to explain that I would sleep with whoever I really liked, not feeling able to use any of the normal terms—if I slept with a man, I would be being straight for me, but legally gay, if with a woman a lesbian and legally straight—then there are the questions of gay male imperialism and radical separatism, which make both gay and lesbian uncomfortable labels.

—Kate More

AG100: How do guy guys (in general) respond to you? I meant *gay* guys, not guy guys!

OutlawGal: ::slow smile:: Well, most gay guys I meet get confused at first. They end up attracted to what they think is a woman and that throws them way off then when I come out (as fast as possible, usually) we have a good laugh, and they ask me out!

AG100: When you said gay guys were first "attracted" to you as a woman, do you mean attracted as a friend?

OutlawGal: ::chuckling:: Nah, attracted sexually. I'm *not* a woman, and not a man, so I've got qualities of both.

> **Louise:** re: gay men attracted to Kate . . . I'm lesbian and at first drag show was surprised at being attracted to men dressed as women, a revelation at age 18. :-)
>
> **OutlawGal:** I think the point here is that sexual orientation is currently tied to gender. We name our desire by the gender of whoever we're attracted to, and gender is tied to a binary. Are we saying our hearts fall into the same corny binary lockstep?

⊚ Sorting Out Love, Sex, and Desire

There was a call for submissions on the Net, recently. These folks were putting together a Web site on the subject of "Love, Sex, and Desire." They asked some pretty good questions; I'd recommend answering them yourself. Here's what I wrote in response.

> *What are the ways that love/sex/desire make it possible for you to survive in your society?*
> Love is what I live for, it's a place where I can let down the barriers I've built to protect myself from all the harm that's been done to me, and all the harm I've done. It's where I can climb out of the shell I live in to protect myself from all the pain I've felt, and all the pain I've inflicted. It's that space where my heart and spirit and body all come together with someone else. It's the only place I know where I can be the most of me that I am, and allow my loved one to be the most that she or he can be. Sex is a doorway to love. Desire lets me know I'm knocking on the right door for me. Those connections, that freedom of expression, that all adds up to joy, and it makes the rest of life bearable.
>
> *How does the society/community prevent you from fully expressing your sexual self?*
> I think most people need to create for themselves the illusion of an identity: a self-identity that matches up with others in the world. I think that's sadly silly. We are *so* unique, each of us, that each time we try to say, "hey, I'm just like you, let me join your club," we lose a little of our individuality. People have known that for a long time, but what hasn't been talked about is the stunning fact of our doing that with gender (identity), sex (the act) and desire (the longing). We dim down our desire, so we can say "Oh, I'm heterosexual," or "Oh, I'm gay." We dim down the act of sex because we don't want to be perceived as kinky. We filter down our self-expressions to fit into

someone's idea of MAN or WOMAN. We do all of this stuff, I think, because we're *so* afraid of not belonging, *so* afraid of being alone. And we institutionalize all of these dumbing-downs of ourselves, and we call the result society or culture. At least that's the way we've done it to date, I think. The oppression of love, sex, and desire are built into the very nature of the kinds of communities in which we huddle.

What are your hopes and fears about love/sex/desire?

My fear is that the oppression of anything other than socially sanctioned desire has gone on for too long, and has nestled in too deep for us to turn it around with anything short of confrontational action. My hope is that enough people will, in their personal lives, name their desires, fuck the way they've always wanted to, and love more and more people each day for the rest of their lives.

EXERCISE: Now it's your turn. On separate sheets of paper, answer each of the following questions:

1. What are the ways that love/sex/desire make it possible for you to survive in your society?

2. How does the society/community prevent you from fully expressing your sexual self?

3. What are your hopes and fears about love/sex/desire?

⊚ Know Yourself, Know Your Desire

It seems that some sort of identity is necessary for love, sex, and/or desire to exist. To the degree we know who or what we are, it becomes more or less easy to pinpoint our desire. For example: "I'm a woman, and real women love men, therefore I love men." Conversely, to the degree we can name our desire, it becomes to that degree easier to *become* whatever is necessary to *attract* the object of our desire. To follow the earlier example, "I love men, therefore I need to find out what men are attracted to, so I can be attractive and wind up with the man of my dreams." I've come to see *attraction* as the key concept here.

Attraction Depends on Traction

Caitlin Sullivan developed the theory that in order for attraction to occur, there needs to be some form of *traction* for each of the parties involved: each person involved in the attraction needs someplace to stand, some-

I have tentatively decided that my "gender" role is "San Francisco gay male sweater queen somewhat-less-than-butch but not fem." I stick pretty solidly to my role, although it does differ somewhat depending on whether I am wearing a business suit at work or casual clothes in the Castro. I play just a little around the edges—you know, a little eye makeup at Halloween can do wonders.

I often think that I would have a very boring, normal, middle class, midwestern life if I were not gay and (therefore) live in SF. I even have a very old-fashioned marriage. I am the breadwinner, while my spouse stays home and cooks, cleans, decorates and does volunteer work; he just happens to be male.

—Edward Langley

place to dig their feet into, something about themselves to point to and say, "This is me . . . do ya want it?" Traction can take many forms, depending on the dynamic within which the attraction takes place. Within some lesbian communities for example, it's a comfortable and easy thing to move into *butch* and *femme:* it's a well-known dance. In a leather community, a *master/slave* relationship provides traction. And romance novels abound with the *strapping hunk/damsel-in-distress* model. Once we move into any of these or other established identities, we know what to do, we know who we're supposed to be. And more importantly, we make it easy for the person we want to attract to relate to us.

EXERCISE: 1.) Write down a list of five of your identities. These can include things like man, woman, boy, girl, college student, executive, househusband, rock star . . . any five identities you can claim. 2.) Next to each one, write down what kind of person the culture thinks you should be attracting romantically or sexually just by having that identity. 3.) Now write down the kind of people, if any, you really *are* attracting with that identity.

	My Identity	**What I *Should* Be Attracting**	**What I *Am* Attracting**
1.			
2.			
3.			
4.			
5.			

Some of Us Need Less Traction Than Others

But traction doesn't always equate to a fixed identity. Rob Sweeney sent me this email which ze graciously allowed me to reprint:

So, C's dying and I'm needing to vent a bit about what s/he's meant to me, and here's a good place to do it. . . .

We've known each other less than a year, but immediately bonded. It was hard not to — I was in her bedroom, rebinding my tits and rearranging my mustache, swearing a blue streak, and realizing I look like Teddy Roosevelt when I'm in full cross-dressed glory — bears are in, every one likes pudgy guys, at least I'm well-endowed, maybe someone at this costume 1920s speakeasy event will have a Teddy Roosevelt fetish I kept telling myself — when she came in to change for the party. Wolfie introduced us, and I took her hand, kissed it and told her I was enchanted to meet her. All this while holding my chest down with the other hand. . . . Fer a fag, I can charm the ladies when I want to, and I wanted to charm C.

She looked me up and down, told me I'd look better dressing left in those trousers, and stripped. She was already incredibly skinny, and the KS splotches were covering her chest, but she looked at me, both of us tucking our selves into our undergarments, and said "If you can be becoming yourself in front of me, I can become myself in front of you." We talked about tucking dicks to hide them — hir PA piercing helped — and making a decent basket, and she envied me my cleavage. (I love drag queens. . .)

And the rest of the night was swell, with much charming of C. And puzzling of other folks in drag, some of whom were trying very hard to grok the idea of a drag king. And then there was this boy I wanted . . . but I digress.

And C's been sick and sicker ever since. I show up every so often, watch TV with her, talk with her, and generally be as sweet a prince as I can to a very brave princess. Sometimes we're just queers of a certain graduated from high school in the 80s age together, sometimes we've bonded over being disabled, sometimes we've talked about being artists. But there's always been a level at which we've been very comfortable and happy with our otherness together. I'm a guy with her, and C's a girl with me. Despite bio-parts to the contrary. Its been fabulous to have that in my life.

And she's on the last bit of her life, and I am so sad. Her mom's gotten cool, and we've achieved gender DMZ — mom calls her C, not [C's male birth name], and we call her him, to mom, at least — and I've said good-bye, but I'm just heartbroken.

Heartbroken for a lot of reasons — damned plague, she's only 25, I never, she never . . . y'all know — but, especially, my life as an odd

> sorta odd guy, who has gotten so much validation from another odd
> sort. . . . So, hey. Thanks for letting me vent —Rob

An interesting exercise might be to review this letter and count all the ways that Rob and C are attracted to each other; what identities they occupy that provide traction through which to connect to the other's many identities; and finally, how many of those identities are modified by what we're calling gender.

Here are some good questions to think about today:

- Who do you love?
- What quality in a person turns your head when you're walking down the street?
- Have you ever been surprised by the kind of person you've fallen in love with?
- Were the answers to any of the above questions affected by who and what you are? If so, how?

Whom Are You Allowed to Fall in Love with?

Given that you've gotten this far in the book and allowed for your own possible gender outlaw status, who can you fall in love with? Must we follow the unwritten law that "real men love women and real women love men?" Who, then, would fall in love with you or me? To whom does your attraction really lead you? Whom do you attract simply by being the gender you are? Are there many questions more important to an individual than these?

Sure, I think there are more important questions. Questions of freedom, health, access to power, access to knowledge and wisdom, these are all more important questions. I have this quote by Olive Schreiner up on my wall:

I saw a woman sleeping. In her sleep, she dreamt Life stood before her, and held in each hand a gift—in the one hand Love, in the other Freedom. And she said to the woman, "Choose."

And the woman waited long: and she said, "Freedom."

And Life said "Thou has well chosen. If thou had'st said 'Love,' I would have given thee that thou didst ask for; and I would have gone from thee, and returned to thee no more. Now the day will come when I shall return. In that day, I shall bear both gifts in one hand."

I heard the woman laugh in her sleep.

I try to choose Freedom over Love whenever the choice presents itself. But Love *is* an important question, and Love or the absence of Love are large factors in our lives. So, let's put these two factors together and talk about the Freedom to Love.

What If Desire Were More Than Loving Men And Women?

Even within the binary gender system, gender and desire are so deeply entwined that by changing one, we're perceived as having changed the other. For example, I've loved women all my life. Changing my identity was supposed to change my desire? I remember the disbelief on Geraldo Rivera's face when I proposed a show about transsexual lesbians. "There's more than just you?" he asked incredulously.

Defining one's desire in terms of gender is not an invalid way to go. Is that how you name your desire? If so, these might be interesting questions to ponder:

◎ If you love women, do you love all of them?
◎ If you love men, is it every single man you love?
◎ If you call yourself bisexual, loving both men and women, is there room to love someone who's neither?

In the same way that gender is not simply measured by two or three aspects of biology, desire is not simply measured by the two or three aspects of genders currently in vogue. When my ex-lover Catherine became David, we stopped being a lesbian couple, and continued living together as a heterosexual couple. That opened a lot of doors for me. That got me looking at men in a whole new light. That made me put down my borrowed sword of lesbian separatism and start to examine my own desire as opposed to the one that was defined for me by the community of lesbians I'd joined.

Take a moment and answer these questions in your mind:

◎ When a lesbian tells you she's attracted to you, do you find that flattering? Frightening? Exciting? Disgusting?
◎ What if a heterosexual man asked you out on a date? Is that the normal thing for you? Or would it call into question your identity?
◎ Does the gender you were assigned at birth, or even the gender you've taken for yourself now, in and of itself monitor the way you act on your desire?

◎ A Possible Dynamic of Attraction

As a bi/poly/pan-sexual, I view others, especially potential erotic partners, through other primary lenses than gender. Sure, if a person seems to have a gender, I notice it; but the basis of my attraction to and possible connection with them will have more to do with spirit and humor and erotic energy and chemistry than gender. Since gender differentiation and separation is so intimately involved with compulsory heterosexuality and monosexism, I consider my eroticism a modest blow against the gender empire. I also do not view men and women as "opposites." What the fuck is that supposed to *mean*?

There are moments when my consciousness inhabits a body whose gendered characteristics are so irrelevant that I can forget them. While sometimes I identify with femaleness (and sometimes in fact with maleness), often I don't identify with either. My spirit is almost always ungendered. Gender is a system of social control, and I would prefer to be in most respects uncontrollable.

—Carol Queen

I don't think attraction is some static *thing* that happens between two or more people. I think all parties involved in attraction *work* at it, so attraction can be seen as a dynamic phenomenon. Most of us begin our dance of desire by establishing each other's genders.

I've no idea what's going to happen to this dance of desire as the culture comes to embrace a multitude of genders, but I have every confidence in humanity's ingenuity in these matters. I'm sure we'll develop signals and mating rituals that will reveal our chosen genders (if any) at the proper time in the dance of attraction with one another. Until then, there are some things we need to remember as we march out into the world with a brave new gender and a brave new desire.

Gender-free or gender-bent presentation is something new again in the world. Not too many folks are up to speed on it yet these days. It behooves us to be compassionate and supportive of someone who's just coming to grips with the complexities of their own desires, especially if we ourselves are their first exposure to people like us. The way I see it, I was pretty scared of this freewheeling genderplay when I first went through my gender transition; so I just expect others to have similar fears, and I try to treat people the way I'd have liked to have been introduced to all this gender stuff back when I was a kid: with some kindness.

I believe that identity and desire *are* linked. I believe that we shift our identities in order to become more attractive to whomever we desire. We tell someone "Oh yes! I *adore* sushi!" Or we'll say "Go see a Schwarzenegger triple-feature with you? I'd *love* to!" Of course, we've been avoiding both raw fish and Arnold for years, but we go and maybe we like it. Maybe our identities shift to sushi-and-Schwarzenegger fan for the duration of the relationship with that person or even beyond that. On the other hand, maybe we only confirm our dislike of both; but the fact is we shift and we try, if only for a moment. Personally, I enjoy shifting my identity, seeing the world a bit differently for the sake of love. I'm deeply touched when a lover tries something on my behalf. It's a dance. A relationship can be seen as identities in motion with one another, dancing to the melody of a mutually perceived value system.

What scares me is stasis: being immobile either in my identity or in my desire. What scares me is the prospect of an entirely predictable and endlessly repetitive series of romances, affairs, sexual encounters, flirtations, and relationships.

Because identity and desire are linked, and because I want my identity to grow to encompass more love for more people, I want to keep widening the parameters of my desire, which results in expanding my identity. It's dizzy-making, and I do rather like it.

> It seems to me that butches and femmes are people whose erotic identities are right out there. It's not a bad life. We get to wear funny clothes and hang out with our friends. It may not be *totally* satisfying, but there are moments of delight that make it all worthwhile.
>
> —Red Reddick

EXERCISE: Looking back on any past relationships you might have had, have you acquired any new tastes or skills from any? If so, list those skills or tastes here.

Might the acquisition of those new tastes and skills have resulted in a shift in your identity? If so, name the identity you were and the identity you subsequently became.

So ... What Floats Your Boat?

Examining what's really worked in terms of fulfilling my own desire, it's been whatever has gotten my attention focused into the right-now moment. It's whatever keeps my brain from trying to figure out what's going on while it's going on; and I'm there, right there in the present, experiencing what I'm experiencing.

Stuff like dancing, orgasms, pain, bleeding, endorphin rushes, amazing good food, performing, writing, a really good conversation, listening to great music, doing great sex, being present for a work of art, working out.

My he/she girlfriend says she has no feeling in her breasts. By day they are bound tight: you can hardly make out a curve. It is not until night, running my hands under the oxford shirt she insists on wearing to bed, that I feel her recoil when one hand lingers on a nipple. I drop my hand quickly to cup the heart, knowing that attention to her breasts makes me some kind of traitor, her an impostor.

Still, on my way to her heart I pause to kiss. I am never sure they will be there on next pass. In trying to love her breasts I am defying God.

—L. Rafkin

This is a fraction of the continuum of my desire that grabs my attention, keeps me from trying to figure out who I am or what I need to be.

I think the trick would be to live our lives so that *anything* we do is done with that kind of attention to detail in the present, that kind of focus on the right-now moment. But there are quite a few distractions. Most of us have so much stuff going on in the background of our minds that it becomes difficult to pay attention to what we're actually doing. I find I'm happier and more fulfilled when my focus is on *values* and on *doing* things, rather than on *identities* and *having* things.

Given that it's important to pay attention, how can we remain deeply entrenched within *any* identity, the maintenance of which demands a great deal of time and attention? Time and attention we could be spending with what really turns us on? I think that's another good reason to make any identity, including gender, a conscious choice. We can *choose* to spend our time on it, honing our uniquely gendered self-expression in such a way as to attract that to which we are attracted, and leaving ourselves free to experience our attraction without the intrusion of some gender-maintenance problem.

If we stop our obsessive search for either being or being approved by The Perfect Gender, which obsession demands we do our best to masquerade as real men or real women, then how on earth are we going to find traction through which we might realize our true desire? However, if we expose the possibilty that we are not being real men or real women after all, if we strip ourselves of one of these imposed identities, we're also going to strip ourselves of all the possibilities for socially sanctioned attractions. It means we must truly come face to face with all our longing, our loneliness, and our need to connect. It means we need to name, down to the fingernails, our desire. Otherwise, we're stuck with a desire named for us by whatever culture we happen to belong to at the moment. And what might the focus of that desire be?

◎ Stepford Men and Women

There is the idea romantically and wistfully circulating in transgender and even some outsider circles that by being born a man, one can become a "better" woman; and that by having been raised female in this culture, one can eventually be a "better" man. This is not entirely mythic, since each of the two main gender categories has evolved over time as a representation of the other's fantasy.

```
Subj: question
Date: Thu, Jul 13, 1995 5:40 PM PST
From: Montana
To: outlawgal
Dear Kate,
   While enjoying a momentary diversion from thesis writing, I found
your book. I only had time to page through it, but I saw that you wel-
comed questions regarding transsexuality. I'm curious about a very
visible subset of transsexuals. It seems that there are many who
frame their femininity in terms of a male fantasy of women as sexual-
ly available, love bimbos. This image is very popular in the sleazy
daytime talkshow forum, however, I've encountered it elsewhere. I
know that the media and personal experience do not constitute a ran-
dom sample, however, it seems that a disproportionate number of
transsexuals gravitate towards the sex industry as strippers, pros-
titutes, etc. I'm curious about how prevalent this really is and per-
haps your opinion on the matter. Do you think that this image plays a
role in feminists' reluctance to embrace transsexuals either indi-
vidually or as a group? I look forward to your response. M


Subj: Re: question
Date: Thu, Jul 14, 1995 2:15 PM PST
From: outlawgal
To: Montana
   . . . Yup . . . quite a few male-to-female transgendered folk, like
the majority of the rest of the culture, tend to opt for identities
that conform to the male ideal of whatever identity they're opting
for.
   I did try to cover that pretty thoroughly in Gender Outlaw, this
tendency for the majority to fall into the male-defined roles of
whatever, but I frame it in terms of appearance, role, and manners,
not so much on economy. And I think it's for reasons of economy that
so many transgendered women are visibly present in the sex industry.
That's one reason why *I* work in the sex industry. The trouble with
being transgendered is the issue of passing, and since so few TG
```

folks feel they pass, there's very few avenues in which to make a living. As to feminism and sex work, most of the sex workers I know are learned, practicing feminists.

Additionally, drag has been a mainstay of the borderline sex industry for*ever*, and a lot more folks have chronicled that. So, sex worker has been a visible role model for many TG women.

I could counter with the fact that a disproportionate number of TG women I know are computer programmers. ::grin:: In fact, there's a joke going around that says exposure to computer screens causes transsexuality.

Back to the point though, to really test these waters, we'd have to factor in the other 50% of the TG population: female to male. That group seems to have a very low presence in the sex industry. Would you say that's surprising?

Warmly, Kate

Here's what I think. I think we construct ourselves into an identity that attracts what we desire. As our desires change, or as our perceptions of our desires change, our identity shifts. If that's the case, then the following is also true: no prefabricated, prepackaged, marketed-for-the-masses mono-gendered identity like "real man" or "real woman" will attract our very personal and unique desires. Taking on such a prefab identity may very well attract something we *don't* desire. When it comes to ready-to-wear genders, you get what you pay for.

The Stepford Man, Stepford Woman model of gender, on top of being a lie that masks the more pyramidal structure of gender and power that exists in the world, kills off not only our self-expression, but also any hope of speaking out loud, let alone pursuing and achieving, our heart's desire.

So what is the nature of your attraction? How do you go about attracting?

EXERCISE: List out five things you do in order to make yourself more attractive.

1.

2.

3.

> 4.
>
> 5.
>
> Do any of these five things bring you closer to the dominant culture's definition of a "real man" or a "real woman"? Do any of these five things you do in order to make yourself attractive take you closer to your *sub-culture's* definition of a "real man" or a "real woman"?

⑥ Looking for Love, There Are No Wrong Places . . .

. . . there are only wrong identities, given the place in which we're looking. But where *do* we look for love? So far, this discussion of desire has centered around the desire to have a particular type of person in our life. But our desire may not necessarily be stated most strongly in terms of whom or what we wish to *have* in our lives. Our desires may be more strong in the areas of what we wish to *be,* or what we wish to *do,* or it may simply be the desire to understand.

Depending on the nature of our desire, we shift our identities in order to fulfill that desire. Depending on where we stand in terms of gender and power, the possibilities for that shifting and that fulfillment become more or less important and/or plausible. But do we know our desire?

People in the fields of advertising and public relations assume *they* know what we want. They know they're marketing to "real men" and "real women," and they know what those two categories want to have. They *should* know, they invented us! But let's break free of their grip for a moment. Let's look at what we really want, and what we need to be in order to attract that to ourselves.

I first "came out" (and still am out) as bi(pan)sexual 4 years ago. I started to identify as a feminist about 1 year prior to that. having been uppity all my life, it's only been recently that i've come to consider what it means to be a "gender transgressive," it's something i still ponder daily. i feel less and less like the word "woman" belongs to me . . . like every other identity, it was something i learned. and it's exciting to let go of it a little each day. All of my identities have undergone several meta-morphoses and I hope they continue to do so.

I don't ignore [the labels butch and femme] completely, but I don't "identify" as either of these things either. I guess I "invoke" them at various times—usually in parody or satire. My identity is a very fluid thing—only every great once in awhile does it occur to me to explore the butch and/or femme identities. And to me, there is no one "pure" way of being either of those things—it's the exploration itself that proves worthwhile.

—Shannon Coulter

EXERCISE: In the left-hand column below, list some stuff you'd like to have. (What do you want? A new car? An amazing lover? A successful career? Whatever . . . just list some stuff.)

What I Want   What I'd Need to Be
                                 In Order to Attract That

EXERCISE: Now, in the right-hand column, write down what identity you would have to construct in order to attract that kind of stuff. In the case of a new car, it might be an identity that enjoys the kind of work that would result in having enough money to buy a new car. Or an identity that someone would want to give a car to. In the case of an amazing lover, well, what would you need to be in order to attract that?

Don't you wish it were that simple? I sure do. But it's a first step, and I'm a firm believer in the old journey-of-a-thousand-miles-begins-with-one-step theory. Naming our desires and what we would need to be in order to attract or attain those desires are two fairly big steps.

So is doing your Ten-Minute Gender Outlaw Exercise daily.
::raising an eyebrow:: Have you been doing that?

⊚ Are You Ready to Become That Which You Desire the Most?

Let's tie this all together now. If in fact our desires lie on a continuum that includes but is not limited to sexual or romantic desire; and if there's any truth to the Zen adage "The way you do anything is the way you do every-thing"; then we're left with a wide band of desire that would include desire for ourselves. If our "self" is *also* a wide band, it becomes feasible to trans-form ourselves into that which we desire. Having named what we want, we could theoretically provide that for ourselves. At what point do we choose dependence on others for the fulfillment of our desires over our ability for self-fulfillment? And at what point do we forget it's a choice?

How Do We Get to Pretty and Witty and Gay?

If I am truly seeking to become the object of my own desire, to become in myself that which I most desire in a friend, a lover, a child, a mother, a father, a brother, a sister, a loving aunt, a teacher, a mentor, a student and so many other aspects of my self that I've yet to plumb, I need to know what qualities (within my range of performing them) each of these identities will challenge me to provide for myself.

If indeed one function of a constructed or conscious identity is to attract to ourselves that which we desire, then one way to get in touch with our desires, to understand them deeply, would be to perform ourselves in the world in such a way as to attract *ourselves* every bit as effectively as we would perform ourselves in order to attract some dream-come-true lover. (Maybe that would explain the fascination most gender outlaws seem to have with mirrors.)

In the sex act itself for example, because that seems to be a real down-to-earth practical application of this theory, becoming the object of one's own desire translates into the kind of masturbation where you're as breathless and flying as you'd be with any other lover you might desire. But sexual attraction is only one form of desire. It's only one kind of need. If we really want to get to a point of breathlessly exclaiming "Who's that pretty girl (or boy, or whatever) in that mirror there," we need to become our own seducers and seductresses in each and every area of our desire.

Let's practice this one, shall we? Here are two exercises that should help us become at once the agent of our own desires and the beneficiary of our attractions.

I feel lucky that I consider my gender as wholly mutable as far as social standards go. I love that I can be who I am, that my comfort zone is in Levi's and boots; that I have no desire to wear make up and will never have to; that I find big butch leather fags the sexiest creatures walking the earth and I can!; that because I believe in this dialogue I have a gift that many in this world will never experience and I'm stronger for it; that I no longer feel the shame of a person who went through her entire life being called a boy or a freak (my current freak status has saved my ass on the streets more than once) by strangers; that I can choose when to educate some confused person in a public restroom (I rarely use public restrooms outside of the city); that I love people not knowing "what" I am, there is a ton of strength in this position; that now I understand why it was so important to me to pee standing up when I was 6 yrs old; that I understand why I am more attracted to other butch dykes than femme dykes . . . oh the list could go on (and it already has!)

—Jen Burton

DESIRE FOR SELF, EXERCISE #1: Name something in your life that's being done for you by another person. It could be mothering, income-providing, teaching, or housekeeping. It could be sexual fulfillment. Anything at all that someone's doing for you that you're not doing for yourself right now.

Now go spend the next month of your life learning how to do that for yourself and doing it.

It's all well and good to talk about fulfilling our own desire, but what about the desire for connection with others? How do we manage that one? If gender is one factor that can supply the traction that's needed for attraction, how do we go about beginning and developing friendships, family, and lover relationships if we're living a genderless or nontraditionally gendered life?

The next exercise addresses our need for connection with others through the self-fulfillment of our own desire. Don't you just *love* how paradoxes work?

DESIRE FOR SELF, EXERCISE #2: Make a list of all the qualities you're looking for in a lover. Post it up where you can see it every day, and every day make it a point to take on those qualities yourself.

By maintaining my focus on the self-fulfillment of desire, I've found it surprisingly simple to keep myself happy or satisfied in many areas of my life, and in a much better position to name what I need and want from a lover, friend, co-worker, whatever. One time, I made a list of all the qualities I wanted in a lover, and set about embracing those qualities within myself. I met Catherine Harrison within a month, and we had a wonderful five years together as lovers, through hir gender change and all. So, go on. Give it a shot. Become your heart's desire.

The good news is that some day your prince(ss) will come. Ze may be you, but ze will come. The *rest* of the news is that the really cool princes and princesses are just like us: they don't sit around in one identity for all that long. So, what happens when the object of your desire becomes another object entirely?

⑥ Katie Strangelove, or How I Learned to Stop Worrying and Love the Bomb

The "bomb" was when my lover Catherine announced that ze was going through hir gender change from female to male, and a good deal of my (gendered and well-ordered) world began to collapse. For seven years prior to that time, I'd spent time and energy establishing myself firmly within a lesbian community, building up my lesbian identity, hanging with lesbians in lesbian places. I was out of the closet as a transsexual; I called myself a transsexual lesbian, in the same way one might call oneself a lesbian of color, or a working-class lesbian. And with that little modifier on the front of my identity, I managed a nice lesbian life for myself. That all came apart when Catherine became David, the man he'd always known himself to be.

I had to face a series of self-centered fears like:

⑥ Would my future continue to be a series of becomings, never really arriving?

⑥ How could I ever hope to adapt my gendered history to this non-gendered situation?

⑥ Would I ever be able to fulfill any of my fantasies with this newly-gendered person?

⑥ How would I cope with the power shift?

⑥ If, as I feared, we might break up, would I find another lover?

⑥ Was I going mad in this type of nit-picky analysis?

David broke the rules of our lesbian relationship: he became a man. That was one factor in our eventual breakup as lovers. I'd not been romantically attracted to the men in my life and he was now a man. We went through some hard years after the break-up, as we both struggled to locate a point of connection with each other that was neither sexual nor romantic. Happily, we made it and are now best friends. So what does that say about the nature of good-bye?

⑥ A Parting Shot at Parting

Good-byes are surely difficult, and good-byes of some sort nearly always accompany any change in gender in this culture at this time, be that change radical or subtle.

___

Say for example you're a very large person, and you got together with someone who really is attracted to you for that reason. Then you lose weight. A lot of it. Since weight is perceivable as a factor in one's gender, then a substantial change in weight is a subtle (or not-so-subtle) change in gender, and you risk a good-bye.

___

Growing up queer, I never fit anyone else's model for "girl." I began to think of identity in terms of sexuality (we used to call it sexual orientation) on a linear scale. But after a while the linear scale failed to accommodate me and the others of ambiguous gender that I knew existed. So I began thinking of a big circle with fuzzy edges, and all people fell somewhere within or at the fringes of this.

Now, the reason I like to imagine a picture of this is because I am an artist and very visually oriented. But after reading [*Gender Outlaw*] I realized something else was missing from the fuzzy-edged circle: Time. That is, peoples' identities change over their lifetimes. This is a very comforting thought to me, and I am a little surprised at myself, since change usually makes me nervous.

—Lucky J. (Joann Boscarino)

Well, here's what I think. I think good-bye has gotten a pretty bad reputation in the world of love, sex, and desire. Sure, good-byes are painful, but what's to be learned from that kind of pain? Maybe the value of saying no? That's a pretty good thing to learn.

The next section of this workbook explores where gender comes from, so we know what it is we're saying goodbye to. How does it enter the culture . . . on the wings of what desire does gender fly into our hearts? Nah, that's too lofty a metaphor. How about this one . . . how do we scrape gender off our shoes once we've stepped in it?

Just Say No

I get asked from time to time how to raise a child outside the gender system. And I've never wanted to answer that, having been raised firmly *within* that system. But I think I have an answer now. I think that if we want our children to have the opportunity to live a life free from the chains forged so long ago, we ourselves must break those chains. I think there's some truth to the idea that children have a tendency to grow up to be their mothers and/or their fathers. I think there's some truth to the notion that we seek out our parents in our mates in one form or another. And for most of us, we also grow up seeking to be, be like, or be liked by that Perfect Gender. If we truly want to give our children a new kind of life, then we ourselves must live outside the system that would enslave them.

We cannot expect our children to climb out from under the crushing weight of that system on their own. We must set the examples for children by refusing to bow to the pressure that comes at us from all sides to be one gender or the other. We need to continue to name gender as a combination of a great many sociological, economical, psychological, and physiological factors, and we need to aim for self-realization as opposed to some better-than-the-rest status.

And we've got to set this new kind of non-gendered standard with the same kind of good humor and fabulous taste we've been doing all along. I don't think there's any other way to do it. After all, do we want to be tacky or tasteless? I think not.

The trick I think in refusing to bow to some genderizing pressure is to first name where the pressures are coming from. Once we spot them, then we can learn to deal with them.

When I first introduced my small daughter to A . . ., a transsexual, I explained to her that A . . . was a special person, that sometimes he was a man and his name was D . . ., and sometimes she was a woman, and her name was A . . . . My daughter looked at me in amazement and asked, "How is this accomplished?" She thought it was the most wonderful magic. Ever since, she's called transsexuals 'magic people'.

—Gary Bowen

A three and a half year old girl that Jessica babysits for proclaimed: "I know the difference between boys and girls." (She was dressed in a pink ballerina outfit with tiny silver high heels with pink fluff on them.)

"Well," she explained, "girls have vulva and wear shoes that make noise, and boys have peanuts and wear shoes that DON'T make noise."

Here we are knocking ourselves out and she had the answer the whole time.

—Diane DiMassa

⑥ How to Say No When No Option for No Is Given

```
Kate—
I am starting down the same path you've been thru and have reached
an identity conflict. I have a good, solid, mental image as a woman,
and I'm very comfortable with that. What I have, however, is a very
non-existent image of myself as the biological male that I was born.
In your book you describe how being "male" is the default, and I feel
like I was defaulted into male behavior.
    So this is my question, before I start this journey in earnest, how
do I know that I'm =not= a man? I figure that between you and your
lover, you should have a great time with this one ;-)
    Sometimes Angie \/
    Sometimes not
```

```
Dear Sometimes Angie ::wide grin:: (Sometimes not),
    From my point of view, there's no way that I or anyone else can say
how *you* can tell if you're "not a man." ::gently:: I think that's
the point I keep trying to make, and it's the hardest one to take in:
that our genders, our identities, they're all a matter of personal
choice, not social or peer approval, and the only laws they're sub-
ject to are the laws we impose upon ourselves. I *can* say that by the
culture's laws on this sort of thing, "real" men don't question their
gender identities. ::laughing:: But who cares what the culture
thinks?
```

Social systems, like any kind of machinery, can come in handy at times. Social conventions make our lives smoother, more predictable, generally easier to live. They accomplish this by taking the guesswork out of predictable encounters. Social conventions such as manners answer the question: how can I best honor (or dishonor) this person in such a way that they'll know I'm honoring (or dishonoring) them?

Then there are social conventions of displaying desire: how can I display attraction or revulsion in such a way that it won't be mistaken. One person's flirtations are another person's sexual harrassment, so I think these are useful social conventions.

The problem arises when social convention becomes less of an option, and more of an obligation. As an innocuous example, when I was growing up, it was polite for a seated man or boy to rise when a woman or girl entered the room. Go figure. I don't know why, that's just the way it was. Well, I grew up popping up out of my chair whenever a woman entered the room. I never knew why. I never made the decision to do it. I just did it, because that's what you did when you were a guy. And that's what can happen to social conventions: it becomes easier to say "Yes, that's all I'll do" than it is to say "No, this convention no longer works for me or doesn't work under these circumstances." It's more *polite* to say yes than to say no, and I think that's dangerous.

If we're going to look at gender as a social convention, and if we want to take it apart, we're going to have to begin saying no to the automatic genders we've been being, even when the option for no is not presented. We need to make a conscious, informed decision to step outside of social convention to some place where we're not clearly definable to ourselves, let alone by the culture around us. The social machinery doesn't work in this marginal space. We're going to be misread, misunderstood. Our nerves will be raw a lot of the time while we struggle to make our identities known to others and meet, time and again, the same frightening question "If you're not a man or woman, what are you?" But it's the only way out of the machine itself. We have to learn to define ourselves, for a while at least, by what we're not. It's not pretty, but someone has to do it.

Wait. What am I saying? That's not right. Everything we do *is pretty!* ::*tossing my hair á la Marsha Brady*::

But we *are* going to have to be willing to be perceived as impolite. We're not the kind of men or women that the marketing executives, the church officials, the tax clerks, the old-guard scientific types, or the lords and ladies of big bizniz would like us to be. We're not real women and real men, and we've begun to discover and exclaim that *neither are they.*

All female athletes are gender outlaws. Through sports we become strong and powerful, though society tells us we should be the weaker, more passive sex. Through sports we come to love our bodies for their physical pleasures and accomplishments, though society says we should fixate on how our bodies appear to others. And through team sports we trust, bond with, and sometimes fall in love with other women—though society tells us that women should devote their emotional and erotic energy to men.

All of this is scary, which is why so many female athletes wear hair ribbons, or deny that they're feminists, or deny that some of us are lesbians.

In the act of lunging for a soccer ball or diving into a swimming pool or engaging in most of the other sports that millions of women now enjoy, the athlete goes beyond gender. She is not thinking about whether her tummy is poking out. She is not feeling like a FEMALE athlete. She's just human, just playing, just intensely involved in the physical activity of the moment. She has transcended gender and, even more importantly, sexism. Which explains, in part, why women are so passionate about sports.

—Mariah Burton Nelson

⊚ So, Good-bye Yellow Brick Gender

I spent most of my teen-angst years raging against anything "girly," convinced that feminine meant weak (hence the phrase "pussy," meaning cowardly or lame). I was the quintessential tomboy and I thought the only way to be strong was to reject my own femininity. It wasn't until I began working as a professional Domina that I began to understand the power of heels and lipstick, the hidden strength of the femme archetype. Now, I am no longer afraid of my own femininity. I have finally learned to love my inner girl as much as my inner boy and I enjoy playing with gender in Daddy/boy and Mistress/slut scenes with boys and sluts of all sexes.

—Christa Faust

None of us are that Perfect Gender, and some of us have begun our withdrawal from aspiring to be that or be liked by that. We need to discover the social conventions we've been saying *yes* to, we need to discover who's been pumping those social conventions into our lives, and we need to smile and say no thanks, not for me, call again another day.

And while we're asking ourselves what exactly we've been saying yes to, we're going to have to ask *why we've gone along with it*. Who (which part of ourselves) inside us *agrees* with the gender police, and for what reasons or aims? The following section of this workbook is not intended to be a full in-depth study of how gender enters the culture, because I think gender enters the culture so pervasively that any one of us can only spot a few of its entrance points. But I'm hoping that by examining these examples, we'll be able to spot that stuff on the sidewalk before we step in it.

Since the culture is currently pretending there are two-and-two only genders, I'm going to frame most of the exercises in their terms. You might, however, keep in the back of your mind the questions: How do each of these arbiters of gender forward the idea of some Perfect Gender? How do they mask the multiplicity of genders we are, as a race of human beings, more and more showing ourselves to be?

Okay . . . who are the judges of gender? How do they hand down their verdicts? How do they enforce their sentences?

⊚ My Gender Is My God: Learning Gender from Religion

It's not only religious texts that come down heavily on gender transgression. Religious leaders, in the position of interpreting those texts for their followers, get pretty darned touchy when it comes to messing around with gender in any way, shape, or form. Back when I started my gender change, I tried calling my rabbi. I explained to him that I was going through a gender change, and that I needed some spiritual guidance. He quoted me the Old Testament saw that "A woman shall not put on the garments of a man, nor shall a man put on the garments of a woman." I explained to him that I wasn't a man. He said, "In the eyes of the Lord, you are and always will be."

How touchy can religious leaders get about gender? In the fall of 1995, the United Nations Conference of Women drafted what they called a Platform for Action, a document that drew fire from both the papal palace and the fundamentalist heartland:

> . . . the word gender became a point of contention in several preparatory meetings. The Vatican said that it has won assurances that if the word is used, the meaning is limited to the traditional male and female definitions, and not to "sexual orientation" categories that include gay, lesbian and transexual [sic].
>
> —*International Herald Tribune,* June 21, by Malcolm Gladwell, Washington Post Service

And Tom Strode wrote in the *Baptist Press* on the Platform for Action, a document developed by consensus at that conference:

> . . . critics cite the following as evidence of their charges about the document:—It fails to describe gender as male and female, though the word appears more than 200 times. Some critics have charged the drafters want to include homosexuals, bisexuals and transsexuals under the definition of gender, a position espoused in some feminist literature.

A spiritual life of some sort is an important component of life itself, if not one of the most important components, and many people find spiritual fulfillment within organized religions. The trouble for most gender outlaws, however, is that gender play really worries many religious leaders. Look, I don't want to beat a dead horse. I think most people have some bone or other to pick with organized religions; be it a political, ethical, moral, or spiritual bone, there's something to pick at. It's easy to target "organized religion" as some deadly foe of self-realization, but the fact is there are a lot of good and good-hearted folks who

---

Growing up, I was desperate to find an outlet where I could be a girl; but was greatly disappointed at the lack of available role models. The only visible route were drag bars, but that didn't seem like a safe environment, so I avoided them. Eventually, I finally just started forging ahead creating my own path.

A few years ago, a number of Pagan friends helped me do a ritual where I reclaimed the name Cynthia and had my ears pierced. Since then, I've been introducing myself as Cynthia to more and more circles of people in my life. Even when I dress in boy-drag now I wear women's clothes—slacks and tops in bright colors and silks.

I'm really pleased though at having the freedom to dress totally femme and feel so completely at peace with myself when I do.

—Cynthia

---

preach, practice, or study within both traditional and nontraditional religions. The trick is finding which people you want to associate with, people you can sit down and chew this gender stuff out with on some spiritual level of conversation.

To Catch a Rabbi, Ask a Rabbi

I learned a long time ago that the only way to argue with a theologian is to trade questions—that's the way the old rabbis did it, they asked questions. So I'm going to give you a fun idea. I want you to call three different spiritual leaders, and yes, it's better if they're from totally different faiths—hey, you can even call the Church of Scientology. And I want you to pretend you're someone else (uh huh, make up a name, whatever), and I want you to explain to them you're considering a gender change and you'd like to ask them some questions. I'm sure that if you've gotten this far in the book, you've got plenty of questions, but here are some other ones you can ask.

- ◉ Does my religion let me change my gender?
- ◉ (If not, why not?)
- ◉ How does my religion define a man?
- ◉ How does my religion define a woman?
- ◉ Is one gender more perfect than the other?
- ◉ If so, how?

As this spiritual leader is answering your questions, you can from time to time ask hir "Where's that written?" That'll spice up the conversation.

- ◉ Does my religion allow me to play at being other genders?
- ◉ (If not, why not?)
- ◉ At what moment does my religion say a person's gender is decided?

The good folk of the state of Washington in the United States recently defeated a bill that, among a lot of homophobic things, would have mandated that one's gender is determined at conception. I'm not making this up. At conception. I kinda wish the bill had gone through: we'd all be genderless!

- ◉ Is God a man or a woman?
- ◉ Why exactly did Ze make us men *and* women?
- ◉ Are there any ways the bible (or whatever text) says that a man or woman should act that don't really apply any more?

- (If so, which ones, and why don't they apply?)
- Does it say anywhere that we have to be either a man or a woman, no other choices?
- What if I want to be neither a man nor a woman, then what?
- What if I'm simply neither right now—what does my religion say about that?

It's very important for this exercise that you be genuinely curious. You are, aren't you? Listen to their answers; keep asking them where it's written so you can read it yourself later. And if at any time you're told that God (or whoever) or the Church (or whatever) prohibits this sort of thing, go ahead and ask with all due concern: What's the punishment for doing it anyway? Go on, make those calls. It'll give you a good idea of what kind of tactics these folks use.

If you find yourself a theologian who's really getting into these questions, who's saying things like "That's a good question, let's look at that one together," you've probably got someone you want to keep talking with. You've probably got yourself a religious belief that will support some of the gender stretching you want to do.

When you're done asking questions of these spiritual advisors, it's time to ask *yourself* some questions about the religion you're involved with or the one you're considering:

- Has your religion been instrumental in forming some of your beliefs about gender? If so, which ones?
- Does your religion tell you anything about gender that you *want* to comply with?
- Do you want to continue obeying your religion's stand on gender?
- Are your religion's restrictions regarding gender essential to the spiritual progress you seek to attain through your religion?
- Is there some way for you to reconcile your identity with your religion?

My Gender Is a Fact of Life: Learning Gender from Science

Science is right up there with religion as arbiters of our genders. Hand in hand with the old guard of the world's religions, the old guard of Science has been responsible for how we view the bottom line when it comes to gender, and the bottom line is usually some form of biology or physiology. Granted, since there's a bipolar apparency when it comes to physical gender, it does seem like there are two and only two biological genders.

No, I won't dignify them by calling them "sexes." They don't need their own term beyond "biological gender."

Why's the Sky Blue?

Theologians might argue that "Why?" is not a spiritual question, but when it comes to Science, we need to be little kids and keep asking "Why?" We need to get into a dialogue with the biologists and endocrinologists, the medical doctors, the physiologists . . . any scientist who's trying to tell us what our gender is. Such a conversation might look like this:

You: What makes a man a man?
Mr. Science: A man has a penis.
You: (kid-like) Why?
Mr. Science: For the propagation of the race.
You: Why?
Mr. Science: So we don't die out.
You: Why?
Mr. Science: GET OUT OF MY OFFICE!
You: Okay, okay . . . there need to be people with penises, but why do those people need to be called "men"?
Mr. Science: Because they *are* men.
You: Why?
Mr. Science: Because they have penises!
You: So you really don't know, huh?
Mr. Science: ::sputtering::

Of course, you might find a scientist who's intrigued by these questions. There are outlaws within every field, and Science thankfully has its share of mavericks.

Speaking of questions, are you doing your daily Ten-Minute Gender Outlaw Exercise?

Don't Abandon Your Tedious Search So Quickly. The Answers Haven't Yet Been Found.

Essentialist Science prides itself on its ability to hunt down answers to questions, but the question of gender has eluded science for eons, and gender outlaws are currently bringing that to light. Essentialist Science does not yet have the answers to gender, and it wouldn't take too many questions to get them to realize that. We need to say no to the grip they have on the system. What's more important, however, is the effect that posturing has on our lives. The degree to which "science" is used to uphold moral or religious values is astounding. Check out this press release from the National Gay and Lesbian Task Force:

> Washington, DC—October 31, 1995—Biology may influence sexual orientation according to a new study released today . . .
>
> Dean Hamer, a molecular biologist with the National Cancer Institute, reports that the study found a hereditary predisposition to homosexuality in some men. Hamer suggested that the genetic material in one segment of the X chromosome may increase the probability of homosexuality in some men.
>
> "The Hamer study is an important addition to the growing body of evidence indicating a biological basis for homosexuality in some people," said Beth Barrett, NGLTF spokesperson . . .
>
> "Regardless of the origins of homosexuality, however, discrimination based on sexual orientation is always wrong and must end," Barrett said. "This is especially true to avoid potential genetic engineering if science should ever discover a gene responsible for homosexuality."
>
> "We know that the Right Wing will use any research results against lesbian, gay and bisexual civil rights, because theirs is not a movement based on seeking the truth but on perpetuating bigotry," Barrett said.

I'm sure that biology has some effect on our lives. I know there's a difference between how I act and feel in my current estrogen-based system, as opposed to my former testosterone-based system. Of course science has found out some pretty amazing things about biological gender. The problem stems, I think, from the fact that the culture at large is *selective* about how it uses science to uphold its moral (and gender) boundaries.

Source: Associated Press

San Diego—A species of fish that can change sex, altering genitalia and behavior to suit social circumstances, has been discovered off the coast of Okinawa, Japanese and American researchers report.

The tropical fish normally lives in groups of one dominant male and several females. If a larger male comes along, the dominant male changes into a subservient female; if something happens to the new dominant male, the largest female becomes a male, even if it was a male once before.

It has generally been believed that such changes are irreversible.

Biologist Matthew Grober of the University of Idaho told a meeting of the Society for Neuroscience Sunday that at least three species of fish, a variant of the gobi called Trimma okinawae, had been identified that could change sex repeatedly when required. Restructuring of genitalia and their brain takes place in about four days.

The discovery is significant because the brain region involved in the sex change is the same region recently suggested to cause transsexuality in humans, Grober said.

I love reading stuff like that. It connects me to nature when the rest of the world seems to see me as so disconnected from nature.

I'm curious about the conclusion (or nonconclusion) reached by the researchers. They seem excited because "the brain region involved in the sex change" can be connected to "causing" transsexuality in humans. Excuse me? The changes those fish go through serve a purpose in their lives. Why couldn't the researcher have concluded that maybe gender changes among humans serve a purpose in *their* lives? ::shrugging:: It's all in the spin, isn't it? The point is that the old guards of Science and Religion have joined forces big time on the subject of gender, and that alliance is difficult to break. The question is: How does it affect *us?* How can we avoid falling prey to the pronouncements of Science? I think the solution might lie in linking up with the current outlaws of Science. At this writing, those outlaws are the chaos theorists.

Gender Is Chaotic, and That's the Good News

The idea behind chaos theory is simple: everything is ultimately connected. According to this theory, there are no truly isolated incidents or beings in the universe, rather we're all linked physically (and perhaps mentally) by our actions and reactions. The by-now classic example is the butterfly that flaps its wings in Maine, setting into motion the final bit of turbulence in the air that results in a hurricane in Japan. Scientists have found that experiments conducted, for example, in a vacuum, might indeed prove some points; but that when it comes to predicting real-time behavior, no experiment conducted in a vacuum (i.e., isolated) is truly valid or reliable. There are far too many other real-time factors to take into account. And that, I'm thinking, is where the methodology of chaos theory links up with the methodology of the gender/identity/power theory. That's why I think the pyramid theory of gender, identity, and power works: it takes into account most if not all of the factors that go into gender as gender plays itself out in the world. The pyramid model of gender, identity, and power is no isolated test-tube study of the vast network of cultural and personal phenomena we've dumbed down into biological gender for the sake of our admittedly tired li'l brains; it's got some room to explore.

A good example of some test-tube gender theory would be the scientist who maintains that external genitalia is *the* mark of gender. Ze is not taking into account hormones, chromosomes, or reproductive organs. A scientist who takes all *those* factors into account is not likely to be factoring in family, community, or the culture at large. Very few physical scientists factor in age, race, the economy, beauty and ugliness, and all the other factors that truly make up gender. And no old-guard scientist that I know of at this writing has taken the politics of choice into account: not a bit. So, while science may in fact have some very good notions about *parts* of gender, to date there is no scientific theory that explores gender as part of a system. And that is simply what gender is turning out to be: part of a system. By feeding some of these questions to scientists we know, by encouraging them to begin to view gender as part of a system ranging far beyond physiology, we can play a part in giving them a whole new playground to study.

Before we can question the scientists, we need to question ourselves.

On any given day I am called any or all of the following, "Mom," "Daddy," "Sir," "Grandma Bear," etc. How do I define myself? Blessed, for sure. What I am is a Two-Spirit and what that means is that I have both a male and a female soul in one female body which features, among other things, a beard. I knew that I was a Two-Spirit before I was told by my Gypsy surrogate parents and before it was defined for me by my Cherokee/Seneca mentor. Being a Two-Spirit really has nothing to do with hormones or sexual preferences but when I was younger and I didn't understand myself, I thought about taking hormones and altering my body. For a Two-Spirit, it is not an issue of being a male or a female but of being both. I am a transgendered entity who is most at home as a butch dyke. What is important is that no matter how mean-spirited the world can be, we can find a place of peace within ourselves and extend our loving hearts back out into that world.

—Bear Dyson

EXERCISE: Truthfully, do you now or have you ever believed that there is some bottom-line biological difference between men and women?

_____ YES _____ NO

If yes, what's that difference?

Has anything in your life caused you to question that difference as a valid differentiator between the genders? If so, what?

Do you still believe there is some biological difference?

_____ YES _____ NO

If yes . . .

◎ Are you yourself fully qualified as a member of one gender or another?

◎ Is everyone you know fully qualified as a member of one gender or another?

◎ From what you know about me, am I fully qualified as a member of one gender or another?

◎ My Gender Is How I Act: Learning Gender from Gender Experts

Throughout the history of Western civilization, there have been guide-books that have laid out the proper behavior for men and women, girls and boys.

On the negative side [of marriage], there is the wedding night, during which the bride must pay the piper, so to speak, by facing for the first time the terrible experience of sex.

At this point, dear reader, let me concede one shocking truth. Some young women actually anticipate the wedding night ordeal with curiosity and pleasure! Beware such an attitude! A selfish and sensual husband can easily take advantage of such a bride. One cardinal rule of marriage should never be forgotten: *give little, give seldom, and above all, give grudgingly.* Otherwise what could have been a proper marriage could become an orgy of sexual lust.

–from Instruction And Advice For The Young Bride,
The Madison Institute Newsletter, Fall Issue, 1894

At this writing, the big in-vogue book is John Gray's *Men Are From Mars, Women Are From Venus.* Gray's analysis of the way things are right now on this planet between men and women is obviously a work of love and caring on his part. It's dead-on accurate, but it's close-ended. It doesn't take us any further than the binary.

Men mistakenly expect women to think, communicate, and react the way men do; women mistakenly expect men to feel, communicate, and respond the way women do. We have forgotten that men and women are supposed to be different. As a result our relationships are filled with unnecessary friction and conflict.

Clearly recognizing and respecting these differences dramatically reduce confusion when dealing with the opposite sex. When you remember that men are from Mars and women are from Venus, everything can be explained.

—Gray, page 10

Isn't that comforting? I think that's very comforting. I do. I love the idea that everything can be explained when we accept a simple binary. I also love the ideas of Santa Claus and everlasting love. Don't get me wrong, I believe in a lot of woo-woo stuff. I'm a double Pisces with a Taurus Moon. I was born in 1948, the Year of the Rat. I use several I-Ching software programs on my computer, and I've been reading tarot cards for nearly thirty years.

The way I understand tarot is that it very possibly started in ancient Egypt. The tarot was a book of collected wisdom in picture form, but this was prior to the discovery of bookbinding. The pages were loose, and the result was a "deck" of "cards." When you were stuck in some conundrum, you were supposed to flip through these sheets of pictures and ponder them until something, some archetypal image, shook you loose from your fixation. Nowadays, we'd call it Jungian.

Over the ages, humanity's tendency to grab for the quick fix, the ready answer, the simple solution, bent the use of the tarot to fortune-telling. You picked a card, and that was who you were, or what your future would be. You didn't have to work at it, you were the effect of it. Tarot has lots of choices available to someone who really wants to study them: sixteen personality types, twenty-two levels of spiritual awareness, and thirty-four ways to navigate any given situation. The more cards you use in a reading, the more combinations you come up with. It's a philosophical machine that sees identity as part of a larger system, but it's rarely used like that these days.

Modern astrology suffers a similar fate to modern tarot. David Harrison taught me a lot about astrology. The way he views astrology is similar to the way I look at tarot cards. Most people think that when you're a Pisces or Scorpio or whatever, well, then that's what you are and you can never change. Harrison's understanding of astrology is that sure, these stars and planets and heavenly bodies have some influence over our personalities, but we each inherently have boundless ways of expressing ourselves, unlimited ways to behave in this world. He simply sees a Gemini as someone who has different challenges to overcome than, say, a Virgo.

———

There are even more choices in astrology than in tarot. Sure, there are only twelve different basic types, but you start modifying these types by the position of each of their planets and stars when and where a given person was born, and the variations become infinite. Add that scope of infinite variation to a philosophy that says you're not *stuck* in any particular place, and you've got a system that allows for real self-exploration. We're not talking dial-a-horoscope to find the lover of your dreams here. We're talking about a philosophical machine that acknowledges identity as part of a larger system, a machine that allows for identity in *motion.*

Okay. So, what kind of system has risen today from the ashes of these thoughtful and provocative systems of growth and spirituality? Men are from Mars? Women are from Venus? Gray's findings concerning mono-gendered behavior patterns might be quite accurate within a given social spectrum. The phenomena he's spotted that are "specific" to one gender or another may in fact be reproducible within some close-ended system. But . . .

◎ Of what value beyond safety and security is a close-ended system?
◎ Given the option of an open-ended system, which would you opt for?
◎ Is the gender system you subscribe to currently close-ended or open-ended?

———

Excuse me. I need to get bitchy. Men are from Mars? Women are from Venus?
  This kind of QUICK-FIX ESSENTIALIST view sadly deserves its position as the ultimate distillation of the study of gender that has gone on for eons. It's the MacDONALD'S VERSION OF HUMANITY: "Have it our way." It appeals to the take-a-pill mentality of Western civilization and IF IT WEREN'T SO DANGEROUS, IT'D BE HILARIOUS.
  There. . . that feels better. Thank you.

———

There are other folks writing about "the difference between men and women," and probably the most useful one I've found is Deborah Tannen's *You Just Don't Understand.* Like Gray, Ms. Tannen opts for the binary, but her presentation of the differences is a great deal less confining to people than *Men Are From Mars* . . . . is. Tannen has done an analysis of the speech and communication patterns *common* to men and women in this culture, and that's how she presents them. I found that she does not, like Gray, stretch those observations in order to build a case for some essential binary. The reader has to *think* when reading Tannen's work, "How much of this applies to me?" Gray's work, like that of L. Ron Hubbard, Adolph Hitler, and other fanatics who preach some sort of the-real-you-is-just-like-me-or-should-be doctrine, depends upon complete acceptance of the entire logical, linear, accept-my-first-premise system in order for it to work. It counts on people ignoring other factors of gender like age, race, the economy, et cetera.

Here's the guideline I use for reading books about gender:

◉ Does the theory presented examine gender inclusive of or apart from *all* of its components?
◉ Does it allow for some disagreement?
◉ Does it make promises of a quick fix, or is it more of a challenge, involving some work?

EXERCISE: Name any other criteria you would like to use when judging a book about gender.

Now, using each of those criteria as well as the three listed above, examine and analyze the following expert excerpts.

Keeping people divided—that's the purpose of making people fearful of those who dress differently, or who change their sex, or whose sex is not either-or. That's the function of pitting lighter-skinned people against those with darker skin, nationality against nationality, men against women, straight against lesbian, gay, or bi, abilities against disabilities, young against old. Divide-and-conquer is a crude weapon, but it has proven historically effective—that is, right up to the point where people wake up and realize that they have a material need for unity.

(Feinberg, 123)

It is helpful to remember that sex reassignment does not change the person inside the body. The female-to-male will be basically the same person he was before. What does change is his outer appearance. What does change is how other people act towards him. What does change is the way he feels about himself.

(Sullivan, 24)

The following [are the first two points of a summary of] my conjectures regarding the phenomenon called transsexuality:

1) The transsexual phenomenon is, minimally, a psychological birth defect. I project that genetic and brain researchers will ultimately find a biological basis for this phenomenon.

2) Because transsexuals have this apparent birth defect, they are not "normal." Fortunately, with current psychological, medical and surgical advances, they can be rehabilitated.

(Ramsey, 142)

By the time people reach adulthood . . . it is not just the culture that is limiting them to half their potential. It is also their own readiness to look at themselves through the androcentric and gender-polarizing lenses that they have internalized from the culture and thereby to see every possibility that is consistent with those lenses as normal and natural for the self and every possibility that is inconsistent with those lenses as alien and problematic for the self. In other words, they are limited by their enculturated readiness to constantly ask, "Does this possible way of being or behaving adequately match my culture's conception of a real man or a real woman?" and to answer the question with, "If not, I'll reject it out of hand. If so, I'll consider exploring it further."

(Bem, 153)

Nonsexist counseling is another direction for change that should be explored. The kind of counseling to "pass" successfully as masculine or feminine that now reigns in gender identity clinics only reinforces the problem of transsexualism. It does nothing to develop critical awareness, it makes transsexuals passive spectators of their own decline, it manages transsexuals' intimacy, and ultimately it makes them dependent upon the medical-technical solution. Such counseling destroys integrity and the potential of transsexuals to deal with their problem in an autonomous, genuinely personal, and responsibly social way. The transsexual becomes a kind of acolyte to his doctor and psychiatrist, and learns to depend upon these professionals for maintenance. The baptism of "passing" behavior that is conferred upon the transsexual, plus the administration of exogenous hormones, along with constant requests for corrective polysurgery, turn him into a lifelong patient.

(Raymond, 181)

The struggle has been the right to self-naming and expression of identity, which has shifted in the community to questions about the necessity of passing for typically gendered people. Of course people's experiences vary and many find their sense of gender identity approximates closely to one of the two accepted genders in the binary system. But for others, the experience of crossed or transposed gender is a strong part of their gender identity; being out of the closet is part of that expression. It is not really a debate about privacy and personal safety versus politics, so much as an impulse towards pride and a rejection of internalized transphobia. Some people choose to come out of the closet because doing so will help to educate the general public about the diversity and humanity of transgendered people and so ameliorate oppression in the future.

(Nataf, 16)

My Gender Is My Passport: Learning Gender from the Law

Did you know that in most countries, your gender is recorded as a matter of law? That from the moment of your birth, you're classified into an identity you haven't had the time or experience or intelligence to figure out? There you are, newly born, dealing with all this birth stuff; you don't know the language and can't get your needs and wants articulated, and the first social thing that happens to you is that you're fixed into a legal identity that will determine the course of your life. And did you know that in most countries, it's against the law to *change* that gender once it's been assigned? Is it just me, or does that strike you as a little weird? Does it sound like that sort of legal system is truly representing your best interests as a complete being, capable of some wonderful growth in your life?

Furthermore, the law as applies to gender doesn't come under much personal scrutiny until we become aware of running headlong into some brick wall. Women's rights organizations are active in changing laws as apply to gender, and that's the culmination of centuries of observation and experience on very personal levels. The law as it effects *trans*gender is an important battleground for the women's movement. Most women who are reading this book are already aware of the laws that limit them, laws based solely on gender assignment, which in turn are based solely on external genitalia. But there's an entire range of laws dealing with gender that severely limit our potential for full self-expression and growth, primarily because the law with its emphasis on genital perfection, forwards the notion of a Perfect Gender; not to mention both the legalization of "real men" and "real women" and the subsequent criminalization of anyone who claims to be or is perceived as being neither.

In our more "enlightened" age, many of the blatantly discriminatory laws have been struck down, but what we're left with is an *absence* of laws that protect against discrimination based on any deviance from the Perfect Gender.

———

At this writing, transgender activists with support from the gender community are lobbying politically stronger gay and lesbian groups to include transgender in their agendas. At the same time, these same activists are organizing lobby activities aimed directly at central seats of local, regional, and national governments. The current political goals seem to be framed as getting named within bills designed to protect those within both sex and gender under-represented categories.

———

Ignorance of the Law Is No Excuse

What has always made me identify female is the female's ease in society with being an androgyne. I am not a man. I am not a woman. Latin terms bore me. Yes, there are definite steps to living androgynously . . . steps I take to outwardly manifest my true self to the world, but I vastly prefer to keep my life *out* of the hands of the doctors and scientists and lawyers et al.

—Bonnie

How we become aware of the laws that enforce purity of identity is usually a matter of a personal run-in with one of the folks whose job it is to enforce the laws. Sometimes it's as simple as being daunted by the "M or F" question on most government forms. Sometimes it's as devastating as the case of Brandon Teena, a young transgendered man who lived in the rural midwestern United States. When his biological gender was discovered to be female, he was beaten and raped. He filed a complaint with the local sheriff's office, whose response was laughter. Due in part to their failure to protect him under the law, he was brutally murdered several days later along with his two housemates.

The legal system wants us to be real men or real women. Currently, they're basing their gender designation solely on genitalia. Does that sound like an evolved legal system? The laws are geared to protect those who are most nearly the Perfect Gender, or those who manage to get close to them. Since you're reading this book, I'm willing to bet there are one or two laws that don't protect *you*.

And Speaking of Protection

There are quite a few organizations these days that are doing excellent work to change the legal system in order to redistribute both wealth and power, and to protect basic human rights. There's a snag here, though. I think there's a danger with any specialized civil rights movements, and I'll be going into more depth on this later in the book, but to sum it up: I believe that organizations or groups that fight for the civil rights of some without taking into account the common oppression of the many are doomed to the same fate awaiting anyone who bases their struggle on identity as opposed to values.

We as outlaws need, I think, to become aware of the struggles of all outlaws everywhere. We need to keep looking at this stuff until we find a common bond, some banner under which we all can dance. From my point of view, the common bond could be linked to the gender/identity/power system and the oppression of all but a few who meet the membership requirements of the Perfect Identity club.

> Until and unless we can join in coalition with other groups, I believe the possibility for achieving a genuine sense of community, a genuine sense of equality is unattainable. I believe that sexual object choice alone is not sufficient to connect a community, and, by extension, a movement, and that we must, therefore, look beyond ourselves and base a community and a movement not simply on social identity, but also on shared ideas, on ideology, among individuals from disparate social identities, with like minds, political philosophies, and strategies for achieving their objectives. This is my vision of a movement.
>
> —Warren J. Blumenfeld, from his address to the 15th Annual Lesbian, Gay, Bisexual, Transgender Pride March and Rally, Northampton, Massachusetts, May 4, 1996

EXERCISE: Immerse yourself in your favorite news medium for one week. It can be an online service, public radio, CNN, or your local paper. Really get into it. Take notes on any cases and stories you perceive as discriminatory. They don't have to be specifically about gender. Try to find the common link. Does the gender/identity/power system work as a link? When you've found yourself a link, ask yourself these questions:

⊚ Have you personally had a run-in with the legal system where you felt your rights were violated? If not, do you know of someone who has?

> ◎ Can that violation of rights be traced to some failure of you or that person to live up to either "real manhood" or "real womanhood" as laid out in the gender/identity/power pyramid metaphor?
> ◎ Can that violation of rights be traced to some failure of you or that person to live up to some Perfect Gender?
> ◎ Are you currently involved with or supportive of some civil rights organization that's actively seeking to extend the protection of human rights?
> ◎ Are you speaking about this stuff to people?
> ◎ Please do.

There's little that's more effective in freezing a person into some unwanted or self-destructive identity as making any alternative identity illegal. And if governments can make a transgender identity either illegal or invisible, what are they going to do about all the *other* imperfect troublesome identities that fall further down on the gender/identity/power pyramid?

> LAW EXERCISE:
> 1.   Go through your private papers, your identity cards, your membership cards, insurance forms, all of it. On a separate piece of paper, note down which groups, clubs, parties, organizations, or agencies require your gender as a matter of record.
> 2.   Next to each group you listed, write down what possible reasons that group might have to record your gender.
>
> ADVANCED LAW EXERCISE:
> 1.   Write to each group listed above and ask the reason they want your gender. You can make this a form letter if you've got a lot of groups to write to.
> 2.   When you get a response, determine if you feel they have sufficient reason to record your gender.
> 3a. If they do, then by all means politely thank them for the courtesy of their thoughtful answer.
> 3b. If, however, you feel they've no real reason to know or fix you into some gender, then write them back politely requesting they remove your gender from their records as this is an invasion of your privacy.

4a. If they respond they'll do this, then by all means politely thank them.

4b. If, however, they choose not to remove your gender from their records, you could always ask to speak to your contact's supervisor and repeat steps 3b through 4b until your gender is removed from their record.

5. If that doesn't work, you might want to consider doing the Way Advanced Exercise that just happens to come next.

WAY ADVANCED LAW EXERCISE:
Be or hire a lawyer to organize a class action suit to have your gender removed from the records of all the groups who currently hold that information about you.

REALLY WAY ADVANCED LAW EXERCISE:
In hir book *The Apartheid of Sex,* Martine Rothblatt maintains that a key initial action in a successful transgender movement would be to make illegal the requirement of the M/F designation on all government and public forms, much in the same way that race has been removed as a required piece of information on public forms, including job applications. So, how about doing just that? How about putting some of your political muscle and time behind this one? The sooner this one is done, the sooner the government won't be able to enforce the M/F dichotomy.

◎ My Gender Is My Beauty: Learning Gender from Art

An empty mirror and your worst destructive habits,
when they are held up to each other,
that's when the real making begins.
That's what art and crafting are.
—Rumi

Did you ever see one of those old movies from the forties or the fifties in which a white actor played an Asian? An African or African American? A Native American? Today, we live in a *more* politically enlightened age. More pressure has been brought to bear on our art-makers to knock off the racism. But did you ever wonder why people never gave that a second thought back then?

Let's get a little closer to gender-home with movies from the eighties and nineties. Have you seen *Priscilla, Queen of the Desert?* Or *To Wong*

I break just about everybody's gender conventions. I'm a tranny (snap), a tranny guy (snap, snap), a non-assimilationist, not "just a regular guy" tranny guy (snap, snap, snap) who is taking hormones and having surgery anyway (snap, snap, snap, snap). I've always been queer but I've never been lesbian. My partner is a hormonal intersex with a mostly female body and an androgynous name and appearance. Sometimes people think we're a gay couple, sometimes a straight couple (with either one of us as boy and girl), and sometimes a lesbian couple. I've lost track of how many conventions are broken by now. I know my life has fractured mine.

—Barton Miller

Foo, Thanks for Everything, Julie Newmar? How about *Victor, Victoria,* or the Channel Four Television production of Armistead Maupin's *Tales of the City?* Have you ever wondered why the transsexuals weren't played by transsexuals? Why the Victor/Victoria character wasn't played by a faggy drag king? Why the drag queens in *To Wong Foo* weren't played by drag queens?

Using the metaphor of the gender/identity/power pyramid, why is it that when a person of a higher, more perfect gender, portrays someone of a lower gender, it's not only okay, it's also considered a brave act.

Conversely, why is it that when a gender outlaw manages to portray someone more perfectly gendered and gets caught at being an outlaw, it is headline news? A case in point is Tula, a transgendered woman who for years lived well as a model and actress until ze was outed in both national and international media. Words like "freak" became attached to hir name, and I don't believe "brave" was ever a word the media associated with hir. But Tula was a hero(ine) to me and many other outlaws. Ze fought back, and wrote hir own books about the injustice ze was dealt. Tula is a modern pioneer of transgendered art.

Follow the Money

It would appear that most big, expensive, well-funded, popular art forms re-enforce the gender/identity/power system.

The *craft* of art, and of course art itself, have a wonderful potential to transform both artist and audience. When art sells itself to the highest bidder, the chances are it will lose any edge it might have had, and the odds are it will keep the gender/identity/power system rolling along at a nice healthy clip. The power of transformation in those cases is itself transformed into the power of repression. A lot of what passes for art in the culture today is simply dumping more gender barriers in our way. So, how do we look at this stuff without falling prey to what amounts to its crafty machinations?

Well, I think all art is manipulative. It gets down to the motivation behind the manipulation, and *that* gets down to a judgment call. The only way I've been able to justify my own art is with the hope that it raises more questions than it provides answers or solutions, and that it opens at least as many doorways as it tries to close. The artist working in the area of gender representation could determine what hir own particular transgression of gender might be, and ze could include that in hir art. At the least, ze could take care not to reify any oppressive aspects of gender.

> ESSAY FOR EXTRA CREDIT:
> Using as much or as little paper as necessary, and by whatever means you'd like to communicate it, set down your opinion on the following statement and questions. Given the multifaceted model of gender-as-construct as laid out in the gender/identity/power pyramid, it should be possible for an artist to become, if only for the moment of creation, that which ze is creating, even though that may not be hir home identity or gender. And if that can be done by an artist using some form or medium, could we not do that ourselves? Could we not create ourselves as the artistic representation of our desire, using our bodies and social interactions as our media? Would this be art? Could doing this transcend some art/life binary?

I feel like I break gender rules or laws mostly with my mouth. I have strong opinions and voice them. I look at things and take them apart in ways that a woman is not expected, or really wanted to. Often I am told I am too serious, too abrasive, too critical—all of these comments I think mean overall "too masculine" and its certainly not comfortable for me in some circles to discuss being in "drag" when I put on the skirt etc.

I also break the rules in my artwork. Viewers don't like to be confused about an image that does not clearly state the subject's gender. There are a hundred unwritten rules about how to photograph men and women, when you break these rules the viewers get very uncomfortable. My self portraits are pretty much about my feelings of not feeling female enough and I've been told that they are "too honest" or "too sad."

—P. S. A.

If We Can't Be a Great Artist, We Can Always Be a Great Work of Art

The responsibility of the artist regarding gender comes under scrutiny as more and more artists explore various aspects of gender they may not currently be living out, such as Anne Rice's exploration of sadomasochism in many of her novels. But not all artists exploring identities outside their real time genders have as much popular success as Rice. Isabel Samaras is a San Francisco artist who enjoys doing sexy art. I have several pieces of her work in my apartment. Her images range from a Vargas-like rendering of Batgirl to a delicious gay sadomasochistic depiction of *Star Trek*'s Mr. Spock and Captain Kirk. Fascinated that her own identity has become entangled with the images she paints and sculpts, Isabel writes:

> This [gender dialog] has come up a lot in the course of my work — people being puzzled. Why would I paint two women together, if I'm with a man? Even more outrageous, why would I paint two men together? And the cherry on this frothing heap of turmoil is when I'm barred from being in some show of work because I'm not gay. I just *love* this one. Someone will request my work for a show, say it's something about lesbian and gay erotic work. Then they'll find out I'm living with a man (EEK! A MAN!), and tell me to go away! Pretty frustrating. Shows of hetero erotica don't usually want to mess with the other stuff, and shows of the other stuff don't want to mess with *me* because I'm in a hetero relationship.

Writers have begun to ask me how they might write with transgender identities in mind, and how to write transgendered characters even if that isn't their own experience. I've had to come to grips with this question of art and politics in my own writing. Well, here's what I think.

I think we make too much of a big deal out of writing that "crosses genders." We're crossing some line called gender, and oooooh that's really scary. It sounds like the Fifties, when crossing the color line was sooooooo scary. Ever hear that term, the color line, any more? Not as much. I wonder what the gender line will look like forty years from now.

My point is that every writer writes across gender.

When a butch writes a femme character, that's cross-gendered.

When a sissyboy writes a Castro clone, that's cross-gendered.

When Danny DeVito writes dialogue for Arnold Schwarzenegger, that's cross-gendered.

When Madonna writes a song about virgins, that's cross-gendered.

Gender is a word that means category, that's all it is.

We need to stop saluting to the star-spangled Gender Binary, and the genitals by which it stands.

When we write, our characters have SO many aspects to them, gender is only one. I swear, it's that simple.

Whose Responsibility Is Gender-Conscious Art?

I think the responsibility of any artist is to forge points of connection with those experiencing hir art, and to encourage further points of connection beyond the experience of the art itself. Because the gender binary itself has rarely been questioned before these days, I think art that questions gender and implicates the defenders of the Perfect Gender is art worth making and art worth paying attention to.

———

My preference these days is for art that entertains as well as challenges. I'm thinking that's similar to my fondness for pleasure and pain.

———

I think the responsibility of the audience, those of us who are experiencing the art, is to be aware of our experience. We know it's very likely that the artist has the idea of manipulating us into some frame of mind or state of being, even if hir manipulation might knowingly result in some unpredictable or random effect. So it would benefit us to focus at least some of our awareness, if only retrospectively after the event of the art itself, on exactly which of our buttons are being pushed and in what gendered or other direction we seem to be being shepherded by the artist. In that way, we can separate the politics from the craft and we've got more options to enjoy the experience. I think while as audiences, as listeners to music, as viewers of any art forms whatsoever, we can certainly enjoy the craft of a piece, we need to take more into account than the craft itself. I think we need to take into account politics, race, age, class . . . that old list of qualifiers. We need to seriously ask: Is the craft I'm watching re-enforcing a system that would oppress me? Or is it challenging, in *some* way, that system?

Assuming both artist and audience fulfill their responsibilties, the resulting event should be rewarding for all concerned. Holly Hughes views law-makers in much the same way:

They've been writing the script and directing their action. But we can interrupt their show at any point. We can break character and start acting out our own plots. I think you'll find it easier to perform acts of resistance than you think. I have a hunch you're a natural.

—Holly Hughes

⊚ Can you put the ideas you've been working on into your next creation, whatever that might be?
⊚ Have you seen any art recently?
⊚ Can your gender become a work of art?
⊚ Can you become your own work of art?

ART EXERCISE #1:

1. With what art form are you most familiar?
2. Attend, read, view, or otherwise experience that art form with special attention to any aspects that might be giving off messages about the gender/identity/power system. If there don't seem to be any such messages, keep watching until you find some. If you still don't find *any*, I'd be personally curious to know more about the artist.
2A. If you did find one or more messages about the gender/identity /power system, write them down on a separate piece of paper.
3. Put a mark next to any of those messages which were seductive or appealing to you.
4. Did any of those seductive messages make you think you are more or less of a real man or a real woman? Put another mark next to any of those messages that did.
5. Write down just how the artist got you to think or feel that.

ART EXERCISE #2:

1. Repeat the above exercise, only this time choose some art form you rarely if ever attend, read, view, or otherwise experience, *or* use the same art form, but an artist whose work you don't particularly connect with. Do all the same steps of the first exercise. Write down any thoughts you have on the subject of these questions.
2. Were there more or fewer gender/identity/power messages?
3. Were the messages more or less obvious to you?
4. Were the messages coded in some other language or signage?
5. Were you more or less able to be distant from any manipulation that might be going on toward making you more desirous of being a real man or a real woman?
6. Write down what you think gave you that relative immunity to artistic manipulation of your personal standards of gender, identity, or power.

⑥ My Gender Is Dirty: Learning Gender from Pornography

Subj: Your Book
From: Brenda.XXX@lancaster.uk
To: OutlawGal@AOL.com
So, a question. How do you think gender is constructed through

fantasy? I live most of my time trapped in my own bad "B" movie . . .
Happy days and bye . . .

Dear Brenda,
Thass a real good one! Okay—I think that gender can be seen as a
form of self-expression, existing for the purpose of establishing a
connection with another entity (be that an individual or group).
Fantasy could be said to be the stated or unstated desire for a particular type of connection. It's a longing. Given a strong enough
longing, then certainly the desire would find its way into an individual's identity, no?
Example: if I want a connection with birds, let's say that's my
fantasy, and I see that birds *really* like trees, I might consciously or unconsciously become more tree-like, right? That would get me
my fantasy of a connection with birds.
The problem in this culture comes from a double bind: gender is
nonconsensual, enforced, and fixed; and most fantasy is taboo.
::laughing:: No *wonder* I get headaches!

Pornography has become such a flashpoint, hasn't it? Is there any other art form that sits so squarely in the middle of moral, ethical, political, legal, religious, and philosophical debates? Something *that* controversial has got to be good for people.

I really like good porn. I read it whenever I can. I've begun writing my own. Pornography gives me a chance to see my fantasies played out to their (sometimes logical, sometimes illogical) ends. Pornography, I think, opens a lot of doors for us that are otherwise closed by social convention. If in fact our identity is shaped by desire, and if desire is kindled by fantasy, and if pornography is the textual, aural, or visual (but not actual) realization of fantasy, then pornography actually helps us realize more and more of our own identities through the usually *un*-explored route of desire. If we apply that principle to a culture that defines its desire solely by gender, we're going to learn a lot about our gender identities from the pornography of any given culture or subculture.

Pornography, I think, would be best simply viewed as an art form: a nice, dangerous-to-the-status-quo art form. Pornography as an art raises questions concerning our desire and identity; it implicates those parts of ourselves that are fighting self-expression and self-realization.

EXERCISE: Get a copy of several newspapers that represent different subcultures. Examples of different subcultures would be: gay male, soldier of fortune, home town or city newspaper, etc. Check the papers to be sure they have personals sections, adult services ads, lonely hearts ads, or the like. Read through those sections and mark the ads you would consider in bad taste. Place another kind of mark next to those you would consider an expression of personal desire. Place a third kind of mark next to those ads you might consider close to a fantasy of your own. Write down your observations and conclusions from having done this.

I don't want to get into a debate about the moral, ethical, legal, or any other aspects of pornography-as-art. I don't want to start quoting porn here. I just want to do what I can to help free people from the chains placed on their fantasies, desires, and ultimately identity and self-expression through the overwhelming opposition to pornography in this culture. Most of us fantasize. It's just not been safe to do that in the world at this time, so I'd like to change that. Please try this, just for a moment. Put aside any objections or revulsion you might have about this word *pornography,* and just imagine something.

◉ Imagine for a moment the sweetest, gentlest, most loving sex you can think of. Go on. If there is a partner or partners involved, imagine them as the most perfect partners ever.

Got that? Okay. Not so bad. Now . . .

◉ Please imagine the kind of sex that you would find most thrilling. Really thrilling, we're talking spine-tingling, toe-curling stuff here. Right, not bad.

Now we're going to apply the principle of being willing to become that which we fear most.

◉ I want you to imagine yourself involved in the kind of sex that scares you. It either scares you because you've been told it's bad, or because you simply believe it's bad, whatever, it scares you. Go on. Scary sex, and you're doing it. It's your imagination, and no one's looking, are they? Go on.

I'm going to assume you did that and I want you to write some stuff down now:

> Who were you in the first imagining (sweet, gentle sex), and what were you doing? What were your feelings?
>
> Who were you in the second imagining (spine-tingling, thrilling sex), and what were you doing? What were your feelings?
>
> Who were you in the third imagining (scary, dangerous sex), and what were you doing? What were your feelings?

- Did you notice any shift in self-perception among those three imaginings? That is, did you become a different kind of person in each of the three scenarios, or was there some different facet of yourself highlighted in each scene?
- Did you notice some part of yourself that you don't frequently get to experience outside of some sexual encounter?
- Whether you liked that part of yourself or not, is there anything you experienced in your imagination that you might like to explore further in your imagination?
- Whether you liked that part of yourself or not, is there anything you experienced in your imagination that you might like to explore further in real time?
- How might your gender identity shift if you actually explored that part of yourself?

One value of the art of pornography is that it opens doors to self-exploration and self-definition.

⊚ My Gender Is What I Buy: Learning Gender from Marketing

If I was in high school, and I was out, and nobody cared either way, I would have had pictures of Chris Cornell up in my locker. Instead I had pictures of Heather Locklear, Morgan Brittany, Charlie's Angels. Why did I pick those particular women? I think it had a lot to do with their hair. I was obsessed with long hair. I wanted to have gorgeous long locks like Farrah Fawcett. That was the attraction. I was actually very jealous of them. Women are allowed to have long curly hair, I was not. I remember my very favorite commercial when I was about 14.

It was for Pert Plus, I think, and it was of this beautiful heterosexual couple. They were on vacation and were lazily touring about some friendly Caribbean town when they realized that they were late for their "ferry." They began to run for the ferry and ... oh the build up is so exciting ... and they had to jump on to the back of the ferry as it pulled away. A nice older man helped them on with a huge and very uncharacteristic smile. Then, the best part of all, the woman takes her hat off and "swooshes" her head back and forth, back and forth. Well, her hair was wonderful. It was blonde, curly, long, and just beautiful. I WANTED TO BE HER!!!!!!! Seriously.

—Jamie

I've done quite a bit of sales and marketing in my life. From Time/Life books to Scientology; from somewhat dubious timeshare real estate in Florida (I only did that for a week, honest!) to season tickets to the San Francisco Opera, I've sold stuff. I think I was good at sales and marketing because I understood that effective marketing and ultimately effective sales depend on creating within the consumer an identification (matching identities) with other persons who use or buy a given service or product, or by creating or stimulating some desire within the consumer for some fantasy, ostensibly or realistically attainable by the use or purchase of a given service or product. There are those two concepts linked up together again: identity and desire.

Sales and Marketing 101

It works like this: you have a product or service you want to *market* (get well known or well thought of) and *sell* (get into the hands of some end user). Well, first you have to know a lot about your product. You have to know what it is, what it can do, how it works, and how much it's going to cost to produce. You're also going to need to figure out who's going to need it enough to buy it.

You need to target the market window: you need to nail down the identity or identities common to the different kinds of people who will buy your stuff. Because you're so far away from the consumer of the product or service, you can do things like conduct surveys or hold roundtable discussions. What you're looking for is *the lowest common denominator that will reach the greatest number of people who will buy*. Okay, once you've got that market window targeted, you can figure out how much you can charge for this service or product, and where you can sell it so it'll be easily accessible for your targeted group of buyers.

Yes, this has a lot to do with gender and power. Honest.

Marketing Gender as a Need

The marketing of goods and services in today's consumerist culture manipulates both identity and desire and ultimately reenforces the pyramid model of the gender/identity/power system. Because gender is one of the lowest common denominators of identity, and power is just now one of the lowest common denominators of desire, we've got a match made in heaven for marketing people everywhere. All marketers have to do is divide their goods and services into two categories: stuff for men, and stuff for women. All they have to do is figure out how to convince people that their goods will make us *better* men or *better* women than anyone else's stuff. I think this analysis works. Even in the marketing of supposedly non-gender-specific goods like insurance, soda pop, computers, or cars, the emphasis is on *how* buying those services and goods will make you fit in and be respectable within the community you wish to be a member of. In terms of the gender/identity/power pyramid, the ultimate marketing device would convince us that by buying that service or those goods, we will rise up on that pyramid.

I'm not saying there's some evil world conspiracy of marketing geniuses that has this all mapped out. I believe they're as befuddled as the rest of us when it comes to the ideas of gender and power. But they've stumbled onto this killer combination of identity and desire, and further stumbled onto linking those factors to gender and power. The fact that they probably don't know what they're doing makes them all the more dangerous. Like putting an uzi into the hands of a four-year-old.

So what do you do when confronted with this stuff? Stop buying it? No, no, no. Buy what you want to buy, please. Just know *why* you're buying it, and please don't buy something for the sake of either climbing up that pyramid, or maintaining your position on it, unless that's exactly what you want to do, that's all. Here's a couple of little exercises you might want to try:

EXERCISE: READING THROUGH THE ADS

Go to a magazine stand and get yourself a couple of magazines of different types. They can be car mags, computer mags, fashion mags, social consciousness mags, whatever. Try to get the kind that have a fair number of ads in them. Now, flip through the magazines and stop when an ad attracts your attention. Don't read the ad fully yet.

1. What about the ad attracted you: the product, the image, or the text?
2. Whatever it was that attracted you, do you suppose it appealed more to your sense of identity or was it some fantasy of yours?
3. Read the ad fully, paying careful attention to both text and image.
4. Do you still find yourself attracted? If so
   - Is there something in that ad that you can identify with in terms of being a man or a woman?
   - Is there something in that ad that makes you feel you'd be a *better* man or a *better* woman?
   - Is there something in that ad that matches a fantasy you might have, or gives you the idea that you might be able to attain that fantasy?
5. If you're no longer attracted to that ad, having read it more closely
   - Is there something about it that conflicts with your sense of your own womanhood or manhood?
   - Is there something about it that makes you feel less powerful, either as a man or a woman?
   - Is there something about what the ad is promising that, if you lived it out, you'd find repugnant?
6. Repeat this exercise with a few more ads until you're comfortable with analyzing what attracts you and what repels you.

Advertisements and commercials are only one way marketing people get us to buy things. There's also something called point-of-purchase marketing. That's where people spend months, even years, trying to figure out how to get your attention once you're in the store.

EXERCISE: SHOP TIL YOU DROP, #1

Go grocery shopping. Make it one of those big all-under-one-roof supermarkets, if you've got one in the area. It'd be worth traveling the extra distance to one for the purposes of this exercise. When you get there, notice the packaging that attracts you. These designers are smart, talented people so it's no shameful thing if you admit you're attracted to something. Just notice what you're attracted to. Here comes the fun part. Spend some time examining the package.

1. What about it attracted you?
2. Was there anything that appealed to your womanhood or your manhood?
3. Was there anything that made you feel you could advance yourself upwards in terms of the gender/power pyramid?
4. Was there anything that made you feel good about being exactly where you are?
5. Having done that examination, are you still attracted to buying that product?
6. Repeat this exercise with a couple of products until you develop a way to spot any manipulation that might be going on.

EXERCISE: SHOP TIL YOU DROP, #2:

Go to a department store. Again, try to get to a really big one, one with lots of departments. Pretend to yourself that you have a lot of money to spend, and you want to spend it. Just walk around and let whatever catches your eye draw you in. Remember, expense has nothing to do with it: you have all the money you need. Notice something that attracts you.

1. Why is it attractive?
2. Is there something about either the displays or the goods themselves that would make you more of a woman? More of a man?
3. Is there something that would make you a *better* woman? A *better* man?
4. Maybe there's something that makes you feel very good about being exactly what you are?
5. Something that makes you feel satisfied with your place in the world?
6. Keep walking around, spotting things, until you develop a sense of what exactly it is that's attracting you to purchase this stuff.

The omnipresence of marketing in our greed-driven culture pretty much ensures the omnipresence of pressure to belong to one of two genders, and the pressure to be, be like, or be liked by the Perfect Gender.

⊚ My Gender Is My World:
Learning Gender from Friends, Family, and Clubs

Parental gender stereotypes come into active play immediately upon the birth of a child. Studies of parents of newborns only a few days old have found that parents' observations of their days old infants reflect the common steretypes that females are "soft, fine-features, little, inattentive, weak, and delicate," and that boys are not. Parents, fathers more so than mothers, tend to perceive their infants as acting in these ways despite the fact that female infants at birth are generally more mature, active, and alert than male infants. This once again illustrates that people perceive babies on the basis of their own beliefs about what they are "supposed" to be like, rather than on the basis of what babies actually do.
(Devor, 33-34)

I know. This is a pretty obvious way that gender enters the culture. It's akin to peer pressure, and it's where many social scientists believe we learn most of our gendered behavior, so there are lots of books and essays available that analyze exactly how this transmission of socially acceptable gendered behavior takes place. I want to focus briefly on the nuts and bolts of how that might have happened to *you*.

EXERCISE: Write down up to five gender-specific behaviors you were *actively taught* by the people who raised you as a child.

	Teacher	Behavior(s) They Actively Taught
1.		
2.		
3.		
4.		
5.		

Now write down some of the gender-specific behaviors you're aware of that are or were displayed by the people who raised you as a child.

	Teacher	Behavior(s) They Displayed
1.		
2.		

> 3.
>
> 4.
>
> 5.

⑥ Do you notice any of those behaviors in your own life today?

⑥ Did any of the gendered behaviors you were taught conflict with the gendered behaviors you watched your teachers display?

If It Walks Like a Duck, Then So Will I

We tend to take on patterns and behaviors that will make us feel most part of the social unit to which we belong. Corporations mimic families and friends in this regard when they publish their guidelines for acceptable behavior and dress at work. Unfortunately, most family members and groups of friends don't write down their guidelines for acceptable gender behavior and presentation. Most of us have learned our genders by trial and error.

EXERCISE:

1. Can you recall times when as a child you experimented with some new form of behavior, only to be told or to somehow discover that this behavior was not appropriate for your assigned gender? List up to five of those times here.

2. Can you remember one or more times when you as a child learned a specific gender behavior from an adult family member? List up to five of those times here.

3. Now rate each these learning experiences on a scale from one to five where five would be the best of all possible ways to learn something—gentle, respectful, and rewarding—and one would be a very painful or embarrassing way to learn something.

Did the Devil Make Us Do It?

This gender game, especially when it comes to family, friends, and lovers, is not a one-way street. It's not all about someone pressuring us to be one way or the other. We bring our own preferences and needs to bear in all these relationships. We depend on others to remain stably gendered in much the same way we've known during the time we've loved them. So, take a deep breath and relax, and let's do a little mind-stretching stuff.

EXERCISE: On a separate piece of paper, write down your honest responses to the following scenarios:

◉ What if you found out that your birth mother went through a gender change and is now a female-to-male transsexual man?

◉ What if you found out that your birth father went through a gender change and is now a male-to-female transsexual woman?

◉ What if a close relation told you that hir sexual orientation was different than the one you thought it was?

◉ What if a lover or friend told you that ze wanted to take on a different role in your relationship, a role that *you* have been fulfilling so far?

If your response to any of the above questions was anything less generous than "Fine, I'd be really supportive and I've got no fears or hesitations whatsoever," then maybe there's something you're holding in place when it comes to a fixed gender system.

A Case for Gender as Conspiracy Theory

Finally, it's worth mentioning that like other cultural entrance points for gender, the entrance point of family, friends, and clubs is not isolated from the other entrance points. Here's an example of how the family teams up with legal and medical forces to make sure we're all real men and real women.

Anything that challenges the definition of girl and boy fuels our cultural anxiety around gender. So deep is that anxiety that our government has sponsored many studies and experiments on children who do not fit the norm. Government records indicate that, since the early 1970s, at least 1.5 million dollars was awarded from the National Institute of Mental Health (NIMH) alone for this purpose. For the most part, on the occasions when "normal" children were studied with these funds, it was to determine treatment goals for "abnormal" children.

(Burke, 32)

In this model, the family member who is frightened by and concerned with the gender discrepancies of a friend or relative, contacts the concerned medical professional who *fixes,* with reluctant or no consent from the individual, the problematic gender issue, using funds from the concerned government. As we're obviously in no position to wave a hand and halt the machinery of both Science and Government, our best solution on behalf of a gender-troubled friend or family member would be right now to protect them from the almost overwhelming pressure of those two social megaliths. That's what I think families and friends need to do for each other.

⊚ My Gender Is My Station: Learning Gender from Class and Race

Some interesting questions to ponder:

... in addition to the Ten-Minute Gender Outlaw Exercise that you did today, of course!

⊚ Is there anything about the culture or subculture in which you were raised that makes you the kind of man, woman, or other gendered being that you are today?

⊚ Are you conscious of your gender presentation when you physically enter another culture or subculture?

⊚ Would members of your subculture consider you a real woman or a real man?

⊚ Do you believe that members of the class you belong to now are more masculine men or feminine women than members of some other class?

In developing the pyramid theory of gender, the idea that there's a perfect gender someplace, held in place by the very power it commands, is itself a fluid construct. It became apparent to me that more than a few people wouldn't buy the "perfect" gender as I've got it laid out on top of the pyramid, as either a "real man" or a "real woman."

Someone from a working-class world, for example, might very easily see what I've called a "perfect" gender as an effete snob, a sissy, and in no way a *real* man at all. Similarly, racial prejudices

Venice Beach
and O, i am the luckiest girl
walking arm and arm with my two
packing butches
Does any femme ever get more
stylin' than this?
the people look at my he-shes
i can see it in their eyes
he? she? he? she?
and i am one happy, flying dyke

−K. O.

come into play when looking at gender: women of color, for example, have frequently been exoticized as sexual objects by Eurocentric colonial cultures. Women of color haven't been considered "real women" by many people higher up on the pyramid, but they're certainly seen as the most real women by others at a similar level on the pyramid. Subculture-specific language even includes *names* for people who are more perfectly gendered. *Lady, gentleman, righteous dude, one fine bitch,* are some culturally specific euphemisms for real men and real women.

Katie, the Nice Jewish Boy

I was raised in an upper-middle-class suburban culture. My parents were second-generation Jewish immigrants. My father was a medical doctor, a heavy man, not inclined toward competitive sports. My mother was a school teacher in one of the local grammar schools. My brother grew up to be a successful psychologist. Intellectual success was a sign of real manhood for us, and that's what I fought for in an effort to shove my gender issues under the carpet. There was one major drawback: in our community, Jews were a minority. Intellectual Jewish boys like me who were clumsy, fat and not good at sports were not "real" boys, not in the Christian All-American community I grew up in. As a child, I was torn between wanting to be *real* in the eyes of the larger culture, and *real* in the eyes of my Jewish community. I was pretty miserable most of the time.

Looking back at my childhood, it's pretty obvious that there were pyramids of gender *within* the larger pyramid of gender. Each subculture, whether based on race, class, ethnicity, sexual orientation, or any other factor of identity, has its own definitions of what real men and real women are. More or less isolated communities are more likely to evolve some internal uniformity in their agreement on socially acceptable monogender presentations. Given the generally conflicting notions of reality from one subculture to another, not to mention the conflict between the views of those subcultures and the view of the dominant culture, there's not much of a window in which to develop a cohesive sense of a *personal* gender identity. So, we're left with some options:

⊚ We can choose one subculture's gender definition over another's, thus abandoning any claim to a "real" gender within the culture that we've left behind.
⊚ We can present ourselves as real in *many* subcultures, shifting our gender presentation, chameleon-like, with each culture shift we make.

- 🅖 We can mix and match our gender presentations from many cultures, presenting a gender that's not quite real in any single arena.
- 🅖 We can simply express ourselves as fully as we wish, with disregard for what's considered real or not real in any given subculture.
- 🅖 We can consciously choose to do any of the above at any time, for reasons of comfort, safety, fun, or growth.

I think the key to any of these choices is the idea of choice itself. We all have the capability to make both our gender identities and presentations the result of an informed decision.

It appears that in order to compensate for some lack of individual power within their societies, subcultures tend to tightly define "man" and "woman." Like most definitions of man and woman, these categories generally go unquestioned; they become assumptions; they are seen as "natural." By reason of their unquestioned status, any information about these categories beyond or beneath the cliché level or the stereotype becomes forbidden knowledge. That guarantees the longevity of these two identities as well as their supremacy in the world of gender. That also makes it very difficult to make informed decisions about our own genders and identities. That robs us not only of choice, but of power.

This exercise might open some previously locked doors.

> How has been being mistaken for a boy/man affected me? When I was much younger (adolescent/teenager) it embarrassed me. As I got older in my twenties and thirties, it angered me. Now I'm in my forties, and it humors me.
>
> —Susi Rosenthal

Write down the qualities of a real man in the subculture within which you grew up.

Write down the qualities of a real woman in the subculture within which you grew up.

Now answer these next two questions.

If you live in a different subculture now than the one in which you grew up, write down the qualities that make up a real man in your current subculture. (If you live in the same subculture, write down the qualities of a real man in some other subculture you've observed or experienced.)

If you live in a different subculture now than the one in which you grew up, write down the qualities that make up a real woman in your current sub-culture. (If you live in the same subculture, write down the qualities of a real woman in some other subculture you've observed or experienced.)

Was there any difference between your answers to the first set of questions, and your answers to the second set of questions?

How about these next questions?

Drawing upon your own belief system, your own experiences, your own preferences and desires, what do you now believe are the qualities of a real man?

Drawing upon your own belief system, your own experiences, your own preferences and desires, what do you now believe are the qualities of a real woman?

And finally:

What gendered qualities do you regularly display or perform?

Are there any gendered qualities you possess that you find yourself unwilling to perform? Write these down, and write down the conditions under which you're unwilling to perform them.

Are there any gendered qualities from some other culture that you'd *like* to perform or own? Write them down here.

If you've answered these questions, you've now got a lot of information to work with. Now it's simply a matter of what's important to you. Now you're in a better position to make an informed choice about your gender presentation, given your cultural, racial, subcultural, or class environment. Of course there are the factors of safety, comfort, playfulness, political activism and personal growth to take into account. You can blend in, if that's what you need or want to do. You can stand in the spotlight. You can be the town eccentric. Whatever. It's a *choice*.

⊚ My Gender Is Valuable: Learning Gender from the Economy

Gender is rarely seen in the popular culture as a function of the economy. Leslie Feinberg's work in this field is ground breaking in that hir focus keeps both class and the economy in the forefront when exploring what have been previously considered issues relating solely to gender.

Here are some questions to think about before we dive in.

I'm something of a bitsa. Bitsa this, bitsa that. But I don't know if you can get outside the "gender continuum" altogether. Where would you go, darling? Australia? Come to think of it, there are plenty of examples of non-gendered people here: Leonie Kramer, the entire cast of "Neighbours", Helen Demidenko. . . . I think it's the sunblock. But I wouldn't live anywhere else. (I wouldn't be allowed too!) Gender, you see, has always escaped me. Well, it's better than flatulence. My doctrine has always been "Men can grow as much body hair as they like—unless they don't want to."

Now, does that make sense? Because if it doesn't, it's probably because I'm hanging upside-down like a fruit-bat while water gurgles down the sink the wrong way. And that, as you'll agree, darling, is an excuse for almost anything.

—Alberta Winkler,
Mawson, Australia

- ⊚ Are you wealthy enough to be the kind of man or woman or whatever gender it is that you want to be? Why do you suppose that's the way it is?
- ⊚ Have you ever found your economic picture or job status to be effected by your gender?
- ⊚ Would a radical shift in your job status change the way others perceive you to be masculine or feminine?
- ⊚ If you won the lottery, say six million dollars, would you do things to change the way you perform your gender? What sort of things might you do?
- ⊚ Have you noticed that people of another gender than you, have different expectations when it comes to financial security, wages, and access to health care and education? Why do you suppose that is?

⊚ What do you think the changes might be if we didn't have to tell insurance companies or potential employers what our gender is?

⊚ If you got to call the shots—if you were the one who got to say what gender is in the world, and people would go along with it—what would you say?

Gender: The Final Frontier

I'm a major *Star Trek* fan, a Trekker if you will. In the *Trek* universe of the twenty-fourth century, money and profit do not rule the large organization of planets known as The Federation. Personal needs are seen to (albeit mysteriously: we never get to see *how* they manage that), and no one is without a rewarding job or human (and other-than-human) rights. Sigh. Dontcha just *wish?*

Back in the real world, the size of one's bank account or the total value of one's assets and property seem to be a fairly good indicator of how much power one wields; and if power is a good indicator of how perfect one's gender is perceived in the world, it follows that the more money we have, and the more we own, the more of a real man or woman we are or could be, right? I don't think so. I think the economy is one factor among many, and certainly having the power that money can bring us in the world today will go a long way in helping to construct a real good gender identity; that's a far cry from fulfilling all the qualifications for gender perfection.

The North American Eurocentric culture in which I'm living and working abounds with clichés that seem to prove that money isn't everything when it comes to gender—not if one's gender is truly dependent on how its put into play with other people.

⊚ The wealthy but boorish and perhaps ugly man who needs to buy his love and intimacy (and has no difficulty doing so).

⊚ The elderly wealthy widow who takes on young gigolo lovers, all of whom despise her.

⊚ The image of upper-class effete men, behind whose backs men of middle and working classes snicker.

⊚ The successful female executive in a power suit who has no time for a lover in her life, and whose very presentation as a successful woman intimidates rather than attracts others.

These are all examples of how even a positive economic status can negatively impact one's gender. Of course, to paraphrase Shalom Alechim, it's no great honor to be poor either. The cultural clichés point to the impact of money when it comes to gender presentation: the young male hooker in the movie *Midnight Cowboy* is not a *man* within the circle of his wealthy female clients, he's a *stud*. In cultures where slavery is sanctioned, slaves of any gender are neither men nor women: they're animals, or at best they're sometimes valued only slightly higher than animals. And if you have a criminal record of any kind, your gender status is severely impacted to the point of affecting your ability to raise or adopt children.

> Gender is as important a category to me in selecting friends and lovers as is race. That's to say, it's important, but only because of the power imbalance bestowed upon us by living in an oppressive system. If a potential friend or lover and I can talk about and get beyond that inherited power differential, then we can progress from there.
>
> —Dawne Moon

But all other factors being more or less equal, it's pretty obvious that the two-gender system results in a one-up, one-down dynamic when it comes to economy: people deemed men mostly get the first crack at money and power, and if you're going to be playing around with gender, it would be wise to keep this in mind.

EXERCISE:

1. Make a list of five of your friends or family, each of whom has a different gender (e.g., het white man, lesbian drag king, teenaged boy, female undergrad student, etc.). List each person's name and gender at the top of a single sheet of paper.

2. Now call each person on your list and engage them in a ten- to-fifteen minute conversation about the economy and their status within the economy. Note down the points that seem important or startling to you. Be sure to ask questions like "How does that make you feel?" so you get an emotional take on this. We're not looking for a purely financial analysis here. Gender is part of a system, and this exercise is to discover how gender is integrated with the economy.

3. Write a short summary of what you discovered about gender's relationship to the economy.

Yeah, You're Pretty, but Can Ya Pay The Rent?

A bizarre kind of privilege [to experience] as a gay man was straight male, breeder privilege. I recall pushing a friend's baby in a carriage. Suddenly, people were very warm and outgoing to me. The experience dumbfounded me. I hadn't changed. But somehow I'd become a straight man out on a walk with my baby boy. Very bizarre, and somewhat maddening.

—David C. Southgate

Well-intentioned members of the medical profession who manage the care of transsexual people place a great deal of emphasis on the probability of economic success of a gender-change candidate. As a result, transsexual people are subjected to something called a "real-life test" (RLT) as part of their transition from one gender to another. Prior to any surgical intervention or legal acknowledgment of their status as some desired gender, transsexual people must first live *as if* they're already a member of that gender. We're told by our therapists (most of them) to go underground, to pretend to be this other gender, and to see if we can measure up. Can someone who was raised male in the culture, with a more or less enculturated sense of entitlement to wealth, power, and acquisition, cope with the very real doors that will suddenly close in hir face? Can someone who was raised female in the culture, more or less enculturated with lower expectations and accustomed to taking the back seat when it comes to job opportunities and the wielding of power, cope with the very real demands placed on hir to succeed?

Transsexual people, no matter the direction in which they're heading, prove the existence of male privilege over and over. For example, when I left my job at an IBM subsidiary (at which I'd been hired as a man), and took a *more responsible* job as a woman at a similar Ford Aerospace subsidiary, I took a 30 percent pay cut. The only thing that had changed in my life was the gender I was presenting. A 30 percent pay cut.

But it's not all rosy for the female-to-male side of the coin. While a transsexual man might *appear* to have more privilege in his new gender, that doesn't hold much water when he goes to the hospital or has to produce a resume.

If we believe and forward the idea of a two-gender system, we are forwarding the idea (upheld by those who've got the power to enforce it) that one of the two genders is going to have more access to power than the other. It would seem that a key component to any true economic revolution would be the dismantling of the bipolar gender system.

The Way to a Gender Outlaw's Survival Is through Hir Paycheck

The first thing we need to realize is that when we start playing around with gender, most of us fall out of the economy. So we need to decide whether or not we want to hide our transition. If we do decide to *pass* as another more socially acceptable gender (and that's what I decided to do when I first transitioned from man to woman), things become fairly straightforward: we need to understand the reality of a gender-biased workplace, and we need to prepare ourselves to take a place in that workplace *as* the gender we've chosen. For those with marketable skills, it's not too difficult. As my employer told me when I informed him that I wished to resign my position due to my impending gender change: "Why? You can still sell, can't you?"

> EXERCISE:
> 1. Make a list of up to five jobs you've held during your lifetime. These can include babysitting, sex work, robbing convenience stores, sitting on a board of directors, managing the home you grew up in, full-time studenting, whatever. The definition of job here might be "whatever you're doing in order to make your living or your way through the world."
> 2. Next to each job, note what gender you were at the time, using modifiers from the gender/identity/power pyramid to note more subtle shifts in your gender from job to job.
> 3. Now explore your own economic status in each job, paying careful attention to how each factor (e.g., age, weight, attractiveness, education level, etc.) affected your ability to support yourself in the world.
> 4. Write down a summary of your observations during this exercise.

Katie's Moon is in Taurus, So Ze's Bullish on the Economy

While I'm not transgendered, in the way that I've known this word, I feel that one of my tasks in life has been to fashion a gender identity that makes sense for *me*. Twelve years ago, I had testicular cancer and came out of the experience cured, dehumanized, angry and shy one testicle and the ability to ejaculate. In the process I went from being a functionally bisexual, gay-identified person (deeply closeted) to functionally gay, lesbian-identified person (much more out, but fewer dates) to something a bit more balanced (perhaps, whatever "balanced" is) now.

I had to begin building a new self-concept that was broader than my previous one—what I came up with is a self-concept based on doing no harm and easing others' pains in little ways; finding humor where others might not; and tending my inner garden. I've learned how to listen better and ask questions better so that people sometimes leave me feeling as though they've learned something about themselves. I like that.

—Fred in Walla Walla

If we buck the gender system, we're going to buck what the world's currently built on: power. And if we do that, how do we expect the world we're bucking to reward us in its own currency? However, by doing what we believe in, we'll survive and be able to do more. At least, that's what happened for me. I've eaten a lot of pasta, rice and beans along the way—I still do. Currently, I still do professional phone sex when I'm in a heavy writing period and can't tour my performance work for an income. ::shrugging:: That's the economy. But I feel more fulfilled than in any other time of my life, and each day I find ways to compromise less and less with a world that wants me to be a real man or a real woman. That's what I really want to say about economy and gender play: there's no way to expect today's respectable economy to finance us for tearing it apart just so we can live our lives the way we want to; so we might as well live our lives the way we want to, which will eventually, I believe, help to dismantle the system that's been oppressing us.

⑥ Just When You Thought It Was Safe to Go Back into the Culture

We never know when gender is going to jump up and bite us on the bum. There are as many ways for gender to enter our conscious or unconscious systems of values as there are systems with which we might interact in the world. The trick, I think, is to learn to spot when we're being shunted into a one-or-the-other decision. It then becomes easier to spot the criteria by which we're being shunted. Once we spot the criteria, we can choose to buy into that system or not. Each of us is going to devise hir own methods of ferreting out the pressure exerted upon us to conform to the identities of real men and real women. Each of us is going to develop ways of dealing with the culture's insistence that we be, be like, or be liked by those who are most nearly perfectly gendered. The bad news is that the pressure's everywhere. The good news is there are even more perks awaiting the brave hearts who tackle this hydra head(s)-on.

More Perks of Saying No to Gender Perfection

It's difficult to say no to cultural pressure and insistence. What has become perhaps even more difficult in this world of ours is saying yes to our own hearts. To have lived in this culture under such confinement of our identities for so much of our lives can only result in our having taken on the mantle of *restrainer*, beginning with a conditioned self-restraint. And when we cast off that mantle? When we no longer choose to buy into a system that's been telling us "No," "No you can't be a man and giggle," or "No you can't be a woman with a swagger"? All that's left to us is yes. Yes to everything we've ever wanted to be in our lives. Yes to all the wonderful ways we've always wanted to express ourselves.

But American culture, currently spreading itself and its gender police through the world at breakneck speed, is going to come down squarely against what I'm talking about here, in much the same way as the Third Reich came down so hard on the free expression so abundant in the Weimar Republic. American culture, spawned in part by the Puritan ethic of the Northeastern immigrants to North America, continues to forward that ethic in the form of the archaic bipolar gender system. Right now, however, gender transgression is new enough to go relatively unnoticed while we continue to make some headway.

But what happens when we're noticed? What happens when we call our attention to ourselves? What happens when we men giggle? What happens when we women swagger? In addition to tickling the imaginations of others who may want to do the same, I think we begin to reach a deeper connection with *ourselves*. We begin to connect with the older, more basic issues that have chal-

Why would I want to break a gender convention? I have no fear whatsoever about attending a gender convention. What I do fear is my non-conventional gender identity. Gender fluidity is one thing, but my gender identity mostly resembles "Silly Sand." It's all over the place and it refuses to hold it's shape! When I'm with a partner, one minute I want to be treated like the Goddess I know myself to be, the next minute I feel just like I'm Johnny Depp and I want to fuck 'em silly. How can I expect anyone to keep up with me when I can't keep up with myself? It's exhausting! I'm scared of that.

—Justin Bond

I'm a Sister of Perpetual Indulgence living in New Orleans, a retired psychiatrist, and I love to play with people's heads on the issues of yin/yangs:
feminine/masculine
doctor/drag queen
sickness/health
(I'm also a person with AIDS)

—Aunt Viva

lenged humanity forever. I think we dig way beneath the ideas of capitalism, religion, consumerism, Protestant morality, "family values," and identity politics. I think what happens when we begin to live our lives with mindful nonrestraint is that the resulting joy begins to make us grateful, and we start to find room in our hearts for ideas like inclusion, compassion, nonviolence, sharing, and transformation. It all gets back to transformation.

EXERCISE: What if you could be whatever you've always wanted to be? Describe yourself here. Oh go on, there's no need to be self-deprecating or overly modest. This is a good basic lesson in liking yourself, so go on . . . indulge every noble, kind, and passionate notion you've ever had for yourself.

So how're you doing? Can we take a little stock here? Draw these three pictures. When you're done, compare what you just drew to the earlier time you did this exercise, back on page 42.

Draw a perfectly gendered person

Draw a picture of yourself the way you are.

Draw a picture of who you've always
wanted to be.

And now that we've spent all that time learning how to say no, it's time
to . . .

Just Say Yes

This workbook began with a deceptively simple maxim: look out for where gender is, and go someplace else. Well, we've looked at where gender might be lurking. Now it's time to go someplace else. Now it's time to look at actually creating a brand new gender for ourselves—one that allows us to express ourselves more fully and with less pressure to conform to the either/or systems. It's time to stop looking outward for gender guidelines sactioned by the culture. There's no real challenge in following their guidelines, is there? Besides, all we can do when we look outward into the culture for a gender to emulate is say no, no, that's not *quite* how I want to express myself. The challenging part comes from looking inside, deeper within ourselves, and saying yes. Yes, that's more like the way I've always seen myself to be.

The first look within ourselves may be startling. Kind of like wandering into a storage room that's been closed off for years and years, filled with every point of view we've ever had. We all carry around many points from which to view any given phenomenon, including but certainly not limited to gender. My own take on life in general, and gender in specific, is influenced by, among other things, the following value systems that are each scrambling for ascendency in my spinning head.

◎ A 1950s modernist (essentialist) view of how the world works.

◎ A white upper-middle-class male baby boomer sense of entitlement, and all the privileges accorded thereto.

◎ An American-Judaic sense of being a member of a persecuted minority, with an emphasis for passing as a non-Jew; and the stress placed on the value of questions as opposed to answers.

◎ A sixties hippie accent on peace, love, harmony, and happy endings (not to mention fun stuff to wear).

I do [break any rules or laws or conventions of gender] in a couple different ways. As a male bodybuilder I will often shave my legs, arms, and torso as the urge hits me, even if I'm am not planning to compete. I do it simply because smooth legs/arms/whatever *feels* good to me.

Many people cannot understand *why* a heterosexual guy would do something like this, but it's hard to explain other than it shows the muscle definition better (my standard response), when the truth is I just *felt* like doing it. I also have one acrylic nail. I do it because my right index finger was smashed when I was 2 and it doesn't grow right and I've found an acrylic nail makes it look like a normal nail and protects it. Combine that with shaving, and I get some weird looks from people. Oh well.

—Tom Underwood

⊚ My work with tarot, which I interpret as having an emphasis on the *journey* of life as opposed to *arriving* at any given point.

⊚ A Zen focus (lack of focus?) on the value of paradox.

⊚ A decade spent as a dedicated Scientologist, from which I learned the pitfalls of a system based on greed, the acquisition of power, and the absence of love.

⊚ A Wiccan appreciation for otherwise inexplicable spiritual intervention.

⊚ The emphasis placed by quantum physics, and chaos theory, upon ultimate connectivity and relativity.

⊚ Sufi teaching techniques, which use comedy to get a point across.

⊚ A Taoist focus on nothingness.

⊚ My brushes with academia and postmodern theorists who've developed a uniquely Western approach to positing both paradox and nothingness.

⊚ My career in theater, which taught me transformation, the value of entertainment, and the importance of connecting with an audience.

⊚ My involvement in and love for sadomasochism and dominance/submission play, which has allowed me to understand the idea of service and the responsibilities inherent in the use of power.

⊚ The use of a computer as my primary tool, which has given me insight into the value of order and linear organization as a means to communicating ideas.

⊚ My life in the cyberspace community, which gives me a nonlinear, rule-free, free-form playground to live all this stuff out in.

Put 'em together and what have you got?

⊚ Shh-h-h-h-h! We're Going to Look at the S Word Now

> **kaos:** Buddhist spirituality has obviously been a clarifying influence in your search for "gender peace . . . " Is it possible, since we are a Western culture, to gain similar understanding from a Judeo-Christian perspective?
>
> **OutlawGal:** ::nodding:: I think postmodernism is the Western extension of Zen. Both philosophies concentrate on what really isn't, rather than what seemingly is. But postmodern theory has yet to embrace the inevitable paradox: that by deconstruction of everything, there is a simultaneity of everything and nothing.
>
> **kaos:** yes . . . I think that for folks rooted in traditional Western

thought those will be hard bonds to break, don't you think?
OutlawGal: ::nodding:: That's why I wanna do this Workbook thing
. . . Very little of postmodern theory extends itself into practical application, whereas Zen is nothing if not practical
application.

Let's examine this gender thing on still another level. A great number of people change, mess around with, or challenge gender norms because the gender norm they're having to live up to "doesn't feel right." Even people who *don't* mess around with gender because they're happy just the way they are will tell you when pressed, "I just know I'm a man," or "I just know I'm a woman." Well, what's that about? What's "feeling," and what's "right?"

Beyond Both Nature and Nurture

For whatever reason—DNA, brain structure, social conditioning, or peer pressure—gender has become intrinsic to our identities, to the point where we "just know" what gender we are. I'm talking about the gut level *feeling* that what we've been has either been sufficient for our lives, or that it some-how just hasn't been enough. The gender we're being now simply is or isn't completely congruent with what we *feel* ourselves to be. This is where postmodern theory caroms headlong into an area it has been as yet unwilling to embrace or even acknowledge to much of a degree: the area of spirituality.

The male/female, straight/gay thing is too rigid for me, too, BUT I have trouble reconciling that with the fact that I find great empowerment, great strength in my identity as a lesbian woman. I realize that those are halves of dichotomous categories set up to box us in to "this" or "that," but I still feel as though I would fit your definition of "trangressively gendered" because, while I identify with these labels, I don't necessarily box myself into "I'll never sleep with a man," "I'm going to be butch," etc. (I guess I have a bit to go because I do box myself into the "woman" category, but then, being strong and outspoken, I defy what women are supposed to be . . . ?). Am I catching on here?

—Vickie Johnson

We hear the word "spirituality" and we think we're going to hear nothing but new age-isms for the rest of the conversation. The fact is that for many of us, it doesn't matter *what* the latest theorist or social politician has to say about gender, we simply *feel* ours is either right and complete, or it isn't. All the deconstruction of all the social machinery in the world isn't going to resolve our inner feelings and spiritual belief systems as they affect our identities, gender or otherwise. We need a language to talk about those feelings. Talk of angels and demons and lions and tigers and bears (oh, my!) may be exactly the right metaphor for someone's spirituality, or it may just seem silly to someone else.

I wonder at our need to talk about these feelings, and I'm dismayed at the taboo on that kind of talk. A friend of mine put it very well when she said it's a whole lot easier to talk about sex than it is to talk about our spiritual beliefs.

We need a language that won't scare people off, a language that won't get us laughed at or beaten up. So far in this book we've been practicing saying no. Now it's time to practice saying yes. And maybe the language of yes is different than the language of no.

Those of us who are questioning our genders need that langauge in order to acknowledge the feelings we've got—the ones the textbooks never seem able to describe well enough for us. We need to explore our feelings or we'll always have this nagging *feeling* that our gender exploration isn't quite complete.

> Me? I'm a death-fetishizing urban streetwalking somethingorother in love with sensation and the perpetual worship of the eroto-spiritual whatsis.
>
> —T.R.

I'm thinking the language of yes might be a question, and the language of no might be an answer. What do you think?

◉ Identity As the Bermuda Triangle of the Soul

It's so tempting to arrive at an identity and simply stay there, isn't it? I've done that over and over in my life. The fact is, no single one of my identities, no matter how comforting they were at the time, has been able to sustain the legion I keep discovering myself to be.

> It may be that the satisfaction I need
> depends on my going away, so that when I've gone
> and come back, I'll find it at home.
> —*Rumi*

I've been making a serious effort to avoid attachment to any single identity I'm exploring. My theme song has shifted from "I Am What I Am" to "Be All That You Can Be." And I love all this! It's like a dance, this shifting identities. I'm most attracted to people with whom I can shift and change. It's the fluidity that hooks me, it's the vulnerability needed to express such a wide range of one's self. It starts with the act of letting go of the need to know someone's gender, along with the act of letting go of the need for others to know us as specifically gendered.

What Gender Is That Doggie in the Window?

Let's start with the relatively easy one: why do we need to know someone else's gender? I know I do. Here's an example: I fairly regularly prowl bookstores, searching for new books on gender theory. I weigh several factors before I actually pick the book up to flip through it:

Life without gender? Could you describe how that works for you? Impossible to answer. Trying to figure this out is like trying to detect the taste of the local water. You can only do this when you've been away and tasted the water of another town.

—Mona Sutton

◉ The title: Is it clever? Does it pull me in? Does it assume two genders, or leave room for more?
◉ The publisher: Do they generally publish books that forward the binary or question it?
◉ The author: What's the author's gender? Is this book written by a man, a woman, or a neither?

I use the gender of the author as a reference point to judge the thoroughness of the viewpoint of the book. I hate that I do that; it's something I'm trying to break myself of, but I do it. I assume that a book written by a "woman" will probably have more questions about gender than answers, because women have been in the position of having to question gender longer than men have. And I'll generally buy anything by someone who has defined their gender as up in the air.

So gender can be a *reference point,* a way station on the road to getting to know ourselves or others. It's another use of gender as social or intellectual traction. Ava Apple, speaking of her email, said "Sometimes I need to know whether the person writing me is a man or a woman or whatever. Then I know something about them, and I can take it from there. It's like knowing if a person is a Pisces or a Scorpio."

◉ What's important to know about someone?
◉ What's important for someone to know about you?
◉ Is it hir gender you need to know?
◉ Or is it a series of qualities that we've somehow gendered?

> EXERCISE: Make a list of ten things you need to know about a new person coming into your life. Then arrange your list in order of importance with the most important factor at the top and the least important factor at the bottom.

> Now make a list of ten things you want others to know about you as
> you're first getting to know them. Take care to name these as
> qualities rather than as identities. Then arrange your list in order of
> importance with the most important factor at the top and the least
> important factor at the bottom.
>
> Now compare the two lists. Write a summary of your observations
> and conclusions on a separate piece of paper.

◎ Just Say Maybe

The trouble starts when gender (identity) ceases to be a *reference point* for
connecting with a living growing person and is substituted for the person
hirself. When gender ceases to be a way station and becomes a destination—one of only two possible destinations, at that—then we need to bow
out of the gender/identity/power system by invoking the three words that
system cannot tolerate: "I don't know."

◎ I don't know what a man is.
◎ I don't know what a woman is.
◎ I don't know what my gender is.
◎ I don't know why I have to be one or the other.
◎ I don't know why you expect me to be one way and only one way.
◎ I don't know why I've expected that of you, but I'm working on that
   one.

And because I-don't-know usually opens the door to more questions,
here are some that come to mind.

◎ Have you ever been expected to do something simply because you are
   or appear to be the gender you are?
◎ If so, how did that make you feel?
◎ What, if anything, did you do or could you have done about it?
◎ Have you ever consciously shed a particularly useless or even harmful-
   to-you identity of yours?
◎ If so, can you recall a moment you decided "No, that's not what I am."?
◎ And as a bonus question: Where do you suppose that identity went after
   you got rid of it?

Who Are We after We Leave Ourselves behind?

I found that a simple way out of most identity traps is to positively define myself by what I'm not. By saying, I'm not a particular whatever, an infinite number of possible yes-I'm-some-other-things present themselves. Managing some current gendered identity along with the shadows of some past gendered identities can be pretty tricky until there's an integration of all the qualities of all the gendered identities we've had the opportunity to be.

EXERCISE:
1. Name up to ten of your current various identities, and list them on one sheet of paper.
2. Are you all of those identities simultaneously, and all the time?
3a. Is someone expecting you to be some particular one of your identities *all* the time? If so, write their names down next to the identity they're expecting you to be.
3b. Do you find yourself buying into the pressure to be that identity?
3c. Are you reciprocating by encouraging the other person or persons to continue their perception that you are solely that identity?
4. Imagine you are able to strip away everything about yourself that you didn't like. On a separate piece of paper, write or draw what that might look like: you, but you're only the parts of you that you like.
5. If you were actually able to *do* that, then you should be able to strip away everything that was left. What would you be then?
6. Can you truly be *nothing*?
7. Is this getting close to something a little deeper than gender?
8. Would it be worth it to try to strip away gender in order to get closer to what you really are?

◎ Is Nothing Valuable?

One of the loudest objections I've heard to the idea of doing away with gender (after the desire objection) is the idea that by doing away with gender, we'll be left with nothing. Okay. So? Who says nothing is a bad thing to be left with?

Practitioners of Eastern philosophies have been attempting to achieve something called nothingness for quite some time now, and it makes me curious. In this increasingly Westernized world, it's getting more and more difficult to find a Bo tree to sit beneath. The pressure is on from all sides for each of us to grasp whatever is newer, faster, bigger, and better. That's what real men and real women do, right? Well, how does someone find a glimpse of nothing in the midst of *that* maelstromic value system?

I think it's all very well to talk about "fluidity" and playing around with gender, but then people ask: "If you feel gender is so fluid, why did you feel the need to change your body so radically?"

After a few years, as we feel more at home in our new bodies, and out there in the world, we tend to forget how uncomfortable we used to be. We forget how absolutely NECESSARY it was, at the time, to change our physical selves to more closely match our insides. And had we not done so, we would never be who we are now.

I liken it to being an actor preparing for a role. You have to shed a layer of physical mannerisms — like taking off a coat — and get to "zero." Only then do you have the freedom and awareness to really shape who and what you want to be, and build a "character." Recently I saw myself in a home video, shot several years ago prior to my transition from female to male. It suddenly struck me how foreign this person looked to me, and how throughout my life I really HAD been playing a role—complete with all the learned physical cues. Had I not gone through my gender-change, I would have never fully comprehended that.

—email from David Harrison

Yeah . . . ::grinning:: . . . that's my David. He and I have talked a great deal about this getting-to-nothing thing. In my own experience, every time I go through some gender change I've had to reach a point of nothing: no gender; and I build from there.

EXERCISE: Examine a glass, a vase, a jar, and a bottle. Which part of each object is useful? *(Answer on next page.)*

In the Western world, the concepts of nothing and no gender are conspicuously invisibilized. Getting to that point of nothing is what takes the work.

Bridle the mind, for it is like a wild horse. It needs to be tamed. First one has to know it is there, running on the plain. Then try to catch it, ride it, lead it by the reigns and be watchful of its movements all the time. With firmness, gentleness and patience, the horse will be tamed and the master known.

One has to practice the healthy way daily and unconditionally. Without daily practice, the little progress one makes will wither away quickly. . . .

It will take many years to purify the mind. Have courage and trust the positive nature of the universe and the positive nature of one's own being. Practice daily; never skip a day.
—Hua-Ching Ni, pgs 269–270.

I thought I might take this time to mention that the "never skip a day" part of that quote could be taken as applying to your Ten-Minute Gender Outlaw Exercise. Ha!

**Answer: Which part of each object is useful? The empty space,
the nothing.**

⊚ Is Nothing Everything?

Why all this emphasis on nothing? Because from a point of nothing, really being nothing, we have the potential to be anything, including any gender. Working from a point of nothing is like working on a clean slate. We can draw whatever we like. Here are some questions to think about that might illustrate how this works:

⊚ Has anything in this workbook been disorienting to you?

⊚ Has anything in this workbook caused you to question some assumption you've had about yourself?

⊚ Has anything in this workbook caused you to question the way you've always thought about gender?

I'm going to assume your answer to at least one of these questions was yes. If that's not the case, I'm going to assume you haven't been doing your Ten-Minute Gender Outlaw Exercise regularly. Tsk, tsk, tsk.

so if we can bend gender that much, then what's in the middle, if there is a middle? and if you take gender away, what goes in its place? and how do you live life without gender? i understand that gender is something that patriarchy has a huge investment in, i also understand that we can own our own gender and take it on and off as though its a clothing item. but once you take off gender, are you standing there naked? what do you put on so you're not naked or exposed? or is there an underlying layer? if so what is that? i'm confused about where you put gender when you take it off, and what goes in its place.

—Setafina

Shortcuts to No Gender: Sort of an Exercise

What is Matter?—Never mind.
What is Mind?—No matter.
—Punch, 1855

It's the moment of disorientation, I believe, that signals proximity to nothing.

The supreme paradox of all thought is its attempt to discover something that thought cannot think.
—Kierkegaard

From a point of disorientation, it's a hop, skip, and a jump to a clean-slate way of thinking available to us, if for no other reason than nothing else we know is working.

It's the nothing that makes us something.
It's what we miss that hits the mark.
—7-Up jingle

We've not been schooled to deal intellectually with nothing. Dealing with nothing is no part of our emotional arsenal.

What is truth? I don't know, and I'm sorry I brought it up.
—Edward Abbey

We use terms like *confusing, baffling, disorienting,* and *confounding* to describe our response to a set of conditions or concepts that make *some* sense together. These are very different terms than *bizarre, fantastic, fictitious,* or *maddening,* which describe what we tend to label impossibilities.

Mu: Literally "no" or "not." *Mu* signifies the absence of everything, but it does not mean "nothing"—it transcends the illusory distinction between positive and negative and is sometimes translated as "not two." It is said that once you have grasped *Mu,* you have grasped Zen.
—Jon Winukur

I think that I have somehow managed to nurture an ability to confuse people about what exactly I am. It is sort of a disrupter beam that makes people stop in their tracks and stare in a confused sort of way. They shake their heads and try to regain their gender balance but they can't as long as I am around. It makes some people really angry and even violent at times. They feel like I am doing this to them on purpose. They feel like I am trying to trick them and make them feel stupid. In this culture it is a huge offense to mistake someone's gender. It is so important to get it right because without that information the rest of the social interaction will have no structure and that is scary to most people. Other people are turned on by it. Myself included. There is nothing more exciting in sexual play than flirting with someone who I have no idea what their gender is.

—Elise

⊚ Are You a Man or a Woman?
Well, Yes and No.

Both *paradox* and *nothing* fall under the Western designation of impossibilities. That's Western thinking's loss, because both nothing and paradox do exist, and are either closely approached or experienced by many people every day. I think it's very sad that so many people don't know what they don't know.

One tangible example of proximity to nothing would be my statement that I'm neither a man nor a woman. To many people, that's an impossibility, something to be viewed as a fantasy, a pipe dream, or a perhaps a psychosis. Those people view my gender identity in the same way pre-Columbian navigators viewed the world: you sail too far, you fall off. I'm quite aware of the quandary in which my statement of neither/nor places people with no prior exposure to life beyond the binary. Frankly, I'm no longer concerned with some people's unwillingness to make the leap necessary to discover the reality I and others are experiencing right here, right now. It would be *nice* to be seen or taken as something other than a freak, a fanatical crackpot, or a deviant person, but the world just isn't nice sometimes.

All this to say you *can* experience nothing. You *can* grasp a paradox. The gender/identity/power pyramid could be a tool for exploring these concepts, but on its own, the pyramid isn't quite accurate on the printed page. The static pyramid model doesn't adequately reflect how constantly we shift closer to or further away from a perfect gender, if only imperceptibly. We are all passing through genders, sometimes on an hour-to-hour basis. Many of us confine ourselves to some category like "man" or "woman," but even within that category there's still some range of motion.

I am quite comfortable living between the genders. My therapist, however, along with a lot of people, are the ones scared of my betweeness, and then interpret this as ME being afraid of being "a woman." They are still thinking in binaries, and when I play the game, "why am I so afraid of being a woman?", I am too.

I end up having a similar problem with queers, who want to know why I am not butch or femme or top or bottom. Sometimes I really feel confused, and accused of being confused. But only when asked to define myself. I finally told someone this weekend, "Look, I know exactly what I am, but there just aren't words in this language I can use to describe myself to you, so I'm sorry." It wasn't well received, the person called me arrogant, but she was being pushy and rude to begin with.

I am half mexican (which is already a mix of races) and white (which is as well) and have had to pretend to be one or the other in terms of race as well. One of the greatest Chicano slogans, referring to California suddenly becoming part of the United States is: We didn't cross the border, the border crossed us. It sums up the gender issue for me as well.

—Maria Sanchez

On the brighter side, more and more people are stretching what it means to be a man or a woman. Some people are saying they're neither. Maybe you're toying with that conclusion yourself?

⊚ The Identity Politics of No-Identity

Had another interesting bathroom experience. I went to Denver this weekend for a training seminar and had to drive 7 hours to get there. So of course I have to stop at a roadside rest area for some relief. Anyway, I go into the women's can and do my business and I'm out drying my hands under the dryer and this older woman opens the door to come in and she stops, startled to see me. She looks at the "Women" sign on the outside of the door again and stands there with the door open staring at me like she's really scared to come in. She wouldn't go in until I left— just stood there with the door open. Never said a word to me.

  Gosh, I felt really bad. I mean, I've been yelled at to get out of bathrooms before, but I've never really felt like I made another woman feel unsafe around me before. It was a very odd feeling that I didn't like at all.

—jayneway

What we seem to be doing in identity politics, our need for and formation of community based on some pure identity, is reducing the concept of culture to an extension of identity. I AM becomes WE ARE. And bingo, you've got a culture. One of the benefits of an identity is the culture that the combined membership of that identity spawned prior to one's own membership. The point of arrival at *no* identity is the point of departure from a world that depends on identities. If we admit who we are not, we're going to disappear, because we can only exist in a world that would deny our existence as nothing. Once we admit that we truly exist as being outside the binary, we also begin to suspect that none of us can truly have a pure identity, gendered or otherwise. And if we do come to that conclusion, that's when we disappear. Well, not really. I think what happens is the apparently monolithic WE ARE reverts to a lot of I AMs, and we have the opportunity to forge a culture of unique individuals who share common values. Freedom, compassion, and honor come to mind as some worthwhile values to share. But it begins, I believe, with nothing.

In defense of identity politics, it does seem to be a necessary phase in getting the needs of under-represented groups out into the public discourse. The problem comes when that tactic is used after the needs are known. That's when coalition politics needs to kick in.

I think the human spirit is too large, too free-flowing, too filled with potential and possibilities to be frozen, stuck, or confined within one identity without a great deal of effort. It's sad to see the degree of effort some people exert, most of it quite unconsciously, in order to maintain a mono-gendered identity.

Whoa! Stop, stop, stop.
I think it's time to take a break from all this theory.

⊚ Playing with Words

The **bold clues** are anagrams for the answers that will fit into the cross-word puzzle. Each answer is one word, unless the clue specifies more. That should take your mind away from all this boiling for now. The answers are on page 172.

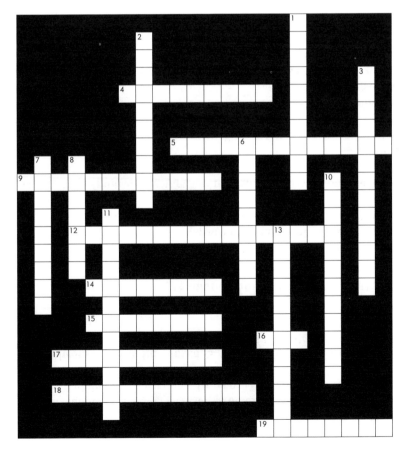

Across

4. Some call it sin. **I say exult!**

5. Personally, I indulge in this pleasurable philosophy whenever I'm in **a smash mood (sic).**

9. Depending on your point of view, this lifestyle could be seen as **a true-hole sex,** *or* **a resolute hex,** *or* perhaps **our late sex, eh?**

12. If you've gotten this far in the workbook, you know what I think about this kind of organizational theory: **It's plenty idiotic.** (two words)

14. Some may not choose this mode, but it's **fine in me.**

15. Your balance of these had better **mesh, or no** real gender for you!

16. This is the only anagram I could come up with for **Zen.** Somehow, it's appropriate.

17. Devotees of this philosophy **ponder most** everything.

18. **No girlie** pics here.

Down

1. If you've got the right combination, you might be able to **smooch more.**

2. These folks are just now surfacing as a unified group. My guess? They're our **next desire.**

3. **Angst rendered.**

6. Some might consider this trait compatible only with **alien scum.** Not me.

7. Using these as the sole criteria for gender assignment has turned out to be **a giant lie.**

8. **Able sin.**

10. We can find these two genders in varying states of **organdy bliss.** (three words)

11. This identity could be **a new-told urge** or **glad new route.** For some, it could even be a **wet organ duel.** (two words)

13. It might appear to some that this kind of person **inverts taste.**

Answers to Playing with Words, page 171

13. transvestite

genitalia 8. lesbian 10. boys and girls 11. gender outlaw

1. chromosome 2. intersexed 3. transgendered 6. masculine 7.

Down

14. feminine 15. hormones 16. Zen 17. postmodern 18. religion.

4. sexuality 5. sadomasochism 9. heterosexual 12. identity politics

Across

Zen and the Art of Gender Maintenance

I wrote this as a workbook because it's been my experience that it takes a great deal of personal work to get to a point of *consciously* changing or even stretching genders. We've spent most of our lives either convinced we were real men and real women, or convinced that we weren't. Sure, we can pretend. We can masquerade. We can slap on a false mustache and bind our breasts; we can tuck our penises between our legs and wear fabulous makeup. And sometimes that's fun and that's as deep as we ever want to go with this gender game. But if we want to experience a deeper level of our identities, freer from the constraints placed on each of us by the omnipresent gender police, it's going to involve some deeper work.

Passing Through

The concept of gender as a journey is a useful one for anyone who's serious about exploring gender from more than a purely academic standpoint. I was on a speaking tour in Duluth, Minnesota. I was trying to express the concept of shifting genders. A woman in the audience raised her hand, and summed it all up in one sentence by saying "I get it . . . it's a matter of passing through identities. I've been doing that all my life." That flipped me out, and I asked her to write me about it.

the next time i see my mother i'm going to tell her that she was right about my sexuality being a phase. shortly after i came out to her [as a lesbian], she said, "Shelly, you have passed through so many phases. You pick up something and give it all you've got and it's

always just a phase. This is just another one. I should know, I'm your
mother." well, she said something like that anyway.

at the time, i responded to her (rather defensively) by saying
that i hadn't been going through phases, i had just been experiencing
life and learning from that experience and moving on to different
stages of my life and growing through the process....at any rate,
she was right.

—Shelly Lynne

We're not accustomed to naming a change from straight to gay a *gender* change. We're not in the habit of seeing large weight gain or weight
loss as gaining or losing a gender. We tend to huff and puff about the difference between girls and women, boys and men; but we haven't dared
called them four different genders. A shift in ideological viewpoint hasn't
been seen as a shift in gender. But given the pyramid metaphor of gender,
identity and power, that's exactly what each one of those examples is: a
gender change. And that's exactly what this section of the workbook is
going to deal with: your journey through genders.

Yeah, it's time to start playing consciously with gender if you haven't
been doing that yet. It's time to put all this theory to the test on a very personal basis. But listen to me: you are far better prepared to play with this
stuff than so many others have been. You've done a great deal of ground-
work and you only have to explore as far as is comfortable for you. Honest. But to have come this far in the theory of it all and not to play with
your gender? Come on, I'll be gentle.

⊚ Have Gender, Will Travel

I've talked with several people about this concept of journeying through
genders. It conjures images of long road trips, traveling thousands of
miles, going through arcane surgical procedures, and never returning. I
want to remind you that journeys come in all shapes and sizes. Yes, there
are journeys that last a lifetime, journeys that are more or less permanent,
like moving to a new town. There are journeys we are forced to make, like
being shipped to a death camp because we don't match up to some Aryan
ideal. But remember, please, that a trip down to the corner store and back
is a journey. A weekend vacation to the mountains is a journey. It doesn't
have to be scary or overwhelming. I want to look at the metaphor of a gender journey from this latter standpoint, as something consensual and
something we can to some degree plan for and enjoy.

It doesn't matter what map or yardstick we use to measure our journey, but yardsticks are useful. So there's an exercise coming up now. We're going to find *some* journey story or metaphor that you like, against which you might compare your own journey through genders. It could be a trip paralleling *The Odyssey,* or maybe you want to travel the twelve signs of the zodiac. You might use Kerouac's *On The Road,* or Swift's *Gulliver's Travels.* Maybe you like the CD-ROM game, *Myst.* Perhaps you have a favorite tarot deck, or the *I Ching* rings true to you. Both *Star Trek* and the stations of the cross are useful metaphors for a journey. So is the Zen koan of *The Ten Bulls.*

Sweetie darling, you could even think of your journey through gender as a dream vacation, planned out in detail with some fabulous travel agent who knows just the sort of things you like to do.

It really doesn't matter what metaphor you choose. What matters is that you find a metaphor that's useful for a journey right now. And if the metaphor you'll be selecting stops working after a while, you can always find another one.

⊚ On the Road to Nowhere

Do you think I know what I'm doing?
That for one breath or half breath I belong to myself?
As much as a pen knows what it's writing,
or the ball can guess where it's going next.
—Rumi

One important note before deciding what metaphor you'd like to use. Some of my friends felt that in order to have a journey, there needed first to be some stated destination. I think that's the trap of a journey metaphor: the need for a destination, stated as "I'll be a man," or "I'll be a woman," or "male-to-female" or "female-to-male." How do we honestly know what it is that we want to reach until we've reached it?

How can we posit our true nature when we've never seen it before, when that true nature we wish to become has been covered up by so much of what the world has told us to be? Rather, let's name this journey of ours as a search for whatever turns up, with no particularly nailed-down destination beyond that.

> EXERCISE: Select a metaphor for the journey you're on. Examine your life so far. At what point in your journey are you? What's next? What do you have to do to get to the next step?

And don't forget your daily Ten-Minute Gender Outlaw Exercise! That's what's going to help keep the path clean in front of you, while sweeping up the stuff you've left behind.

⊚ Is Gender Is as Gender Does?

Okay, we've got some sort of measuring stick for ourselves in terms of our *progress* through gender; so let's start shaking things up a bit. Let's get to that point of nothing, no gender. A good place to start might be examining just how stable our current gender presentation truly is.

EXERCISE: Make a list of three people you know in each category below. Try to put down as many people from whom you're keeping a secret about yourself. For example, maybe your boss doesn't know. your sexual orientation; or maybe someone knows you as a lesbian, but doesn't know you're transsexual; or someone who doesn't know you used to be fat (or skinny). For each person you choose like that, try to include someone who *does* know that secret: maybe a close friend who knows your sexual orientation, but doesn't know that your boss doesn't know. Go on . . . make it complicated; it's not like they're all in the same room at the same time!

A. Family

1.

2.

3.

B. Lovers (past and current)

1.

2.

3.

C. Friends

1.

2.

3.

D. Members of Groups, Clubs, Organizations

1.

2.

3.

E. Peer group (e.g., co-workers, students, interns, unemployed, self-employed)

1.

2.

3.

Now, think of a time you interacted with each person listed. Next to each name, jot down what gender-specific qualities that encounter brought out in you at the time. Remember that gender can mean more than man or woman. Someone might, for example bring out boy or girl in you. Or maybe femme or butch. Or dominant or submissive. There are lots of qualities. Think about each encounter, and next to that person's name, write down what qualities you found yourself expressing.

I'm going to assume that in some of the examples you wrote down, relating with different people brought out some different qualities in you.

Again, the different qualities may not have traditionally been called gender qualities; but take another look at the gender/identity/power pyramid, and how many factors go into gender presentation. I'm willing to bet that shifting whatever qualities you might have listed will result in a gender shift, however subtle.

◎ Guess Who's Coming to Dinner!

Shifting gender on the basis of the company we're keeping at any particular time makes an interesting case for gender being an interactive phenomenon, as opposed to it being some essential component of our identities. Gender might be seen as a form of communication. Maybe we shift genders in order to better communicate with someone. Let's test this one further. Remember what I said about all those folks not being in the same room at the same time? Well . . . guess who's coming to dinner!

EXERCISE: THE DINNER TABLE, PART I

Select nine people from the list you made above. You're inviting these people to a dinner at your place. The more unusual the mix, the better it will be for the purpose of the exercise. For example, invite two ex-lovers, your mother, your boss, and your third-grade English teacher! Make sure there's at least one person from each category, but no more than two from any category. So, there's a total of ten people for dinner, including yourself. Write their names here:

1.
2.
3.
4.
5.
6.
7.
8.
9.
10.

Say you have a choice of a rectangular table or a circular table. Which do you choose, and why?

Now, draw a seating plan for these people: who should sit next to whom, and why.

Let's step into the kitchen for a moment to talk a bit. Your guests will wait for you.

⊚ Splattering

Gender is interactive and relatively predictable between ourselves and another person. We know what gender to perform (be, and present ourselves as being) when relating to any given person. But what happens when we have to perform our gender(s) to two or more people simultaneously, each of whom is expecting a different gender performance (identity, and congruent presentation of that identity) from us? What happens when we cycle through a series of such encounters relatively quickly, without a chance to regroup within ourselves, sort out what we just went through, and come to some relatively controlled balance of self-identity or self-identities?

We've all seen the classic comic or farcical *schtick* where some character is leading a double life and suddenly has to confront people from both those lives at the same time. Wilde's *Importance of Being Earnest* comes to mind. The movies *Tootsie* or *Victor/Victoria* might be more to the point. Unmasked, the central character is faced with explaining how ze has been a man to some people, and a woman to others. My question is: Why do we laugh at that predicament? What experiences have we had in our own lives that enable us to identify with the plight of someone in that situation, to the point of getting relief through laughter?

Last Friday, as an experiment, I was trying to be very conscious of my personhood, presenting as close to *me* as possible not thinking about me as boy or girl, just me. Really focusing on it. In the grocery store I was referred to as "lady" by a woman. This irked me.

The following day, wearing the same jacket, and general clothing (jeans, boots) I didn't think about *it* at all and as I held the door open for a guy at the post office he said "thank you sir."

Within the hour I was at a thrift store buying a couple of men's suits, very conscious of it, knowing that the sign outside said "Today only, Men's Suits 1/2 off. Men Only" thinking I would be gearing up for a gender discrimination battle at the cash register, and again, I was called "lady" but, by the woman at the register. And I got both suits for 50% off.

—David Connor

> Of course your dilemma may be that no one persona fits you all day and all night, inside your persona and out. I think, :::whoa, blinking::: why I don't like to socialize is that it wrenches me into different personae. I just can't make that many transitions. Being a crab [Cancer sign] gives me the illusion that I'm pretty much one person all the time. Hence my sense of splattering when I'm at a party, encountering different people I know.
> —Caitlin Sullivan, from email to Kate

Caitlin Sullivan and I use the term "splattering" to describe what happens to us when we have to be too many identities or genders to too many people at the same time. For me, it's a real moment of personal joy. It's when all the mechanical or automatic ways I've developed for dealing with people simply fall aside, or reveal themselves as the bag of tricks I use to grease the social machinery of my interactions.

It's very much like what happens to me when performing in a stage, movie, or television show. Most of me is absorbed in simply being the character; I've got the lines memorized, so I can concentrate on making those lines come to life by putting myself into the experience of the character. Yet, there's always a small part of me I'll call "the lookout," who's aware of things like someone in the audience sneezing loudly on a very quiet line of mine; so I'll repeat that line to make sure the audience has heard it. It's the part of me that's aware which camera is live, so I know whether I'm in profile, dead-on, or off-camera. This lookout is the voice that tells me the audience is lost or bored or distracted, so I can jack up my pace or volume, or do *something* to get their attention back. It's the voice that says my audience is totally with me, so I can luxuriate in some silences and whispers.

Where's the "me" onstage? The *me* that's being the character, experiencing the highly dramatic situation of the moment? Is it the *me* that's concerned about having eaten garlic for dinner, with a big romantic scene coming up? Maybe it's the *me* that's just recognized an ex-lover in the third row, or the *me* that's spotted an amazingly attractive butch on the aisle, adjusting her suspenders? Is it the *me* who's chiding myself for all these wandering thoughts, directing my performance as I'm giving it? Is it the *me* who knows when my face is well-lit as I'm walking across the stage? Perhaps it's the *me* who remembers my trick knee went out earlier that afternoon, and adjusts the character's walk accordingly? I think I'm all of these things concurrently, and it's what I love about performing: it's an instant splatter into the harmonious and simultaneous expression of all the different aspects of *me,* denying myself nothing. It's more of what I look for in companions, friends, lovers, and extended family: that freedom to be present, unguardedly. It's when we splatter consciously, I think, when we invite it and let ourselves go into it, that we expand our ability to stretch our genders, let ourselves go, lose a sense of who or what we might "really" be, and we're simply there. Certainly a little thing like gender blows away easily in that kind of wind storm.

For an entertaining view of how splattering works, check out the one-act play, "Post Hard," on page 212 of this book.

Okay, I'll stay here in the kitchen. You go on back to your dinner guests. What? You don't know what to say to them? Okay, here's an idea.

EXERCISE: THE DINNER PARTY, PART II.
Think of an amusing embarrassing incident that's happened to you; the more complex, the better. Sum it up in a few words here:

Guess Who's Coming to Dinner!

Now, get some sheets of paper and write down that story as if you're telling it at the dinner table. Begin by telling the first sentence to the first guest to your left; write the second sentence to the guest to the left of hir; the third sentence to the next guest on the left, and so on. Everyone can hear everything you're saying, you're simply looking at one person at a time. Be sure to include at least one sentence for each guest. (You *are* a good host/ess, aren't you?) If you have more than ten sentences in the story, just continue in a circle with one sentence per guest.

Really get into it. For example, if you chose your mother to be one of the guests, what would it really be like to tell her this story in the presence of, say, your lover and your boss?

Read back over what you wrote. These questions are a good way to look at what you just did.

◉ Was there any point in this exercise where you felt totally free to express yourself, without concern for how people might react?
◉ At what points in the exercise did you feel powerful? At what points did you feel less powerful?
◉ What has that got to do with your gender?
◉ Did you have any different underlying messages to each guest? (e.g., flirting with one, keeping something secret from another, trying to avoid yet another, etc.)
◉ What did it feel like to balance the management of your identities like that? What emotions did it bring up for you?
◉ Was there some guest with whom you were more "yourself" than with the others?
◉ Was there some true "me" in all of this? If so, who was that?
◉ Was there some true gender of yours in all of this? If so, what was it, and what made it more true than any other gender you presented or regularly present?

How're ya doin'?

I don't know about you, but when I start getting into this kind of analysis, when I really ask myself these kinds of questions, my brain starts to fry. I lose some degree of certainty about who or what I am.

If anything like that is happening to you right now, this would be a good time to go for a walk or take a nice bath. When you come back, we're going to do what might at first glance seem like a big shift of focus here. So, go relax. Go on, shoo!

⊚ The Name Game

Thus far in the workbook, we've been giving names to quite a few folks out there, but we haven't given any names to ourselves. I've tried to avoid giving names to different identities we might become. Names have a tendency to stick, and I don't want to be the one doing the sticking. But names have a value when we're looking within ourselves to sort out our own identities. Once we've acknowledged what it is we aren't, it sometimes helps to put a name to exactly what we are if for no other reason than to serve as a marker on our journey, a way of saying "Oh yes, I occupied that identity once."

When we don't name ourselves, others tend to name us. A common and usually harmless example of this are the pet names we give to and take from our lovers. A not-so-harmless example would be the epithets hurled at some of us from passing car windows.

> I am not genderless, but rather am gender*ful*. As a creative tool, I can perform gender in fun and various ways. Wearing bright colours and a skirt, I can flounce around gaily; throw on a leather jacket and snug levi's, and I appear to be butch and rugged. Rather than being simply androgynous, I prefer to think of this freedom as a deconstruction of gender standards and expectations. As part of this freedom, I allow people to assume a gender for me based on how they interpret my appearance and behaviour.
>
> I never have been a man. I never will be a man. I never want to be a man. I am a sissy, a fairy, a faggot, and so much more. Embracing gender diversity (what I have called "genderful") has been my liberation.
>
> —Gerald Walton

EXERCISE: Make a list of the names you've used for yourself over the course of your life. Next to each name, jot down a few key words describing the identity you had when you used that name.

Of course, those kinds of names are very personal. There are other kinds of words we consciously or unconsciously use as names. Words like queer, straight, gay, lesbian, black, white, Jew, transsexual, student, professor, doctor, or fool. These words also trigger something inside the person who's been on the receiving end of them. Like proper names, these words can stick to the degree we haven't ourselves named (acknowledged, said yes to) what's been triggered.

EXERCISE: Make a list of the words you've used as names for yourself over the course of your life. Next to each identity, jot down a

> few key words describing what it meant to you to claim that identity as who you were at the time.

I think that the most valuable label or name would be paradoxical. It would be a name that defines the unique essence of who we are, without constructing a definition that would exclude anyone else. It would be a name that would give us unlimited options while at the same time giving us some common ground. Did "transgender" show up in your list of identities for that exercise? Might you add that one if it didn't?

◎ This Will Be the Death of Me

How do I know that loving life is not a delusion?
How do I know that in hating death I am not like a man who, having left home in his youth, has forgotten the way back?
—_Chuang Tzu_

I wrote earlier about death, transformation, and gender; now that we're at a point in this workbook to actually _do_ this stuff, it's time to expand on it. More and more people are playing with the transformation of gender these days. People in all walks of life are saying no to the categories of "real man" and "real woman." They're trying out a gender here and a gender there. These transformations can be purely physical, or they can go deep to the core of our identities. My own style is to get as much as I can out of any identity I find myself in; that leaves me that identity as part of a bag of tricks I can pull up whenever I want to. It means a lot of freedom for me. And of course, there's a cost to all this. Going fully into any given identity means giving up fully the last identity we've been occupying. It's like a death, no?

What image does "death" conjure for you? Some dark figure with a skull's head and a scythe? The queen of spades? A shrieking harpy? Needles and dials all going into the red on some hospital monitor? A beautiful angel with whom, when you finally meet her, you fall in love so hard that your soul is pulled out through your eyes? Maybe death is so common in your life that it's all you can do to flip through the obituary pages of your local queer newspaper. Maybe you're dying right now and don't want to think about it. That's okay. Really. We don't need to talk about those kinds of death, not really.

In the same way we needed to devise a language we could use to speak about spirituality, we need a language to speak about death. Unfortunately, there aren't too many people who've died and lived to tell us about it, so trying to find a language to describe the experience of death itself isn't going to be all that easy. However, there *is* a language in place that describes the process of dying: Kübler-Ross's five stages. That'll do, for starters.

The acknowledged spokesperson in this Western culture for the dead and dying is Elisabeth Kübler-Ross. In her ground-breaking book *On Death and Dying* she lays out five stages we go through during the process of dying. Since we're talking about killing off one (or more) of our identities, it might be good to have a guidebook to getting through the experience. According to Kübler-Ross, the stages we go through are:

Denial and Isolation

Anger

Bargaining

Depression

Acceptance

I never would have thought these five stages might apply to a gender transition, but in reviewing my own life, they most certainly do.

EXERCISE: What was your last gendered identity transition? (e.g., from boy to man, straight woman to lesbian woman, pre-menopausal woman to menopausal woman . . . whatever) Write the two identities here:

Identity A / I left off being this gendered identity:

_____

Identity B / I assumed this gendered identity:

_____

In your transition from Identity A to Identity B,

- Was there a time when you didn't believe you'd really make any transition?
- Did it make you angry to have to be leaving your Identity A?

◎ Did you try to make any deals or bargains about just how far you might go?

◎ Was there a time when it was just all too overwhelming?

◎ And finally, how do you feel about that gender transition now?

Angry? Hmpf. I tell you how angry I am. Almost fuckin ruined this body I'm stuck in. Drugs, razors, torn muscles, I ran from this . . . Prison of the Meat. Fucking dying in my own female flesh. Gonna drown in my own menstrual blood.

Do I hate myself? Naw . . . I hate my position: I hate my prison. Don't hate my breasts because they're breasts. I hate them because they're mine. Like I hate my back. This isn't my body. My body is silicon and solder. My body is CyberSpace. There, I am Shahn, Gareth, Interrupt. Not this fuckin' whining, pissing, lonely, getting-hungry, lame-backed, bull-dagger you see. I'm a fucking synapse. I'm light and heat the very pulse of information you speak.

You want to feel my pain? Put your head on the railroad tracks. Just lay it right down and just wait until you don't have to wait anymore. Just go to sleep and someday, you'll be free.

Don't fucking hug me. I don't want your meat.

—Shahn David Dickson

I'm still working on acceptance. What I want now is acceptance for *each* of the aspects of my own fluid self: the boy stuff as well as the girl stuff, and all the stuff that's neither one nor the other. That's what I'm working on now. I'd like to get to the point of not caring what people think I am. I'm not there yet, but I'm getting closer. Monogenderism is so seductive.

So, gentle reader, please don't despair if it takes some time to get through to the point of saying good-bye to the monogendered identity we've been being, or even trying to be, for so long. Whether that identity has felt more or less right or wrong to us, it *has* been the one we've been living through for quite some time now. What I'm finding out is there really is no rush, it can take years. The more deeply I explore each step of my journey, the fewer times I need to retrace my steps.

The paradox is that even when we fully leave a gender, it stays with us to some degree. I think that's true for every identity we've ever had. Colors of the old identity/gender creep onto the palette of our new identities, often without our being aware of it.

◎ The Shame Game

I'm going to guess you're getting your fill of exploring gender on your own about now. I'm also going to guess that maybe it's time to talk with someone else about all this stuff you've been poring over. It's time to articulate your own ideas about gender, and the best way to do that is to talk with someone else about it, live and personal. It can be pretty intimidating talking like that. I know. I remember when I was beginning my first conscious gender transition, the one from male to

False Pretenses
by Anne M. Griepenburg

Once
What fabulous clothes do you have for me to try on today? The last set didn't fit quite right. But today I'm willing to go further, to make changes. Whatever it takes—I'm there.

Upon
She saw right through me, of course. "You're a man!" she screamed hysterically. The direct accusation shocked me. While a complete stranger on the street might call me "sir," I thought that here, at least, it would be safe to be myself. Still partially aroused, I fled from her attack.

A Time
Her body jerked in spasms. She gripped her cock as jism shot loose, tears streaming down her face. She tried, but no matter what she did her heart was still connected. Darkness held her shaking body.

Can I tell you a little secret? I'm not sure I had a gender before, and I'm not sure I have one now. But I spent over 30 years pretending to be male, and now I'm ready to start pretending to be female.

—Sharon Minsuk

female. It was pretty scary. At first, I didn't even want to talk with anyone about it. It was all I could do to *read* about this stuff, or to take small steps like cross-dressing in secrecy. I remember the first person to whom I said "I think I'm transsexual." I'd chosen a very liberal friend of mine who'd responded, "Oh really? That's cool." I was floored; I was expecting him to make the sign of the cross or something, or somehow get himself rid of me. I *did* get that sort of response from others I told subsequently, but I learned to hang on to the favorable responses, and to use those favorable responses as safety rungs up the side of this identity cliff I was beginning to scale.

One thing that helped me at the time was my membership in Alcoholics Anonymous. Back then, I was attending daily meetings and tiptoeing the twelve-step line. AA was a lifesaver for me; I'd been drinking pretty heavily, and I'd just begun to do a lot of cocaine. Looking back, it was all I *could* do. I really wasn't up to facing my discomfort with my gender, so I drank and drugged my way through it, until even the drink and the drugs didn't work, and that stuff was staring me right in the face. Getting sober took an escape route away from me. I had to deal with gender, and around the time I finally decided to take the bull by the horns I was faced with AA's fourth step: making an inventory of my life. It was a step I'd been avoiding for nearly two years.

The fourth step in any twelve-step program is where you have to write down all the bad stuff and all the good stuff in your life, although the emphasis is usually placed on writing down all the bad stuff. I didn't want to do it. I was busy exploring my gender options in terms of therapy, electrolysis, fashion, feminism, and surgery. I was moving forward, and I didn't want to look back. As part of my research, I put a call into the offices of the International Foundation for Gender Education and spoke with a transsexual woman who answered the phone. We chatted for a bit about transsexuality. She was telling me her own story. Then she asked me to tell her a little about me. I fumbled around for a bit, and managed to say I was two years sober. "Have you done your fourth step yet?" she shot back. I told her I hadn't. She got really gentle with me at that point and said simply, "How do you think you're going to be able to move forward into a new identity as long as you're chained to the shames of your past?"

That hit home, big time. After we got off the phone, I sat down and began writing down all the things I'd done in my life that I was ashamed of. It took me a little over a week to get the bulk of it down, and another week to remember more and more incidents and details. When I finished, I went right on to AA's fifth step: I made a coffee date with a cross-dressing friend of mine, and I shared all this shameful stuff with him. Y'know what? The AA folks were right: I felt lighter and more free than I'd felt in a long time. I got all those secrets out to a friend of mine, and we remained friends. It gets back to the proverb that secrets will kill us.

And no, I'm not recommending you join AA or some other twelve-step program, or even that you start up some sort of twelve-step group around the subject of transgender. (Although I know of some folks in New York who did just that, and they swear by it.) I'm not saying "Get thee to a meeting, go!" I am saying that it would be a good idea right now to do a little housekeeping in terms of all the junk you're carrying around from your past. I'm saying it would be a very good idea, if you're serious about exploring some sort of personal stretch beyond the concepts of "real man" and "real woman," to sit down and list out the stuff you've done in your life that you're ashamed of, if for no other reason than to move forward in this exploration with a much lighter heart.

———

A Note for Those Who Feel They're Transsexual

Look, you may do this gender change thing for real. And if you do, people are going to look at you. You're going to be awkward at first. People are going to laugh and maybe you'll feel ashamed. Some folks will pity you, others may empathize with you. Fact is, some of your shame buttons are going to get pushed. It happens. It's all part of the adolescence that attends any kind of major identity shift. It's why most of us detest being new at anything: we go through an adolescent phase of self-consciousness that's truly painful. I'm suggesting you write up your past shameful stuff now, so that you'll have the energy to deal with your new stuff in the present, and so that you'll be able to sort out what's truly shameful, and what's simply a matter of other people not being able to deal with it. You're not alone. Thousands and thousands of people have gone through a major gender change like the one you're contemplating, and each of them weathered the attendant storms of emotions. You can do it. You've got a lot more information than most of us had when we were in your shoes. You can do it. Many blessings to you.

——

——
A Note For Everyone Else

You may not be going through a radical gender change. The odds are you're going to do nothing of the sort. But I want you to take a moment, please, and think back over some of the things you read in this book. Do you have any wish at all to broaden the definition of your gender? Any wish at all to stretch the boundaries set by the culture for someone of your gender? If you don't, then God bless. Put this book down, or give it to someone who might need or want it. I mean it, no hard feelings. Honest!

However, if stretching your gender identity is something you might consider, then the rest of the book applies to you as much as to any female-to-male or male-to-female or whatever-to-whatever transsexual out there. If you're toying with the idea of being a different kind of man than you've always been, or perhaps another kind of woman than you've been all your life, the rest of the book does apply to you. No, not as dramatically as it would apply to me or many other transsexual folks. But it does apply to you. Please keep on reading. I think you'll find some comfort here.

——

So, you're still with me. Well, I'm glad. Here's an exercise based on AA's fourth step. I hope this helps you, I really do.

> EXERCISE: Go get yourself a notebook that you can carry around with you easily. Start writing down shameful incidents in your life; it doesn't have to be in date order, you can skip all over the place if you want to. But write this stuff down, get it out onto paper. Keep that notebook with you, and as soon as you remember another incident, right it down. Be sure to find out exactly which part of that shameful incident *you* were responsible for, and which parts were truly not your responsibility (it's very rarely an all-my-fault or all-their-fault sort of thing). Just keep writing things down in the notebook; you'll get to a point where there's no more to write, and that's what you're looking for.

Go on, put the book down and do this exercise. You probably need a break from all my ramblings right now anyway. When you're done, pick some friend you can sit down and share all that stuff with. Make sure you get hir agreement to do that *before* you start spilling all of it out at hir. Go on, you'll feel a lot better. Honest.

⑥ Just Dying to Do It?

All right, I've tried to lay out as many cautions and precautions that I could think of. I think we've gone as far as we can go intellectually, emotionally, and philosophically, so . . . let's die a little. I'll tell you right now, there won't be any make-up tips or voice lessons in this next section. It's all about where to do things, not what to do. There's no shopping advice, no sample letters to your boss explaining how you might be changing. There's not even a suggestion of exactly what the very next step in your gender journey might be. Those kinds of details are up to you. Maybe you want to shift the kind of man or woman you already are. Maybe what you really want to do is become more of a man than you already are, or more of a woman. Perhaps you simply want to polish your already fabulous gendered performance. Maybe you want to explore another gender entirely. Some gendered identity you've read about, or saw walking down the street, some character you saw in a movie or on TV or read about in a book, some movie star you always wanted to be like.. Maybe you want to revisit a gendered identity you only dipped a toe into years ago. Maybe you want to explore several genders simultaneously. It's all up to you. You've got a wide spectrum of genders and other gendered identities to play with. I'm going to let you know where some nice places might be to play with them.

I feel a lot like Red Riding Hood's mother here.

Okay, Red, stay out of the woods. The next section of the workbook is going to give you some better ways to get to grandma's house. Places where there are very few if any wolves. Bring a warm sweater.

The Playgrounds

Remember when you were a kid, and you went into a new playground for the first time? Remember you didn't know how all the equipment worked? You didn't know if you'd make any friends there? You didn't know all the games, or if you'd be good enough, or if they'd like you enough? Well, playing with gender is like that. When you make changes in your gendered identity, it's just like going into some new playground where you don't know the rules.

Are We Having Fun Yet?

I keep talking about the fun involved in gender play, and yeah, it's a lot of fun . . . eventually. At first, it can be pretty intimidating. There's danger lurking in the most banal situations, as Diane has so brilliantly illustrated on the following pages.

One of my favorite quotes is this anonymous Zen saying: "All roads in life lead nowhere; so you might as well take the road that has the most heart, and is the most fun." And Gandhi was supposed to have said something like "Everything you try to do is futile, but that shouldn't stop you from trying." I use both of those sentiments on a daily basis, especially when it seems like it's no longer worth the effort it takes to be something new under the sun. I'm going to assume you've got the heart for this journey, or you wouldn't have gotten this far into the book; you're following your heart, and I have a great deal of admiration and respect for people who do that. Well, I think we deserve a little fun for all this trouble we're going to, don't you?

I found that by discovering what gives me joy in my life, real joy, I could find ways to discover that kind of joy in my gender journey. The deep joy in my own life stems from things like finding missing pieces to philosophical conundrums; or being able to express love for someone; or the freedom to be what I want to be, when I need or want to be that (which very often means being quite alone). I find joy in spending time with people who like the same joys. It gives me a great deal of pleasure to be useful in my life, to be of service however I can. I enjoy art or other forms of communication that reach my heart and raise new questions; I love new

Rest Room

OUR HERO

questions of any kind. I like being silly, and in the rare times I allow myself, I enjoy being very small.

———

I also like brown-paper packages wrapped up in string, for these are a few of my favorite things. Did I mention I also adore those little blue boxes from Tiffany's? And those pink shopping bags from Betsey Johnson? And those almost tacky sacks from John Fluevog Shoes?

———

I'm saying all this now, because I think it's a good idea to form some concept of the kind of *fun* we'd like to have, before actually going into the playground to look for it.

> EXCERCISE: Looking over your life, what gives you joy? If it's something specific, like horseback-riding or playing chess, watching movies, reading, or simply sitting on the front stoop on a nice sunny day, then go a little deeper: What about that experience do you enjoy? Displaying your expertise? Meeting a challenge? Giving yourself a moment without the usual pressures of your life? Go deep on this one; it's going to help you in the long run by giving you something to look for in playing with gender. Write your answers here:

———

Okey dokey, we're ready to play now!

———

⑥ Katie's Guide to Some of the Gentler Playgrounds

This section is definitely written with "advanced students of gender" in mind. Many readers of this book are not going to need information about where to go in order to appear to the world as a totally different gender. However, I think that any gender play, even the most subtle, requires attention to both personal safety and comfort, so this section may even come in handy to you some day. You never know, do you?

These playgrounds have stuff in common. They're mostly:

- ⑥ relatively safe
- ⑥ peopled by like-minded or open-minded folks
- ⑥ relatively anonymous
- ⑥ filled with lots of opportunity for fun
- ⑥ accessible
- ⑥ inexpensive

So, let's go for it!

Home Alone

If you're fortunate enough to have a space of your own, that's a wonderful place to start experimenting with different elements of self-expression. One of the most common elements used to distinguish a gendered identity in our culture is clothing. You might try cross-dressing behind closed doors. Of course, you have to go *get* the clothing with which to cross-dress first. That can be a wonderful growing experience all by itself. Have you ever done that? Bought yourself some article of clothing that is obviously not for the gender you're presenting right now? Well, I think it's time to try that one out even if the thought of doing this has never crossed your mind before. Go on, this is safe.

> EXERCISE:
> **Part I.** Name five articles of clothing you'd *never* wear because it's for the "wrong" gender? (if you're a boy, a butch, or a man you might name a dress or some frilly negligee. If you're a girl, a femme, or a woman, you might name a rather plain three-piece suit or a too-tight T-shirt that flattens your breasts completely.)
> 1.
> 2.

3.

4.

5.

Part II. Pick *one* of those articles of clothing and go buy it for yourself. Yes, you can tell the clerk it's for someone else if you really want to. But don't be surprised if that clerk gives you a knowing smile. They've seen it all before. If you live in a small town and feel your safety might be jeopardized, you may want to use a mail order catalogue.

Part III. Once you've got that article of clothing, arrange a time alone for yourself when you won't be interrupted. Take off all your gendered clothes, and put on the item you selected above. What feelings come up for you? Write those feelings down here:

Part IV. Now trace those feelings back to where they came from. For example, if you felt ashamed wearing a dress, where did you learn that shame from? If it was a thrill to wear a padded jockstrap, what's the *basis* of your thrill? Write your answers here.

Part V. Did tracing back your feelings change the way you now feel about wearing that article of clothing? If so, how?

Home Alone Pros: If you have a home or room where you can experiment like this, you're very fortunate. Many of us went out and rented cheap motel rooms alone to experiment like that.

Home Alone Cons: I think it's a very good idea to take a first step with gender play while alone. However, since gender is interactive, there's going to be very little experiential reality of that gender if you don't eventually go out and interact with others.

Support Groups

Even though *Gender Outlaw* came out several years ago, I still get email from readers, some of whom are lonely on a very deep level, bone-deep lonely. The first interactive playground I'd suggest is a support group of like-minded or similar-minded people. If you live in a big city, or even a medium-sized city, one should be easy to find . . . or to put together. Ten years ago, when I started going through my first conscious gender change, there was no support group for transsexuals. My therapist suggested I get together with some other transsexual folks and start one up. I wailed that I didn't *know* any transsexuals, and she offered to mention the idea to some of her other clients. She did, and we managed to get together and hammer out some guidelines, which included a weekly meeting where we could talk about the stuff we'd never dare mention outside of session. It was great. So, yes . . . join or start a support group. There are a lot of good listings of support groups available. The magazine *Transgender Tapestry*, from IFGE, always has a long list of active groups around the world. You can even go online (for free at your local public library) and do a Web-wide search for "transgender + groups," and that'll give you a good number of groups with which you might connect.

Some groups are meetings only. Some also throw parties for their members, so you can explore your new gender in a more social, less angst-ridden context. There are even *online* support groups; there are newsgroups; there are pen pals. And if you absolutely can't find or put together some people, those are valid alternatives. Whatever . . . an easy first step is to get connected with some kind of support group where you can sit down with folks and talk this stuff out.

Support Group Pros: Most members are likely to understand your loneliness, shyness, apprehension, and excitement, and in all likelihood they will welcome you, giving you a place to talk about your feelings. They'll probably have a list of community resource contacts, tip sheets from other members, and a list of transgender-friendly stores, bars, restaurants, and such. You can make some great connections here, and maybe even find some deeper friendships.

Support Group Cons: Nearly every support group comes with its own standards for membership; its own guidelines for "correct" behavior; its own system of values when it comes to who's "real"; and its own ideas about the "right" path to take on a gender journey. These guidelines might conflict with your own ideas, or some members might take umbrage with a more free-wheeling approach to gender play.

Out-of-Town Trips

If you live in a cosmopolitan area where there are a lot of butch lesbians then it's going to be much more difficult for you to pass. One way to help distinguish yourself from them is to dress preppy and conservative—leave the leather motorcycle jacket at home for a while.

—"FTM Passing Tips," posted on the Internet

Many people who start cross-dressing or exploring another gender or genders on a very physical level leave town to do it. I did. I took advantage of business trips to cross-dress, and to simply experience walking around the streets of a different city where no one knew me. I figured if they laughed, they laughed; it was sort of like testing a nuclear weapon way off in the desert: I had the illusion that there would be no real effect from doing it. I needed that illusion of security to build up my self-confidence. No one likes to screw up, and screwing up is exactly what *needs* to happen. Let me explain that.

When I'm directing actors in a play, I encourage them to make all the mistakes they can in a rehearsal. That's my theory; if you make mistakes in rehearsal, you won't make them on stage; or if you do, at least you'll be prepared. I'm not even talking about trying to pass, unless that's what you want to do. I'm talking about learning to comfortably express yourself in some new identity, with all the attendant new attitudes, physicalizations, and methods of relating with different people. Out-of-town visits can come in mighty handy for "rehearsal." Why do you think so many plays go on the road before opening on Broadway?

Out-of-town Pros: Nobody knows you. You can goof, slip up, and make a general fool of yourself, and it's not likely to come back and haunt you in the circles within which you feel safe and at home.

Out-of-town Cons: It's expensive. It also could be dangerous, so it pays to check out the neighborhood first.

Conferences and Special Events

There are more and more conferences, conventions, and get-togethers held for gender outlaws these days. They run the gamut from scholarly to smutty, from follow-the-rules to no-holds-barred. The Internet is a good place to find out where and when these get-togethers are held. They're also promoted regularly in the mags, newsletters, and zines that cater to gender outlaws. I enjoy going to these because frankly, I can be whatever I want to be on a day-to-day basis. I can show up nicely conservative, and explore riot grrrl the next day, followed by a foray into male drag at a dance, and capped off by glam high femme, kissing my friends good-bye.

The benefit of a conference is that it combines the anonymity of an out-of-town trip with the understanding that comes from support groups. There are usually many informative panels covering everything from the latest postmodern theory, to make-up tips, to which new prosthesis makes the most realistic penis when worn inside your boxer shorts or jockstrap. Support groups often distribute their literature at these events, and vendors sell all kinds of books, clothing, accessories, and paraphernalia.

In addition to the learning experience, there are usually social events planned, such as dances, dinners, and outings to shows. Shopping trips are generally built into these types of get-togethers, and for those starting out in a new gender, it can be quite a relief to shop in numbers.

Conference and Event Pros: You get to be anything you want to be, with no excuses! These are good places to find out information that might not be available locally. You'll probably make some lasting friendships with like-minded outlaws.

Conference and Event Cons: They're usually on the expensive side, but the better conferences have scholarship-for-work programs and sliding-scale entrance fees, so it's worth checking.

Friendships

You're going to have to do it *sometime.* We all do. You're going to have to come out to your friends. As you continue to play with your own concepts of real man and real woman, something's going to leak through and someone's going to spot something unusual about you. When you tell them, or when they find out, some of your friends are going to drop you like a rock; some will deal with their own issues and continue being a great friend to you; some maybe even more of a friend because you've taken a step toward a greater intimacy in the friendship.

Ten years ago, when I first came out to my friends before my transition from male to female, the way I'd do it was to bring up the subject of transsexuals in general. It was more difficult ten years ago, because there

I just came out as an FTM to an on-line friend with whom I have been corresponding for months about choral stuff. I finally had the opportunity to meet her. This was a small part of her response to me, and it touched me so much I wanted to share it with others. I hope it inspires and uplifts you as it did me. I look forward to the day when everyone's reaction will be like this woman's.

—Reid Vanderburgh

<< In case you need any assurances, I have REALLY enjoyed talking to you, and I see absolutely no reason for that to change in any sense. I think you're an excellent person, intelligent, funny, and interesting, and now I've found out something "extra" that's very interesting about you, and I look forward to more conversations. I appreciate your "dropping the bombshell" on me; I bet you've had quite a bit of experience in it, but I'm sure it's still a bit frightening. >>

weren't as many socially acceptable representations of transsexuality to which I could refer. I'd say things like, "Hey, did you see that *Donahue* show yesterday, the one where he actually wore a *dress?*" It's easier today. You can get into a conversation about movies like *The Crying Game,* or *To Wong Foo,* or *Victor/Victoria.* Or you could be casually reading this very book while waiting for your friend to show up for coffee. There are lots of less obvious but equally important books you could mention: *Stone Butch Blues,* by Leslie Feinberg, or *S/He* by Minnie Bruce Pratt, or *Nearly Roadkill* by Caitlin Sullivan and yours truly. You could suggest going to a drag king or drag queen show. There are some good queer public radio and cable television shows that regularly give airtime to transgender topics. I used to draw pen-and-ink sketches with a transgender theme, and I'd casually show them to friends to catch their reactions. Whatever you choose to do, I think it's a good idea to bridge into the subject. Unless you're quite intimate already with your friend, it's probably not a great idea to lean over your Caesar salad and immediately launch into "Hey, guess what . . . I'm going to be playing with my gender starting in, oh . . . (look at your watch) . . . four minutes."

One thing I found useful in coming out to my friends was *compassion* for their probable shaky response. Chances are they haven't had the means or reason to examine this gender stuff as deeply as you have; be prepared to deal with questions. I always invite questions when I'm making a new friend. I try to make allowances for enculturated fears on their part, so I try to be as gentle and understanding as I can be. I try to remember when *I* had similar negative feelings about all this stuff. Patience is a big factor, and it nearly always pays off. For those who say good-bye, yeah, that's sad; but better to find out sooner than later. Most friends will treasure your trust in them.

Omigod, I had this sudden flash of someone reading this stuff fifty years from now and chuckilng at these tip-toe predictions of mine—kind of like that 1890's marraige guide I quoted. Sigh. Well, this is the reality of our day and age.

Friends-as-support Pros: Friends are likely to call you on any of your old patterns.

Friends-as-support Cons: Friends are likely to call you on any of your old patterns.

The Bar Scene

I'm going to tell you the story of when I first realized I love butches.

There was this one drag bar in Philadelphia that I used to haunt when I first started cross-dressing in public. It was pretty sleazy, but then again, so was I. I was in my Madonna-wannabe phase, and honey, I did Madonna to the *teeth*, all five feet eleven inches of me (well, taller in heels, of course!). In the drag bar context, I got more than a little validation and admiration for my over-the-top presentation.

Later, when I had decided to go through with a full gender change, and I was being hippie chick femme lesbian, I would hang out at a local girl bar. I was pretty defensive about my self-proclaimed womanhood in those days, and I'd sit off by myself, nursing a Diet Pepsi. Most of the crowd were younger lesbians who for the most part ignored me. I watched and watched and watched. I wanted to know how those grrrls interacted with one another. I was starved for that kind of information. It wasn't until I finally got up the courage to use the bathroom that I ran across the butches.

The bathroom was upstairs, and I remember wading through the crowd of young women to get to the stairs. When I reached the top of the stairs, I did the grade-B movie thing of stopping and staring. I'm guessing my mouth was hanging open in a mixture of surprise and delight. There were these way cool older women in suits or shirtsleeves, playing pool, smoking cigars, and having a great time with one another. When they saw me standing there, one for one their faces lit up. "C'mon in, honey," one of them said to me. They held out a chair for me, treated me like a princess. They taught me to play pool; I tried their cigars, and they laughed when I coughed. They knew I was transgendered, but they saw this other gender identity that I wouldn't see until years later: they were butch, and they saw femme. We had a wonderful time of it, back in the eighties when butch/femme was scorned by the more politically correct androgynous set. And that's why I love butches.

The bar eventually closed, and I lost touch with those women from upstairs at Sneakers. If you see any of them, please let them know they made a baby femme very very happy, and I'm so grateful.

Nowadays, I still spend time hanging out in the bars. Some women's bars, however, attract a clientele that doesn't cotton to gender outlaws, be they male-to-female (MTF), female-to-male (FTM), or something else entirely (SEE?). I don't go to those places. In Seattle, I mostly hang out at The Easy or the Wildrose; in fact, I wrote most of this book at The Easy. I still don't drink; the bartender at The Easy came up with "my" drink: a Diet Pepsi with a shot of Hershey's chocolate syrup, and three cherries. It feels like home.

I'm beginning to identify with the vampires. I only appear at night, take on many forms, it's mostly a secret, most people would "kill/destroy" me if they new my alter identity and trying to find my image in the mirror—hmmm! (Oh yeah—blood red lips often!)

—posted on the Internet

I don't do straight bars very much, not unless I'm doing boy drag and taking a girl friend out slumming. It's not that I'm not interested in men; I'm just not interested in most straight men who hang out in straight bars, and their (usually) attendant poor attitude toward gender outlaws like me. Hey, I saw *The Crying Game,* and what's worse: so have they. As I play more and more with the idea of doing male drag, I've begun to venture into the gay male bars. I haven't gone alone, yet. I've got a few FTM friends who go with me, and our courage grows deeper each time we step inside that most-male of all male bastions. What better place to explore a male identity? And there are *plenty* of bars and clubs that cater to gender-play. The Goth bars, for example, are filled with most wondrous androgynes!

Bar Scene Pros: They're great places to people-watch. If you're into cruising, nothing I know beats a bar scene. If you're not into cruising, people will eventually leave you alone.

Bar Scene Cons: They're not the best places to go if you've got a problem with alcohol. They're *really* not good places to go if you're not willing to be totally up front with your gender ambiguity. (That's what I love about drag kings and drag queens—their "Get over it!" attitude.) Too many passing people have been beaten up or killed for what's taken as a betrayal. At best, you stand the chance of being blackballed from that bar if you're seen as someone who's just there to take advantage of the customers by trying out your new-gender flirting techniques.

Lovers

After I got out of Scientology, I became romantically involved with a woman. I was a guy then, and I decided to tell her up front about my gender quandary. She chewed that over for a week or so, and then one night when we were making love, she began touching my chest while murmuring "What beautiful breasts you have, girl." Our love making that night proceeded like that; the two of us fantasizing a gender-switch. It was wonderful. Afterward, she told me she'd found it distasteful; that she'd thought it might "cure" me; and then my shame kicked in and I never did tell her what a giving lover she'd been that night.

Lovers, even more than friends, need to know. The probability is that your relationship is based on, or has nestled itself into something based more on the relationship between two identities than on the relationship between two people. That's what we're taught: man/man, woman/woman, woman/man, top/bottom, butch/femme, man/woman/man, etc. We're never taught person/person. That's what the bisexual movement has been trying to teach us. We're never taught that, so we fall into the trap of "you don't love me, you love my identity."

The problem arises in an identity-based relationship when one of the lovers decides to switch or shift identities; it throws the basis of the relationship way off. I'm not even talking about a radical gender change here. Any shift in a gendered identity within an identity-based system can put a strain on the system. People need time to adjust to new ways of relating to each other. If the relationship, for example, had been man/man, and one of the lovers decides to become a woman, the other lover is thrown into an identity crisis not of his own choosing. Fortunately, as more and more of these issues are being discussed, as gender identity is becoming grudgingly acknowledged as possibly being fluid, more and more people are riding through that sort of change and are remaining together as lovers.

It's still a danger to the relationship, and it's still scary, and it's still something you need to tell your lover.

The big fear is "Ze would never love me if ze really knew me." Get over that way of thinking—please! And fast!

All right, what if that's true and ze leaves you? What kind of love was that, anyway? You weren't being honest about your desires, and maybe ze wasn't leaving you room to be honest. Sure there's heartbreak, and sure that hurts way deep; but both of you will get over it, and you will find someone who loves you for who you really are, if that's what you want.

On the happier side of the coin, I know quite a few folks who've embraced their lover's gender change and gone on to have wonderful, new relationships. You'll never know until you come out. The principles I'm talking about here apply equally to family members as well as to lovers.

Lovers-as-support Pros: It's the best. Your closest, most intimate friend and sexual partner and you have the opportunity to move your relationship into much deeper waters than identity-loves-identity.

Lovers-as-support Cons: There's a danger of the two of you sliding into some stereotypical relationship, based more on what's "right" according to the culture, than what's "right" according to what the two (or three or more) of *you* decide. There's also the danger that you just may not want to be lovers anymore, as was the case with David and me. Hey, what guarantees come with *any* relationship? However, if you persist with love, you'll have a true friend for life . . . as is the case with David and me.

I love you, David.

Sadomasochism, Dominance & Submission, Bondage & Discipline

Uh huh, I've heard all the arguments for and against it.

The way I relate with people in these matters is through informed consent. This kind of play is where we can start to pull apart gender (the category or identity) and sex (the act), by doing something about *both* these phenomena, sometimes at the same time, and becoming conscious about which is which.

I've been called a femme in butch clothing/ sir on the street and Sir in the bedroom. I've also been called Daddy/ dyke/ butch heart throb/ faggot/ Top/ bottom/ switch/ stud/ pervert/ butch/ bitch/ Master.

Who am I? What am I? Can you tell? Are you sure?

—Kitty Tsui

S/M for me is the consensual act of two or more adults who play with pain: giving or receiving. They transform pain and pleasure. D&S is the consensual act of two or more adults who play with clearly defined power roles, usually some form of master/mistress and servant/slave. It's the concept of owning and belonging. B&D is the consensual act of two or more adults who play with the concepts of punishment, restraint, or imprisonment. Any of these forms of play can be combined with any of the others. Any of these forms of play might or might not involve what's usually called sex, genital or otherwise.

One thing I enjoy about S/M, D&S, and B&D (I'll lump them all into the category "leather" for simplicity's sake) is the opportunity for the players to actually *talk* about their needs and wants, their limitations and boundaries, their fantasies. Even relative strangers who play leather games with each other can reach an intimacy in a few hours the depth of which would rival on some levels the intimacy of many long-term married couples. So . . . here's another exercise.

In my sex fantasy, nobody ever loves me for my mind.

—Nora Ephron

EXCERCISE: Make yourself very comfortable. That can mean alone, or with someone you trust; it's up to you. Comfy? Okay. Now, read these questions and really answer them for yourself. You might want to get some paper and write these answers down. If you know you're hedging on any of them, you can imagine someone you trust, gently saying "Tell me more." Your answers don't have to have anything to do with sadism, masochism, dominance, submission, bondage, discipline, or role-playing; but if they do, well, just let them come.

- What's your fantasy? Really, the deep one.
- How would you like to meet someone to live that out with for a while?
- What kind of time limit on the fantasy would make you comfortable?
- How would you articulate that fantasy to someone who might want to do that with you?
- How would you explain your physical limitations to someone?
- How would you explain your psychological limitations to someone?
- What, exactly, would you be willing to do?
- What, exactly, would you be unwilling to do?
- What, exactly, would you be willing to learn?
- What, exactly, might you try (assuming you knew you could stop if you didn't like it)?
- Is there something you've always wanted to be? If so, what's that?
- Is there some exciting situation you've always wanted to live out? If so, how would you describe it to someone who might want to do that with you?
- What would it take, do you think, for you to actually tell someone all these things?
- How could you get yourself to that point?

There's a bit more to negotiating a leather scene than simply these questions, but these questions are a good start. If you were able to answer them, you could possibly live out a fantasy or two or three. How about that? Even if your answers had nothing whatsoever to do with S/M, B&D, or D&S, you could live out your fantasy. Nifty, huh?

The trick now is where to look for playmates, right? That's a tough one, no matter where you are, but there are a few leads you might want to check out. For factual information about the leather world, Pat Califia's work stands out like a beacon. Pat has several how-to books out, all of which are worth owning and using. For fiction, more of a flavor thing, there's Pat Califia again, Laura Antoniou (writing also under the pen name Sara Adamson), and John Preston's S/M classic, *Mr. Benson.* For actual social groups, potential play partners, and connecting with people in the leather scene, once again I'm going to suggest the Internet newsgroups and Websites devoted to various aspects of the leather community. There are also numerous newsletters, zines, and other publications devoted to helping folks find connections, which you can find at your local underground or sexual minorities bookstores and newsstands.

S/M, B&D, D&S Pros: Playing can be a transcendent experience for all involved. With trustworthy partners, you can really fly up and out of whatever gender you've been being, and take on entirely new identities.
S/M, B&D, D&S Cons: Playing can be dangerous if the players are inexperienced or just plain mean. Please, please, if you're going to do this stuff, start out with someone you trust, and be prepared to do a lot of learning.

Cyberspace

This is the playground that ties 'em all together. As playing with gender does tend to break up our comfortable binary approach to the world around us, maybe it's time we learn how to *think* in new ways, ways other than binary thought. One approach to learning some new way of thinking would be to actually *live* outside the binary, outside one of the two socially-sanctioned genders. Maybe freedom from that system would result in a new nonbinary way of thinking and acting in the world. So, where in the world do we go to experience that?

At first glance, it might appear to be an impossible task to locate a place where gender "is not." I think I found someplace, though—someplace that has almost no rules concerning identity, and is accessible to a great number of people. I'm talking about cyberspace: the wild, wacky world of online life.

◎ Where Gender Isn't

One of the truly wonderful things about cyberspace is that it hasn't been around long enough to fall utter prey to the two-gender system; the lack of physical cues available in cyberspace makes falling into that system actually difficult to do online. Since there aren't any true physical cues, one would have to go to an awful lot of trouble to *put* them there virtually.

My question is: Why bother?

⊚ It's Not Only "The Bad Guys" Who Try to Put Gender There

When I first went online in 1990, I was astounded by the freedom it gave me. I didn't need physical cues to pass! I felt I could finally participate in discussions *as a woman*. However, when I wanted to participate in a particular women-only live chat group, I found they had something called a Voice Verification (VV) list. The head of the list would phone you, and make sure you had a woman's voice; then you were acknowledged as a woman, and could participate. It happens that I "passed" that test, and was welcomed "as a woman," but I felt awful about it, and outed myself a short time thereafter. About a year later, VV was dropped as a qualification.

One reason people need the presence or virtual presence of body cues online might be that many people believe there's truly something *essential* about the body and its relationship to gender, and the socialization that comes with growing up gendered in this culture.

For almost a year and a half now, I've lived in Virtual Reality (Text-based, on the Internet—LambdaMOO and other MOOs) as an Irving, which is another choice in gender.

There are several choices in gender available on the MOO, but I chose Irving because it was a new one . . . my gender pronouns are "e" (subjective), "em" (objective) and "eir" (possessive). It was a hard fight, I admit, to get established—even in such a flexible, virtual reality, there's still resistance among the populace against others' genders not being at all obvious.

Recently, I've begun living in real life (among friends and family) as Irving—I ask them to use the pronouns; language, I know, enforces reality to a measurable extent. Perhaps some time in the future, I will fight for a right to use Irving as a legal gender, though I realize that my odds will be very poor, given the present legal state of gender in the United States.

Irving

⊚ The Missing Piece Is Nothing, and We Can Find It Nowhere

As I said, I get a great deal of joy from putting seemingly unrelated pieces of philosophical puzzles together, and that's what I've been doing around this gender-and-culture stuff. I've come up with this theory that I'm putting together piece by interesting piece to use as a bridge to cross into who-knows-what. It has to do with a lot of things going on in the world right now, the very simultaneity of which will lead, I think, to a cultural splattering of sorts. It wasn't until I went online and discovered a nowhere, a no-place where gender was a no-thing that it all began to make sense. Here are a few other chunks of this puzzle.

◉ The amount of information available to the average citizen is greater than ever before; some people call this the "Information Age." If it is, I think it's less about information itself than how our thought processes are going to evolve in order to deal with or make *use* of all this information.

◉ Postmodernism is converging with Zen in a new no-East, no-West world facilitated by the geography-free nature of cyberspace, and the (at present) extant ideological soup resulting from the framework of hypertext. This merge of postmodernism and Zen seems to be driven by our inherent desires (urges to connect) and fueled by an acceptance of our spiritual nature (urges to exist beyond physical borders).

◉ Political activism on behalf of human rights has for the past century or so been attempting to dismantle binary after binary held in place by the powers that be, whether by legal statutes, religious doctrines, commercial tenets, or social convention.

◉ The transgender movement is the first civil rights movement to grow up in cyberspace, and has not remained unaffected by the nonlinear borderless nature of both the identity it claims and the medium used to communicate those claims.

◉ Children today are growing up to grasp the concept of nonlinear communication as can be found through the use of hypertext on CD-ROMs and the Web. They're going to reach adolescence and adulthood looking for ideologies that most nearly match their (nonlinear) thinking processes, systems that advocate connectivity without borders; and they'll find, among other systems, postmodernism, Zen, and transgender.

Now, if you put all those pieces together, what do *you* come up with?

I come up with postmodernism of the West coming together with Zen of the East at a no-geography point where desire, technology, and spirituality converge. The exact point of the convergence of all these phenomena could be called a state of no-identity, a state that will be actively sought after by future generations. That's what I'm looking forward to.

⊚ But Is It As Good As Real Gender and Real Sex?

Okay, enough philosophical musing. Let's get down to some practical stuff about our cyber-playground. Binary gender, monogenderism, and the myriad social taboos on sex and desire don't yet hold sway online; nor do social taboos about spirituality. Add to that the nonlinear nature of cyberspace, its inherent lack of boundaries or borders, and we're looking at one *heck* of a playground.

I've done a lot of both research and socializing on the Net using my OutlawGal screen name; I'm there to simply be me, so if you ever catch me online under that name, that's who you'll get. But when I go online to surf the chat rooms, I very rarely want to go online as the identity I most usually present in my day-to-day life. Boring! It's simple to negotiate genders online. In this next interchange, I'm using the more gender-neutral screen name, Kachoo.

Remember, in cyberspace, the words that take place between double colons are actions, not speech; as in ::grinning::... I'm not saying the word, I'm doing it.

> **TomCat:** Hi! Are you m or f?
> **Kachoo:** ::laughing delightedly:: Well, what would you be looking for?
> **TomCat:** Female! I'm a real guy.
> **Kachoo:** ::purring:: I like to think any of us can be anything in this space.
> **TomCat:** Well, sure, but I'm a real guy and I like woman.
> **Kachoo:** Have you ever surfed in another gender?
> **TomCat:** What do you mean?
> **Kachoo:** ::laughing lightly:: I can tell from your pause that you have. Were you being a lesbian?
> **TomCat:** Well, yeah.
> **Kachoo:** ::softly:: And were you beautiful? All soft and curvy? Maybe hot and horny?
> **TomCat:** ::breathless:: uh huh
> **Kachoo:** ::leaning over, whispering in your ear, leaving just a trace of lipstick:: Wanna be a lesbian with me just for tonite, sweet thing?
> **TomCat:** Oh, yes!

He signed off, and signed right back on with the screen name AmyDear.

She and I had a lovely evening together. ::laughing delightedly:: So, it's simple to negotiate genders; it's even simple to evade the "m or f" question. All it takes is a little patience, some compassion, and a good sense of humor. It's simple, but it's not always easy. It doesn't always go that smoothly. Some folks hold fiercely to their offline genders and identity. In fact, sometimes reason just won't open a crack in the door.

Brknstock: You sound like a man to me.

Kachoo: ::raising an eyebrow:: What makes you say that, Brk?

Brknstock: You talk too much, take up too much cyberspace.

Kachoo: ::laughing:: Okay . . . how's this? ::crossing my legs at the knee, sitting demurely with hands folded in my lap and speaking quietly only when spoken to::

Brknstock: That's not funny!

Kachoo: ::gently:: Brk, I agree. My point is that here in cyber-space, we can be anything. I surf in a *lot* of different gen-ders, and learn things from each of them.

Brknstock: That's deception, and very cruel to people.

Kachoo: ::nodding:: Agreed. *If* it's important to the other per-son that I be one or the other, and *if* it's gonna be more than a cyber-fling.

Brknstock: You're definitely a guy and don't belong in this room. I'm not going to talk with you any more.

Needless to say, Brknstock and I didn't have a lovely evening of it. ::sigh::

This point of online deception is an interesting one. I don't agree with the idea of deceiving someone with an assumed identity, gender or otherwise . . . not if it's going to be any kind of ongoing relationship beyond hi-how-are-you-let's-have-some-cybersex. A viable, and I believe honorable, alternative to deception is agreed-upon anonymity.

Then there's cybersex itself, where two or more of you get down to it. To me, cybersex takes pornography to a whole new level by adding the factors of being immediate, real-time, interactive, and fully consensual. The *value* of cybersex in terms of switching genders is that it gives us a good place to try out our fantasies, experience them on one albeit primar-ily textual level, so that we'll be perhaps a bit more willing to suggest them to an *offline* sexual partner. For example, I always wanted to flirt, but I was too shy to even try. After a year of flirting online, you should ::blush:: see me now! I've also managed to learn quite a few new things to do with a sexual partner. ::Cheshire Cat grin::

ⓖ It's So Much More Than Sex and Gender, Honest!

You don't even have to *do* sex or gender switches online; you can opt to simply talk about it. I went online one night, set up a chat room called CYBER IDENTITIES, and waited for folks to come in and chat about it. Folks did, and the conversation went on for four hours. I had such a great time discussing ramifications of polygenderisms in cyberspace, mostly with people who would never have called themselves gender outlaws of any kind.

On several of the major online services, there are regular weekly chats for people interested in discussing matters genderal. At this writing, for example, the Transgender Community Forum on America Online (keyword GENDER) has a weekly live online discussion group Sundays at 6 P.M. eastern time. Each week has a different topic, ranging from philosophical discussions to the nuts and bolts of gender change and transition.

Playing with gender and identity in cyberspace can be cathartic, educational, and fun. I heartily recommend it!

Cyberspace Pros: It's a great tool to learn to overcome shyness, no matter one's reasons for social abstinence. It helps to remember though, that it *is* a tool, not your life.
Cyberspace Cons: The safety of cyberspace can become addictive; and cybersurfing can overtake offline life as a predominant forum for ones connectivity. There's nothing wrong with that, but the fact is that while cyberlife is a great meeting ground and rehearsal space, it doesn't stand alone to match up with the benefits a full offline connection with another human being. And yeah, you might get stuck in cyberspace for a while. Go ahead, but remember that little Hallmark greeting card about ships and harbors.

One more thing: Projection and transference have a much better chance of holding sway in cyberspace than in real life. We tend to project the "perfect partner" onto whomever we're with, and in cyberspace there are few clues to the contrary. I've found it pays to be wary of doing that to others, and to be conscious that someone is probably doing that to me.

How're you doing? Time for a little entertainment? How about a play? Hey, do I take care of you or what?

⑥ Post Hard: An Online Play in One Act

Post Hard is a piece I wrote, based on the style that Caitlin Sullivan and I developed for our cyberspace novel, *Nearly Roadkill*. Live chats in cyberspace are not literature. They're not even writing, in the strict sense of the word. They're best described as written speech, and that makes a big difference. Words come tumbling out of people; they're real and they're urgent. Much of the dialogue in this piece actually transpired online one night. I changed the names, did some editing, and tweaked it to make it pretty. ::grin::

In cyberspace, it's easy to carry on simultaneous conversations with two or more people. Each two-way conversation appears in its own window visible only to the two participants; if you choose to be something different in each exchange, you can experience a wonderful splattering of your identity!

EXERCISE: If you're feeling particularly playful, you could either read this script out loud, getting into each of the different characters, or you could get together with a number of friends, with each of you taking one or more parts.

Post Hard

original version written for Rebecca Brown's *Post Heart* benefit

at Red and Black Books, Seattle, February 15, 1996

```
To: Mythter
From: Gyrl
Subject: Splattering!
```

Honey, Honey, Honey,

It happened again last night! I guess it was fitting, cuz it was Valentine's Day. But this time I logged it all. I've got it all sitting in front of me in one amazing file.

My screen name was NiteGyrl. That's Nite with a I, and Gyrl with a Y.

Why?

Cuz I'm an online, wired-up, plugged-in kind of gyrl. Heh heh.

I post frequently, and I post hard.

And last night, I splattered. I splattered big time. It'll go down in history as the St. Valentine's Day Splatter. Darlin, there were shreds of my ego everywhere!

Okay . . . this was the profile I used. Anyone else online who wanted to know who I am could punch that little get-the-profile thingie, and this is what they'd see:

Name: NiteGyrl.
Location: Which way's the wind blowin' today?
Sex: Whatever
Hobbies: Blood. Mine, or yours.

Let me tell you: it got me noticed! Singled me out. It drove people crazy cuz they had to know: What sex? Whose blood?

Okay, you ready? Here we go. I was cruisin' the online dungeon scenes. One of those private windows opened up on my screen. Her name on my screen is MstrssMegan.

MstrssMegan: Hi, looking for a mistress?
NiteGyrl: ::grinning ear to ear:: Just so happens yes, ma'am . . . but this one is kinda picky.

I could see what she was sayin', And she could see what I was sayin' back. And no one else knew what we were doing. Let me tell you, I'm glad for those li'l private windows, cuz she was ready for action, and frankly, so was I.

MstrssMegan: Undress and describe yourself.

Okay, so I kinda warily step out of my boots and jeans, and she's just waiting there, tapping her foot. I stand straight, shoulders back.

NiteGyrl: Ma'am, I'm tall ma'am . . . 5'11", about 150 pounds, ma'am.
   Short dark red hair, ma'am. green eyes, ma'am.
MstrssMegan: Not bad. What about your figure?
NiteGyrl: ::shyly:: Built kind of small, ma'am.

> **MstrssMegan:** ::frowning:: I prefer full-figured. You'll have to be
> punished for that.
> **NiteGyrl:** Y-y-yes, ma'am.

Just then another private window opens up on my screen.
It's some guy who calls himself Angel Boy. Really sweet.

> **Angel Boy:** The wind blows to thee NiteGyrl where a young male model
> and student dreams of your lilting words, and approaches, as
> daintily as a sixth grader looking for a dance, wondering how he
> might get your attention this evening.
> **NiteGyrl:** ::purring softly:: Gentle poet, my attention is yours.
> **Angel Boy:** Ahhh, how I wish I could hear your voice.

> **MstrssMegan:** ::flicking a single-tailed whip:: Do you enjoy pain,
> gyrl?

Whoa! She knows how to get attention, know what I mean?

> **MstrssMegan:** Answer me!
> **NiteGyrl:** Yes, ma'am. This one enjoys pain, ma'am.

You know I like that kinda stuff, right?

> **MstrssMegan:** ::slow smile:: Then perhaps I need to withhold that
> from you for a while.
> **NiteGyrl:** Oh, ma'am!
> **MstrssMegan:** The mark of a good slave is patience, dear.
> **NiteGyrl:** ::eyes cast down:: Yes, ma'am. Patience, ma'am.
> **MstrssMegan:** ::laughing softly::

> **Angel Boy:** Might I inquire as to your station in this dungeon?
> **NiteGyrl:** ::eyes sparkling:: I'm becoming many things to many peo-
> ple this evening, Poet.
> **Angel Boy:** Ahh, but what are you to yourself? That is a tricky ques-
> tion, tred carefully.
> **NiteGyrl:** ::smiling:: I live to serve, to bleed, to lie at the feet of
> one who can master me.
> **Angel Boy:** That, perhaps unfortunately, is something we share—for
> this evening at least. The blood in your profile could have

bespoken dominance or submission, although there is always that gray area in between, yes?

NiteGyrl: ::eyes sparkling:: Just so happens my favorite position is the middle . . . bottoming to one, while topping another, little one.

Angel Boy: That I had never even conceived of, NiteGyrl. I guess you really do learn something new everyday. Where exactly do you see your poet?

NiteGyrl: ::smiling:: A lad as dainty as yourself, and with such a fine sensibility deserves no more than to be my handservant. ::laughing lightly:: Handservant to a slave! Can you obey orders from a slave?

MstrssMegan: Practicing your patience, little one?

. . . says MstrssMegan, drawing forth a cane. I go very still very quickly.

NiteGyrl: Ma'am, yes ma'am!

MstrssMegan: Go on, gyrl . . . present your thighs for a proper caning.

NiteGyrl: ::whimpering:: Please, ma'am?

MstrssMegan: Please what, gyrl?

NiteGyrl: P-please, ma'am, may I have your very best?

Angel Boy: Please, ma'am, what exactly are the qualifications for a handservant, I have never been one.

NiteGyrl: ::smiling:: Have you ever been in service, Angel Boy, or bottomed to a woman? Real time?

Angel Boy: No i have never lived this fantasy, but it has begun to pervade my thoughts. It is a peculiar sensation that I can't even judge because it seems so inevitable.

NiteGyrl: ::softly:: Like destiny calling to you with a voice as soft as flutes.

MstrssMegan: My very best it is, gyrl.

NiteGyrl: ::shivering in anticipation of the blow::

MstrssMegan: But not just yet. ::laughing merrily::

I am *really* squirming now, right? I mean, I love that kind of teasing, hon! But then *another* private window opens up in front of me. Marius speaks in a voice, he says, filled with despair and foreboding. Is this getting cool, or what?

Marius: R U a woman of the night?

NiteGyrl: I've been accused of that and worse.

Marius: Just curious. Thought you were one of my own. Do U like to drink?

NiteGyrl: ::smiling:: Not particularly.

NiteGyrl: Unless the drink is stronger than wine.

NiteGyrl: Darker than the earth.

NiteGyrl: And headier than all the storms on all the seas of all the planets.

Marius: Please come to Boston . . .

MstrssMegan: Have you learned your lesson, gyrl?

I can't speak. I mean type. I mean speak. I drop to my knees before MstrssMegan, shivering.

MstrssMegan: That arouses me, pretty one.

She lifts me gently to my feet, and . . . well . . . starts doing things. ::wide grin::

NiteGyrl: Ma'am! Thank you, ma'am!

MstrssMegan: ::smiling:: Ah, you have manners. Perhaps there's some hope for you.

Angel Boy: ::beseechingly:: What can I do to prove my desire to please you??

Cute boy, huh?

Angel Boy: Shall I call you Mistress??

NiteGyrl: ::smiling:: That'll do for now. ::laughing:: So you want to be the slave of a slave, do you? Low, low, little creature.

Angel Boy: It would herald the start of my transformation and it would be my pleasure, Dear Mistress.

NiteGyrl: ::shaking my head:: You don't get it, creature. Your pleasure is the *least* of my concerns.

Marius: Do U love the night?

NiteGyrl: ::closing my eyes smiling:: It's my comfort and strength, Marius.

Marius: Childe, the night is no longer my friend.

NiteGyrl: How is that possible?

Marius: I am lost somewhere beyond night and day, childe. . . . I'm an old one. . . . Time is short for me, and only one thing can save me . . .

NiteGyrl: ::bright eyes:: Oh, let me guess: the kiss of a younger, more impudent member of our tribe, right? ;D

Marius: More than a kiss, childe. More than a kiss.

MstrssMegan: Gyrl!

NiteGyrl: Ma'am?

MstrssMegan: On your knees, gyrl. I'm going to look for a third play partner.

NiteGyrl: ::dropping to my knees, hands on my thighs, head bowed::

MstrssMegan: ::chuckling:: You stay like that.

NiteGyrl: Ma'am, yes ma'am!

So, off she went in search of who-knows-what! ::laughing:: Y'know how just when you're getting into something, just when it starts to take you outta your head, and into whatever other part of your body you wanted to really feel, just then someone interrupts you? Right. So, PrettyPam's window opens up on my screen.

PrettyPam: hello

NiteGyrl: Hello indeed, PrettyPam.

PrettyPam: like girls

NiteGyrl: ::smiling:: Was that a question or a statement?

PrettyPam: both

NiteGyrl: ::smile broadening: And what are *you* this evening?

PrettyPam: a sub, a slut

NiteGyrl: ::nodding:: And how much experience have you had, little one?

PrettyPam: married to master 5 years

NiteGyrl: Answer properly or do not answer at all.

> **PrettyPam:** yes mistress. married to master 5 years, mistress.
> **NiteGyrl:** Better.

You still with me? Hang in there, okay?

> **Angel Boy:** How may I serve you, Mistress?
> **NiteGyrl:** Is it service you seek? Truly service?
> **Angel Boy:** Yes Mistress. It is a true longing I've never given voice to before this evening.
> **NiteGyrl:** ::smiling:: I think you really like this. That's good. Tell me . . . what are your fantasies about me?
> **Angel Boy:** Yes Mistress. I fantasize about your haughtiness, augmented by your wit, your intelligence. I dream of you putting me in my place. A vague dream since I know so little but a complete one none the less, Mistress.
> **NiteGyrl:** You're quite sure it's the service, and only the service?
> **Angel Boy:** Yes, Mistress!

> **Marius:** I am the original one . . . the others are mere phantasms.
> **NiteGyrl:** ::narrowing my eyes:: Tell me more, Marius.
> **Marius:** I thirst, living in the 90's. Bloodlines have grown weak over the centuries.
> **Marius:** Tell me, do U have fangs?
> **Marius:** Long black hair?
> **Marius:** Flowing white gown?
> **NiteGyrl:** ::grinning:: Told you, Marius . . . I'm a young one, old man, one of the Abandoned Ones. I've got no tribe. My hair's short, the color of dry blood, I wear combat boots.
> **Marius:** I'm looking for someone to bring me back from . . . did you say *Combat* boots?
> **NiteGyrl:** ::chuckling:: Very nineties . . . stick around and you'll find out about this time period.

Okay, so I'm a brat. But now, another dude who calls himself MASTER4YOU has got his little window jumping onto my already crowded screen.

> **MASTER4YOU:** Hello there!!!! How are you?????
> **NiteGyrl:** I am crawling my way out of a *mess* of these private windows! Eeeeeeeeeek!

> **MASTER4YOU:** I see you're popular, huh
> **NiteGyrl:** ::ear to ear grin:: Sir, I feel like a one woman circus!
> **MASTER4YOU:** good......got any room for another person?
> **NiteGyrl:** Yessir! I'm sliding your window to the FRONT of my screen, Sir!
> **MASTER4YOU:** good......I will give you a reward now!!

Oh goodie! Grinning, I sit up and beg, looking awfully cute. You know how cute I can look when I want to, right? Well ::tossing my hair back:: I *can*! ::laughing and laughing::

> **MASTER4YOU:** I'll let you lick my leather boot for now!!
> **NiteGyrl:** Yessir!

Something about this guy. He uses too many exclamation points.
Anyway, I drop to my knees at his feet, pressing my face against his boot . . . soft, then harder, til it hurts my cheek. Slowly, I turn my face, licking leather . . . and a moan escapes my lips, unbidden.

> **MASTER4YOU:** Good slave. . . . . make me want you!!!

> **Angel Boy:** Mistress?
> **NiteGyrl:** ::softly:: Patience.
> **Angel Boy:** Yes, Mistress.
> **NiteGyrl:** Think on this, slave of a slave: you know not who you serve.

> **Marius:** Only a vampire can make a vampire. And only a vampire can save a vampire.
> **NiteGyrl:** Where'd you get that one? Some Transylvanian fortune cookie?
> **Marius:** I am in need of someone who can bring me back. How old R U?
> **NiteGyrl:** Obviously younger than you, you old fart.
> **Marius:** I can only laugh at a response like that . . . .
> **NiteGyrl:** Uh huh. What did you mean, it's going to take more than a kiss?

> **MstrssMegan:** Gyrl, are you still on your knees?
> **NiteGyrl:** Ma'am, yes ma'am! ::fighting the desire to look up into your eyes::

> **MstrssMegan:** You're becoming such a sweet girl, I might keep you.

Ummmmm, you're still okay with this, right? But you're seeing what's going on, right? I'm everywhere, honey . . . I'm everywhere, everything at the same time. This is what I've been trying to describe to you. Okay, I'll shut up and let the log do the talking.

> **Angel Boy:** Mistress, a favor please?
> **NiteGyrl:** ::softly:: Yes, slave of a slave?
> **Angel Boy:** Mistress, are you male or female?
> **NiteGyrl:** ::deep, rumbling laughter:: What if I told you I was a man?

> **MstrssMegan:** Slim pickings tonite, gyrl. Not too many real players. You may relax now and lie down.
> **NiteGyrl:** Yes ma'am. ::curling up at your feet::
> **MstrssMegan:** Tell me . . . are you truly a woman?
> **NiteGyrl:** ::softly:: Now, why do you want to spoil a delightful evening with a question like that?
> **MstrssMegan:** You're a man?
> **NiteGyrl:** Nope.
> **MstrssMegan:** Good . . . because *I* am.

> **PrettyPam:** Mistress, I want to be whipped in a room full of naked women, to serve all with my body, covered with welts.
> **NiteGyrl:** How close have you come to living this dream, ma petite Pretty Pam?
> **PrettyPam:** I served master and another couple.
> **NiteGyrl:** ::snapping:: I *said* answer properly or do not answer at all!
> **PrettyPam:** Yes mistress. I served master and another couple, mistress.

> **Marius:** We creatures of the night exist apart from humans . . . apart from old or young, black or white.
> **NiteGyrl:** Apart from male or female?

> **MstrssMegan:** Are you still there?

> **Angel Boy:** You're a man?
> **NiteGyrl:** You never can tell, can you?

Angel Boy: ummmmmm . . . you *sound* like a woman.
NiteGyrl: ::grinning:: Sometimes I *am* a woman.
Angel Boy: You're a woman?
NiteGyrl: No, I'm not a woman.

MASTER4YOU: now . . . . . . assume your position . . . slave. . . .
   I'm going to do you doggie style!!!!!!!!
NiteGyrl: ::gently:: Hon? Let me ask you a question.
MASTER4YOU: you may...but it better be good!!!!!!!!!!!!!!
NiteGyrl: How old are you?

MstrssMegan: Look, should I just sign off? I'm sorry.
NiteGyrl: Sorry, I had too many messages. Sorry ma'am.... Sir?
MstrssMegan: No, I'm sorry . . . I didn't mean to mislead you.
NiteGyrl: You're really a guy?
MstrssMegan: Yes. I'm really sorry.
NiteGyrl: You're really good is what you are!

PrettyPam: How may I best serve you, mistress?
NiteGyrl: ::nodding:: Describe your current service to your master,
   Pretty Pam.
PrettyPam: total servitude, i am always naked or in lingerie, i cook
   clean, bathe him, dress him . . .
PrettyPam: i service him sexually every morning, whipped if he's not
   pleased
NiteGyrl: ::gently:: You're a guy, right?
PrettyPam: no, check my profile . . . it says female!

Angel Boy: I've never done anything with a guy before.
NiteGyrl: Come here, boy. Wanna hold you, boy. Wanna wrap you in my
   strong arms.
Angel Boy: Mistress?
NiteGyrl: ::gently:: Is it truly service you seek? If that was so,
   would it really matter what I am? Would service itself not be
   enough?

MASTER4YOU: I'm 45, slave!!!!!!!!! Now, turn over!
NiteGyrl: ::softly:: What year were you born?

NiteGyrl: Hello there?

MASTER4YOU: That is an impertinent question, slave!

NiteGyrl: ::very gently:: What are you . . . 14?

MASTER4YOU: 1950!

NiteGyrl: Younger than 12?

MASTER4YOU: I'm 16. Are you angry?

NiteGyrl: ::smiling:: Thanks. Thanks for being honest . . . but I think we need to stop this kind of playing, okay?

MstrssMegan: I need to leave. Are you angry?

NiteGyrl: No ma'am . . . no . . . Sir? ::laughing:: I kind of like you, whatever you are.

MstrssMegan: You've pleased me, NiteGyrl, and I'm happy to have allowed you some pleasure. What's your name?

NiteGyrl: ::smiling:: Kate, if it pleases you ma'am.

MstrssMegan: It does. I like you too, Kate. Will you serve me again?

NiteGyrl: ::softly:: Yes, Sir. Yes, ma'am . . . Yes, you.

MstrssMegan: ::just as softly:: Glad I found you. We freaks need to stick together.

Angel Boy: I don't think I can do anything with you, mister.

NiteGyrl: Why not, boy?

Angel Boy: I'm not into guys.

NiteGyrl: This is cyberspace, boy.

Angel Boy: It's not that.

NiteGyrl: What is it, boy?

Angel Boy: I'm not a boy. I'm not a man. I can't stick around here . . . gotta go. Bye.

NiteGyrl: Wait!

Marius: Yes . . . beyond male and beyond female.

NiteGyrl: Sorry . . . sorry . . . I lost my place here, hon. Where were we?

Marius: What are you?

NiteGyrl: Ummmmm . . . wait . . . you're the old blood-drinker, that makes me a young blood-drinker.

Marius: Do you always measure yourself by the identity of another?

NiteGyrl: ::smiling sadly:: Always. What else are identities for?

Marius: Please come to Boston . . . .

PrettyPam: I am not a man!
NiteGyrl: ::continuing gently:: I don't mind if you're a guy. I like
   boys who become girls. I just like to know the truth.
PrettyPam: No i'm female
NiteGyrl: Describe yourself.

Angel Boy: What do you want?
NiteGyrl: I never said I'm a guy, darlin.
Angel Boy: You said you're not a woman.
NiteGyrl: And that's true. But that doesn't make me a guy.
NiteGyrl: Angel Boy? You still there?
Angel Boy: I have to chew this one over.
NiteGyrl: Confusing?
Angel Boy: No, no . . . it's pretty clear. And all too close to home.
   Gotta go . . . I'll see you again, Mistress, Master. ::grin-
   ning:: Maybe next time, I'll turn the tables.
NiteGyrl: Wait! Please!

PrettyPam: 5'7" brown hair and eyes 113 pounds, 36C-26-28, shaven-
   pierced.
NiteGyrl: What sort of work do you do?
PrettyPam: Aerobic instructor
NiteGyrl: Describe your master.

MASTER4YOU: I want you to be my slave!!!!!
MASTER4YOU: Please?
NiteGyrl: ::gently:: Stop that, honey . . . I'm old enough to be your
   grandmother.
MASTER4YOU: NO WAY!!!!!!!!!!!!!!!!!!!!!!!!!!!
NiteGyrl: Way.

PrettyPam: My Master is 6'0" 210 very muscular, blue eyes/ brown
   hair, magnificent body. He makes me take him into my mouth all
   the time.
NiteGyrl: Gnite, hon. You practice the girl thing a little more,
   okay?
PrettyPam: Okay. Good night.
NiteGyrl: G'nite, sweetie.

MASTER4YOU: Oh, gee. You're really that old?

NiteGyrl: Uh huh, full of wrinkles and bad knees. Why don't you find the teen board and look for someone to explore this stuff with there.

MASTER4YOU: They're all KIDS!

NiteGyrl: I'm sure you can find someone. And look . . . just a little advice?

MASTER4YOU: Yeah?

NiteGyrl: More love . . . fewer exclamation points.

MASTER4YOU: Whoa! Are you a hippie chick?

NiteGyrl: Sorta kinda. G'nite, darlin.

MASTER4YOU: Wow, you're good.

NiteGyrl: ::grinning:: I really hafta be going now. Maybe another time, we can chat and get to know each other.

MASTER4YOU: Yay!!!!!

NiteGyrl: But no more playing.

MstrssMegan: Would you do me a favor?

NiteGyrl: ::grinning:: Fly out there and sleep at the foot of your bed, ma'am/sir?

MstrssMegan: Perhaps someday. But now I would like you to send me some erotic email. I'll email you the details of what I like.

NiteGyrl: ::wriggling happily:: As you wish, ma'am/sir!

MstrssMegan: That's MA'AM to you, girl. I look forward to enjoying you again soon.

NiteGyrl: ::melting:: Thank you, ma'am. Nite, ma'am.

Angel Boy: Whattaya want? I'm *trying* to sign off.

NiteGyrl: Gee, it's taking you a while.

Angel Boy: ::growling:: I'm new at this.

NiteGyrl: That's sweet.

Angel Boy: Whataya want?

NiteGyrl: What did you mean, you might turn the tables?

Angel Boy: Heh heh heh. I'm not new at *everything.* G'nite.

NiteGyrl: ::gulp:: G'nite, Poet.

And I sign off.

My screen goes dark.

And everyone I was, all the different roles I was playing, they're floating out in front of me. All of my identities, everything I can be, is ready to pick from some amazing tree called me that never bears the same kind of fruit twice.

That's what I've been talkin' about, honey. That's what happens when I post hard.

⊚ Back into the Classroom: Three Gender Performance Workshops

Note: *This next section is not for casual reading. It's not for reading of any sort, really. It's for doing. So, if you're reading this book cover to cover, you would do very well to simply skim these workshops to get the idea of them. Then, when you want to do the drills, come back and read them with the intent to learn them. You can pick up with the text of the book at either Chapter 10,* Cautionary Interlude, *or Chapter 11,* This Quiet Revolution.

I developed and coached the following three gender performance workshops on campuses and in theaters across North America, and in several places in the United Kingdom. They were originally designed for acting students, but I've led them for quite a few nonactors and it worked out just fine. There's no prerequisite to any of this stuff other than a desire to explore your gender and your identity.

Gender Performance Exercise #1: On the Outside, Looking In

Purpose: To familiarize students with their bodies, and some of the major limitations of the kind of bodies we have.

To free students from some of the fixed ideas they might have about their bodies by giving them another perspective on looking at their bodies.

Setup: Give yourself at least one hour of free time, away from telephones, email, alarms, beepers, and unexpected visitors. You *can* do this exercise yourself, but it's really best in a group of people (at least you and one other person), with one of you acting as a coach.

You'll need space for each student to lie down on the floor without touching another student. The coach should be comfortably off to one side, preferably out of sight of the students. There's no physical contact between the coach and any of the students, except as indicated in the exercise.

To the students: Wear comfortable clothing, stuff you don't mind lying around on the floor in. This exercise is nonverbal on your part; you don't ever have to say anything. You simply get to observe and examine.

To the coach: You're setting the scene verbally, and then asking the questions. Try to speak in a gentle manner. No barking orders or issuing commands. This is more of a guided meditation, okay? So you need to be aware of your responsibility to the student(s), gently coaxing them to move further and further into the visualization. No, you don't need to stick to this word for word. In fact, it's going to be a *lot* better if you use your *own* words.

———

For more information about coaching, I'd suggest the book Improvisation for the Theater *by Viola Spolin. There are some wonderful exercises in there for actors and nonactors alike.*

If there is no coach, I'd suggest you read the coach's dialogue several times, so you can speak it to yourself in your mind as you're doing it. I suppose you could tape record yourself saying this stuff, but I don't trust the timing of a taped coach; there's bound to come a point where you want to explore some aspect of this, and the tape is going to be inexorably urging you onward.

———

The warm-up: If you're familiar or comfortable with good versions of relaxation, grounding, and protection exercises, then do those. If not, here are the versions I use and enjoy. Yes, it's a lot of words; I decided to write them all down for the benefit of readers who might not be familiar with relaxation techniques like this.

The students are lying comfortably on their backs on the floor. Pillows or cushions can be used under knees, neck, or head if that's more comfortable. The coach uses roughly the following warm-up talk, at a very relaxed pace, allowing plenty of time for the students to go ahead and do what ze is asking them to do.

Warm-up coaching: I want you to get yourself very comfortable. Just move around on the floor for a bit until you're comfortable on your back, and raise your hand to let me know you've gotten to a comfortable position.

Okay, now I want you to relax. Feel the weight of your body against the floor. There's no need to move, just feel how heavy or light the different points of your body that are making contact with the floor. Your heels, maybe. Or your calves. Are the backs of your knees touching the floor? If so, how heavily or lightly? If not, try to feel how much space there is between the floor and the backs of your knees. How about your thighs? What's the weight of the back of your thighs against the floor? Breathe nice and easily while you're feeling all this. Breathe in through your nose and out through your mouth if you can. Can you feel the whole of both your legs touching the floor now, or not touching? Just be aware of it, there's no need to move. Staying still is what we're looking for. Okay, what kind of weight is your butt pressing against the floor? Is the small of your back touching? How lightly or heavily?

Now, as you're breathing, I want you to imagine you can actually breathe in to the area of your body I'm talking about. If I'm talking about your upper back, I want you to imagine that as you're breathing in, you can see your breath actually reaching your upper back. Try that now. Feel your upper back against the floor. How heavy or light does it feel? Can you feel your breath reaching directly into your upper back as you breathe in? When you breathe out, can you imagine your breath leaving your upper back and then out your mouth?

(Coach: Continue in this fashion with different parts of the body: upper arms, elbows, forearms, wrists, hands, fingers, neck, head, face, etc. Be thorough.)

Now become aware of your entire body, all at the same time. Just be aware of where your body is touching the floor, and where it isn't. Be aware of the weight of your body. And breathe. Look for places in your body that might still be a little tense, and breathe directly into those places. Each time you breathe out through your mouth, that tension leaves your body with your breath. Keep looking for any tension left in your body, and just breathe it away. Keep on doing that for a while. Look for tension, and breathe some good air into it, breathing the tension out.

(Coach: Give them some time with this, especially if they've never done any relaxation exercises before. You can occasionally break the silence with "Breathe," or "Look for any tension," or "Enjoy that relaxation"; just encourage them. When they're relaxed, go on to the next part of the warm-up.)

Now that you're all free of all that tension, and nice and relaxed, we're going to do a grounding exercise just so you don't go flying up to the ceiling and hurt your head. I want you to take an internal look at your spine. Just look at your spine, from your tailbone right up through to the base of your skull. Just be aware of your spine. Got that? Okay. Now I want you to imagine your spine growing. Have your spine grow down into the floor from your tailbone. Just picture it as something like a tendril or a root. See that spine of yours growing down through the floor into the room right below us. Don't worry about upsetting people in the room downstairs, they'll get over it. Just keep growing your spine down, down, down, through the basement of this building, through the foundation, and into the earth beneath us. Imagine you can feel the earth with your spine. You can even say hello to the earth that way, you know. Just have the tip of your spine say hi to the earth. Right. Now, have the earth say hi right back. Let your spine keep right on growing until it's at a nice, deep comfortable place down in the earth. Remember, that part of your spine is still connected to you, all the way to the base of your skull.

Okay, now there's something interesting about roots and the earth. They give stuff to each other, it's true. The earth gives all these nutrients to the root system of plants, and the root systems give the topsoil something to hang on to so it won't blow away. There's a give and take. So, I want you to see that part of your spine that's in the earth as giving something for the earth to hold on to. And the way the earth is going to say "thanks, pal" is to send some nutrients, some goodies, into that part of your spine. You can see those nutrients from the earth as small sparkling points of light. They come into your spine deep in the earth, and travel up up up to the very top of your spine at the base of your skull, and they burst into your head, and they shower down through the rest of your body. And that's grounding. That's connecting with the earth on a give-and-take basis. And that's what you're doing right now. You're giving the earth something to hold on to, and the earth is giving you all this wonderful light that's giving you a lot of energy wherever those little points of light land inside you.

Finally, we're going to make sure you feel very very safe in this exercise. Try this: take one of those little light bursts, and let it settle into the very center of your heart. It's warm, and it's pulsing in perfect time with your own heartbeat. Just feel that little light there. Now, if you look closer at this particular light, you'll see that it's a tiny mirror-ball, it's a ball that reflects everything away from it. What this particular mirror-ball is reflecting is any fear or danger or interruption of your own comfort and relaxation and groundedness. So I want you to breathe now. Breathe right into that little ball in the center of your heart, and as you breathe in, that ball begins to grow. And as it grows, it's going to reflect right out of your body any fears or doubts or shame you might have about doing this. Just breathe and let that little mirror ball do its work. Let it grow 'til it fills your heart, reflecting all that other stuff right out of your body. Keep on breathing, nice and gently, and let that mirror grow to fill the trunk of your body. That's right. Keep on breathing. And that ball is still growing, and you don't even have to think about it, it's just making it nice and safe for you to be right where you are, doing what you're doing. Let it keep on growing past your arms and legs, and even your head, and it's washing all those fears out of its way by reflecting them back to where they came from. Now imagine that ball has grown right out of your body, and it's formed a perfect sphere around your body, and it's reflecting away anything that might hurt you. And you're safe there. Just enjoy that feeling for awhile.

Workshop set-up: When the students are relaxed and grounded, the coach then sets the scene as follows. Students continue to lie comfortably on their backs on the floor.

All right, I want you to close your eyes. Good, now imagine yourself an inhabitant of a planet far far far away from earth. Maybe you're lying outdoors, and you're warm and comfortable. It's a beautiful day, and there's no pressure on you to do anything but enjoy yourself.

You should know something about yourself, and about all the other inhabitants of this planet: your natural body is completely formless, shapeless, and weightless. Can you imagine having a body like that? What would it be like? Just picture that kind of body. Got it? Okay, here's something else: you have the ability to change your body at will. You can look like whatever you want to look like. If you want sixteen arms and three heads, bingo, you've got it. That's just the way things are on this planet of yours. You can change your shape whenever you want to. What's more, people on this planet change their shapes all the time, sometimes several times a minute if that's what they want, and since so many people do that, nobody thinks it's a big deal. So I want you to picture what that world might look like with people constantly shifting. You'd get to appreciate people's imaginations, wouldn't you? You'd get into fun games with other people on that planet, almost dances of shape-shifting with one another. Picture yourself doing that with some other folks. Picture yourself shifting shape along with someone else. What does that feel like? There's no need to answer me out loud. Just think the answer to yourself. Is it fun? Is it erotic? Does it make you smile?

What's more, you can create objects or change them or make them disappear at will. There's no shortage of anything. If you want an apple, it appears in your hand. If you want to change that apple into a peach, then it's done! If you've eaten the peach and you want to get rid of the pit, well, you can vanish it. So picture this world constantly shifting color and shape, and it's all beautiful, and you're able to shift right along with it. Let your imagination run with this, and picture what a few minutes on that planet might look like.

(Coach: Give the students a few minutes to picture this. You can occasion-ally help them out with statements like "Remember, if there's something you don't like, you can always change it," or "You can always stay in some shape you like for as long as you like, there are no rules about that sort of thing.")

The mission: After giving the students some time to enjoy themselves as inhabitants of that world, tell them the following:

Okay, now word's come out from the Interplanetary Sociological Insti-tute on this world that they need volunteers to go explore another planet. You volunteer for this job. So you uncreate yourself wherever you are, and re-create yourself at the launch pad at the Institute. Can you see the ship that's going to take you off-planet for the very first time? What does it look like? There's no need to answer me out loud. Just think the answers to yourself.

Now you're getting your final briefing. You'll be going to this other planet, and you'll be taking on the body of a typical inhabitant of that planet for ten minutes. Your job will be to experience what it's like to have that kind of a body, and then return home to the homeworld, and describe it. Do you understand your mission? For ten minutes, you will be, for all intents and purposes, an inhabitant of that planet. Got it? Okay. So, you climb aboard your ship, and wave good-bye, and you're off! Can you see yourself aboard the ship? Right. Now, days and days go by. A long, long time. Finally an announcement comes over the comm system that you're approaching your destination. You're excited, and you look out the view port to see a system of nine planets circling a small yellow dwarf star. You're headed for an M-class planet, the third one from the star. It's small and blue and green and white, and it's circled by one moon. Can you see that planet? How is it different from your homeworld? Is it larger? Small-er? Anything else that's different?

The comm system instructs you to lie down on your back in preparation for your landing, and you do. It's a gentle landing in a remote, uninhabit-ed region of the planet. And now, you've landed. And you can feel yourself taking on the body of one of the planet's native inhabitants, right there, lying on your back on the floor. That's the body you're to observe for ten minutes.

The observation: Now, keeping your eyes closed, I want you to become aware of this body. What does it feel like, lying there in that body? Are you aware of its general shape? Do you have a sense of its weight? Just be aware of your body right now, just lie there and be aware of it. What points of your body are touching the floor? How warm or cool is your body? Now I want you to notice what parts of your body are moving all by themselves. Air seems to be moving in and out of your body without you thinking about it, right? How's that happening? There's also some sort of regular beating rhythm throughout your body. Can you feel that in different parts of your body? Where? Where's that beating rhythm coming from?

Now, keeping your eyes closed, I want you to explore moving different parts of your body. This should be easy for you: you're used to thinking about something and it happens, so think moving part of your body, and feel what happens when you do. Just lie there with your eyes closed, and move different parts of your body: big parts and little parts.

(Coach: Give the students some time to move their arms, legs, fingers, toes, head, face, chest, butt, shoulders. Watch them. If you notice they've not moved something, you can say something like "Okay, I'm going to gently touch a part of your body now, and I want to see if you can move it." Very gently touch some part of their body. Repeat this as necessary.)

All right, how do you suppose people see things on this planet? What part of their bodies do you think they might use? Experiment with that body you've got until you find which part of it makes it possible for you to see things.

(wait until they open their eyes)

Okay . . . now look at your body. What does it look like? Was it what you imagined it to be? What color is it? Is it interesting? What textures does that body have? Use some part of your body to touch another part of your body. What does that feel like? Keep on exploring what your body looks like, and what it's like to touch your body.

(Coach: Give them some time to do that.)

Okay, I want you to notice that this body you're in has four long-ish appendages. Take a good look at them, and decide that you'd like two more. Think yourself into having two more appendages. Did you notice that nothing happened? Decide that you'd like to have a different color scheme to this body, and think that into happening. That didn't work either, did it? Interesting limitations, aren't they? Okay, it's time to move this body around and see how that feels. How do you suppose these people move their bodies from place to place? Suppose you wanted to be three feet from where you are now. How would you get there? Go ahead and try to move your body. Try a couple of ways of doing it.

(Coach: You can give them some hints like, "Would you roll your body across the floor?" "Maybe balance it up on some combination of those four appendages? Do you think it would be safe for you to balance yourself upright like that? Try it." If there's more than one student, you can now get them to look at each other, and touch each other with curiosity. Keep getting them to explore different uses of their bodies for a total of about fifteen minutes, then wrap up the exercise by having them lie back down on the floor, and travel them back to their home planet. Once you've got them back there, tell them the following:)

Okay, we're going to end this part of the workshop now. I want you to open your eyes and just enjoy being right here, right now, in the body that you have. Just lie there until you're comfortable enough to get back up on your feet and have a seat.

Discussion: I've found it very helpful for the coach and students to discuss the workshop. Here are some useful questions to get the discussion started, and to keep it moving:

- What did you learn from this exercise?
- Does your body feel any different now than it did before the exercise? If so, how?
- Did you learn anything new about your body?
- Did you learn anything new about some attitude you might have about your body?
- Was there anything that was uncomfortable for you? If so, what was that? How are you feeling about that now?
- What emotions came up for you during this exercise?

- ◎ What did you find most useful from doing this exercise?
- ◎ Is there anything you learned from this exercise that you might be able to carry over into your day-to-day life?

Gender Performance Exercise #2: The Gender Walk

The central part of this exercise is taken from an old Zen exercise I learned from a theater director who'd studied in Japan. The original exercise went like this: You were woken up in the morning, just before sunrise. You were taken to an outdoor platform, maybe thirty or forty feet long, and you stood at one edge of the length of the platform. As you perceived the first ray of sunlight, you began to move across the room to the other side. You had to keep moving forward, you couldn't stop; there was no zigzagging from side to side permitted. And you had to reach the other side of the platform as the last ray of sunlight disappeared at sunset. Uh huh, that long a time. You learned to move verrrrrrry slowly. You learned a lot about your body. The director who taught this to me had us do this Zen walk from one side of the room to the other in ninety minutes, and even *that* felt like an eternity. I still do that exercise from time to time, and it no longer feels like an eternity; it's begun to be simply time like any other time.

I first adapted the Zen walk to gender performance in 1989, while working with a group of students at the Del' Arte Theater in Eureka, California. Rather than concentrate the exercise on the walk itself, I opted to use the forward motion as a body-level physical metaphor for a journey through gender, requiring the student to perform some interesting mental gymnastics during the journey.

This exercise is best done with a coach the first time, but I don't see any reason why it couldn't be done solo after that. In fact, if you have no coach available, I don't see any reason you couldn't do it solo the first time.

Purpose: To give the student a means by which ze can achieve no-gender. To provide a framework in which a student might strip off their current gender, and construct within themselves the gender of their choice.

What you need: A longish open space, free of obstacles. I've done this exercise in a room that's only fifteen feet long . . . it gets interesting. If there's more than one participating student, the space should be wide enough for the students to stand at arm's length from each other.

A large sheet of paper and felt-tip pen for each student.

Exercise requirement: The students should be familiar with the basics of gender found in the early chapters of this workbook. NOTE: It's okay to do this exercise one time only, but it does get better after a few tries and with longer time periods.

Warm-up: Relaxation, grounding, and protection as in Workshop #1, or by your choice.

Pre-walk: Hand out the paper and pens. Ask the students to draw a line lengthwise down the center of the paper. Now, ask them to list on the left side of the paper whatever qualities or aspects about themselves they feel define their current gender identity; these can be physical, emotional, psychological, social, whatever . . . it's up to the student. You're looking for the gender they're being most of their lives, the one they walk around in, the one they either feel they are or the one they wish to change out of.
Be sure they include:

◎ **physical center:** what part of their body feels central to them right now. For some, it might be the chest; others might feel their center is in their spine, or legs; still others might choose their heads, hearts, bellies . . . it's up to the student to choose that physical center for the gender they're being right now.
◎ **weight:** while standing, do they feel their weight solidly on the full soles of their feet, or do they tend to feel lighter, more up on their toes.
◎ what **oppression** do they feel in their current gender and how does that affect the way they stand or move?
◎ what **privilege** do they have in their current gender, and how does that affect the way they stand or move?
◎ something about their current gender that **they don't want to give up** (ask this one three times, and get three different answers from each student)

Now, ask the students to use the right-hand side of the paper to list the qualities or attributes that will define the gender they wish to become. Again, these can be physical, emotional, psychological, social, whatever . . . it's up to the student. Be sure to include, as above, physical center, weight, oppression, privilege, and (three times) what they'd most like to have in this new gender.
(Note—we haven't given either of these genders a name. Check in with the students to make sure they're not planning to move "from female to

male" or from "man to woman" or some broad terms like those. You're looking only for attributes and qualities; naming any genders at this point will only obscure the details, and the details are what's important.)

Ask the students to read over the two lists, to study them carefully, and get a good idea in their minds of what they'll be leaving behind, and what they're going to be taking on. You can make sure they have enough time to do this by asking them to raise their hands as soon as they feel they've got a good picture in their minds of these factors.

The Demo: Ask the students to line up against one wall, an arm's length from each other. Explain the concept of the Zen walk: for this exercise, they'll be moving forward without stopping for a total of thirty minutes. Any forward motion, like extending a hand slowly forward, counts as forward motion. Tell them you want to give them an idea of the passage of time by a demo, and that you'll time them for three minutes just to give them a taste of what it might take to do the exercise. Explain there will be no speaking during the walk.

Give them a START, and let them move forward at their own pace for a total of three minutes. Say nothing during this time. At the end of three minutes, give them a TIME'S UP. Have them observe where they are, making sure to make no judgments yourself.

The Walk: Have the students take one more look at their sheets of paper; then have them set the papers down and resume their positions against the wall. Go to the center of the room, and let the students know that this is the center point. Explain to them that for every motion forward they take for the first half of the room, they're to consciously think of dropping behind them some aspect of the gender they've been performing. It doesn't matter if the aspect is an attitude or body part or whatever. They're to simply visualize that quality or attribute (possibly including the three they didn't want to give up) dropping away from them as they move forward and leave that aspect behind them. Explain that this will happen until they reach the center point of the room, at which point *they will have no gender.* From the center point of the room to the opposite wall, they are to visualize *taking on* qualities and aspects of the gender they wish to perform; with every forward motion, they'll take on some aspect of that new gender until they reach the opposite wall at the end of the thirty minutes, at which point they will be fully within their new genders.

Remind them that there will be no speaking during the walk, except for your own coaching.

Check your watch, and give the students a START.

You can coach from the side with statements like, "You're moving forward, there's always *some* forward motion," or "See those aspects of the gender you've been being dropping aside with every motion forward."

Keep track of the time, and from time to time, you can let them know "Three minutes have passed," or "Six minutes have passed, check how far you've gone and how far you have to go."

During the first half of the exercise, you can walk the width of the room at the center point, saying aloud to the students, "This is the center point of the room. This is where you'll be when all that stuff has dropped away."

As each student reaches the center line, go up to that student and softly let them know they now have no gender, and that from here on to the end of the exercise, they are to take on qualities of the new gender.

When all the students have crossed the center line, you can coach the group by letting them know how much time has passed, and how much time remains; remind them to keep in constant motion, and that as they move forward, they are taking on more and more attributes of the gender they've selected.

When all the students reach the opposite wall at the end of thirty minutes, encourage them to walk around the space in their new genders by coaching them to:

◉ feel the physical space around them, and how much or little space are they taking up now?
◉ feel the space between them and the other people—how much space do they need now?

While encouraging them to continue moving around the space in their new genders, ask them the following questions, instructing them not to answer aloud, but rather silently to themselves. This part of the exercise should take between five and ten minutes.

◉ Where is your strength?
◉ Where is your center?
◉ Where is your comfort?
◉ Where is your pride?
◉ Where is your safety?
◉ What's dangerous?
◉ What's frightening?

⊚ Where is your comfort?

⊚ Where is your joy?

Ending the exercise: Tell the students to find a comfortable place to sit or lie down, and ask them to close their eyes. Tell them that this is the end of the exercise, and that you want them to take a moment to be aware of the differences between how they're feeling now, as opposed to how they felt when they first began the walk. Give them a few minutes to look that over, then tell them that it's time to let go of the new gender, and return to whatever gender they'd like. You can give them a visualization of having all the added attributes and qualities sinking out of their bodies and into the floor, leaving them clean and whole and refreshed. Ask them to raise their hands when they're done.

Discussion: Ask each student to discuss hir experience during the exercise. If they're having difficulty expressing themselves or knowing where to begin, you can ask questions like these to get them going:

⊚ Tell me about the walk itself. How was your sense of time and distance?

⊚ Did you find you were able to let go of most of the attributes of your first gender?

⊚ Were there any attributes you weren't able to drop behind this time?

⊚ Did you find you were able to take on most of the attributes of your second gender?

⊚ Were there any attributes you weren't able to take on this time?

⊚ What difference do you feel between right now, and when you began the exercise?

⊚ What would you like to do differently next time?

Gender Performance Exercise #3: Acting As-If

This is another exercise I developed for acting students, this time for John Emigh's senior acting class at Brown University.

The more I think about it, the more I'm convinced that acting skills are indeed life skills when it comes to the performance of identity. It might not be a bad idea for anyone who's really serious about exploring new genders to take a class or two in basic acting technique.

This particular exercise may seem fairly advanced, but if you've studied the basics of gender in the earliest chapters of this book, and you've done the first two exercises in this section, you should get quite a bit out of this one.

Purpose: To train the student to be conscious of gender cues, and their use in managing gender attribution.

What you need: A minimum of three people would be best; two to be students, one to be the coach. You'll need some area in which you can move freely during the scene. Despite the number of students participating, only two will be "on stage" at any given time; you will, however, need rehearsal room for as many pairs of students as you have.

Exercise requirement: Completion of Exercises #1 and #2 above, plus a familiarity with the basics of gender. The gender cues referrred to in this exercise are explained in detail in the book *Gender Outlaw,* pages 26 through 30.

Warm-up: Relaxation, grounding, and protection as in Exercise #1, or by your choice.

Setup: Students pair off into groups of two.Students are given these two lines to memorize from the movie *Batman Returns,* by Tim Burton:

> **First Student:** "You're just jealous because I'm a real freak,
>   and you have to wear a mask."
> **Second Student:** "You may just be right."

As these are the only two lines permissible in the exercise, the students are instructed to come up with a context in which the use of those two lines would make sense, as follows:

To the students:
- Decide who says which line.
- Decide together *why* you're saying these lines.
- The text may not be altered except during drill three, and then only as specified.
- Be willing to modify the scene as the performance of gender demands.

⊚ Select a gender to perform. Feel free to invent a gender. There is no need to be restricted by the binary male/female.
⊚ Agree together on the gender of each of your characters.
⊚ Your character's gender should be different from your own gender for the purpose of this exercise, but it's important to note that these drills would apply in the performance of your own gender, as we all perform gender differently.

Drill One: Simple performance

The coach gives the paired students time to set up their scene as above, and time to rehearse it off by themselves. Then, one by one, the coach calls the paired actors up to the stage to perform their scenes, using the other students as an "audience."

There's no critique of the scenes in terms of acting ability. The coach will ask those observing to note to themselves:

⊚ What genders did you see performed?
⊚ Given those genders, did the scene make sense?
⊚ How did you decide what genders you saw performed?

Drill Two: Perform a behavioral gender cue

The coach goes over the concept of behavioral gender cues, and asks students to give some examples. The coach then instructs each of the students to select *one* behavioral cue to perform that would make the scene more interesting. The coach asks the students to notice how that behavior is similar to or different from some behavioral cue you normally perform.

Note: For a more detailed performance of a specific gender, more than one behavioral cue can be layered into any given drill, but for purposes of this exercise it's best to do one cue at a time.

The coach gives the paired students time to rehearse, and then calls them to the stage one by one to perform their scene again. The coach asks the observers:

⊚ Were you aware of some new gender cue being added?
⊚ Did that change your mind about what gender was being performed?
⊚ How did the addition of those cues enhance or detract from the performance of their genders?
⊚ How did the addition of those cues enhance or detract from the performance of the scene?

Drill Three: Perform a textual gender cue

The coach reviews the concept of textual gender cues, and calls for examples from the students. The coach then asks the students to select one textual cue to perform that would make the scene more interesting than it already is, reminding the students to notice how it's similar to or different from the cue they normally perform.

Note: If that cue is a name, salutation, or title, it may be added to the text of the scene.

Note: The performance of cues in this exercise is *cumulative*. The performance of each drill in this exercise includes the performance of the cues developed in the previous drills.

The coach gives the paired students time to rehearse, and then calls them to the stage one by one to perform their scene again. The coach asks the observers the same questions used to follow Drill Two, above.

Drill Four: Perform a mythic gender cue

The coach reviews the idea of mythic gender cues, and calls for examples from the students, asking how each example might affect a character's attitude.

The coach asks each student to select a myth to which the character subscribes that would result in hir character having an extremely interesting attitude in this scene; the coach should remind the students to notice how that cue is similar to or different from a myth to which they might normally subscribe.

The coach gives the paired students time to rehearse, and then calls them to the stage one by one to perform their scene again. The coach asks the observers the same questions used to follow Drill Two, above.

Drill Five: Perform a power dynamic as a gender cue

The coach reviews how power dynamics can be used as gender cues, and calls for examples from the students. The coach asks the students to select between them some power dynamic that a) makes the scene more interesting than it already is and b) enhances each of their gender performances. The coach reminds the students to notice how that power dynamic is similar to or different from some power dynamic they might themselves use in a similar situation.

The coach gives the paired students time to rehearse, and then calls them to the stage one by one to perform their scene again. The coach asks the observers the same questions used to follow Drill Two, above.

Drill Six: Perform sexual orientation as a gender cue

The coach reviews how sexual orientation might be used as a gender cue, reminding the students that sexual orientation may or may not be based on the gender of one's chosen partner.

The coach asks for examples of different groups, cultures, or communities that have a preferred or imperative sexual orientation, and follows up each answer by asking for examples of how the pressure of that imperative or preferred sexual orientation would affect a person's behavior in a given situation.

The coach asks the students to select a sexual orientation that a) makes the scene more interesting that it already is and b) enhances their own gender choices; the coach should remind the students to notice how that orientation is similar to or different from their own sexual orientation.

The coach gives the paired students time to rehearse, and then calls them to the stage one by one to perform their scene again. The coach asks the observers the same questions used to follow Drill Two, above.

Drill Seven: Perform the awareness of gender

The coach goes over the concept that every person is aware to some degree of their own gender, and that one's own gender awareness impinges on some level of their performance of gender. An example might be a lesbian woman deciding to be more femme than usual, or more butch. Another example might be a heterosexual man deciding to jock it up for a day. There would certainly be a degree of self-consciousness involved with their performance of those genders. The coach calls for examples of gender awareness as a factor in gender presentation.

The coach then asks each student to decide exactly how aware hir character might be of hir gender, stressing that the student make the most interesting choice possible, and reminding the students to notice how that awareness might differ from or be similar to their own awareness of gender.

The coach gives the paired students time to rehearse, and then calls them to the stage one by one to perform their scene again. The coach asks the observers the same questions used to follow Drill Two, above.

Drill Eight: Perform a physical gender cue

The coach reviews physical gender cues, and asks for examples of these from the students. The coach then asks the students to select *one* physical cue to perform that might make the scene more interesting, while enhancing the gender attribution of their character. Students are reminded to notice how that physical cue is similar to or different from some cue they normally perform.

The coach gives the paired students time to rehearse, and then calls them to the stage one by one to perform their scene again. The coach asks the observers the same questions used to follow Drill Two, above.

Ending the exercise: After all the students have done the cumulative performance of all eight drills, the coach calls for a discussion of what happened, asking questions like:

- ⊚ What did you notice about the performances as more and more cues were added?
- ⊚ How did it feel to perform more than one cue at a time?
- ⊚ Are you more or less aware of the gender cues you're performing right now?
- ⊚ What do you think you might do differently next time?

These workshops may certainly be done over and over in order to reach deeper levels of gender performance. But now it's time to move the performance of gender out of a controlled exercise environment, and closer to some real-life situations.

⊚ Stepping Outside the Playgrounds

There's *so* much to learn, isn't there? I think the biggest thing that's happening with me at this writing is that I'm finally getting in touch with my body. I've had this internalized phobia about being transsexual for so long. It took me long enough to like myself for being not-man, not-woman; now I'm finally getting to like my *body* for what it could be seen as: a "feminized" "male" body. I'm finally able to start peeling the words *feminine, masculine, female,* and *male* off my body, and the resulting loss of psychic weight feels terrific.

My therapist during my transition from male to female wisely steered me away from pinning too many hopes on my genital surgery. "It's not going to answer all your problems," she told me, and I believed her. What I didn't know at the time was that I was pinning one hope on the results of that surgery: that I'd like my body. I'd bought right into the physiological gender stereotypes. I didn't take into account the very human response to the world of advertising: "My body doesn't measure up."

::shyly:: Well, today I'm starting to hear people when they say I'm attractive; and I'm letting myself get more and more into *enjoying* body stuff. ::blushing to roots:: Well, anyway . . . I hope that makes sense. It's a delightful neo-pubescent feeling. I get to be the movie stars I longed to be. I get to do Holly Golightly from *Breakfast at Tiffany's*, and I get to be Tank Girl. I get to walk in this world, expressing my delight, and I get to see the delight that others express. It takes courage to name your joy and put it out there in the world. I'm able to do that more and more these days. It makes people smile. I like that.

Except on bad days.

That's what this next section is about: the bad days. It would be a good thing to read before setting foot outside these playgrounds.

Cautionary Interlude

Life is a glorious cycle of song,
A medley of extemporania,
And love is a thing that can never go wrong,
And I am Marie of Roumania.
—Dorothy Parker

The reverse side also has a reverse side.
—Japanese proverb

So far in this workbook, we've been practicing genderplay either by our-selves, or with those we trust, or in locations (playgrounds) peopled by more or less open-minded folks. Now it's time to walk into the world embodying the questions you've been asking and the world view you've been forming for yourself around this topic of gender. It doesn't matter if you're doing a radical gender change, or simply deciding to become a man who cries and giggles, or a woman who swaggers and spits—this applies to *you*. Now that you're faced with the very real option of consciously step-ping outside the boundaries of "real men" and "real women," it's time to examine the downside in some depth.

Look, I need to say that most of the time this genderplay stuff is *won-derful*. It's an apex of truly free self-expression. Most of my life these days *is* a "glorious cycle of song." There's a lot of joy at work here. However, there are still bad days. The self-consciousness and depression, the shame and the rage. They happen. This next piece, and the graphic art by Dianne DiMassa, are our respects to those days. We both call it:

Angel on a Bad Body Day

I'm having one of those days when I didn't want to walk out my front door. It's sort of like a bad hair day, only it's more of a bad body day.

Do you feel attractive?
pretty girl?
handsome boy?

I'm too tall, I think to myself.
I joke about my "gorilla arms," my knuckles scraping the sidewalk.
It's no joke, not on a bad body day.
And my hands on bad days?
I do my best to hide my hands,
mask them
these broad paddles of hands I have.

How'd ya look in the mirror this morning, sport?

I'm too long, too flat, I think to myself.
On bad days,
I use smoke-and-mirrors as best I can
I'm a sleight-of-hand artist.
"Here . . . lookit these legs . . . they go on forever, huh?"
(just don't notice these shoulders of mine, please?)
"Here . . . look me in the eyes, fall into my forest green eyes."
(not my broad brow and my square jaw,
not on bad days)

Do you feel pretty? Good looking?

Running my hand over my face on a bad day, I figure I'd better shave. I could only afford half my electrolysis, and that lets me go two days without having to scrape my face, but that means a day of not letting people touch my cheek.

"Please," I'm cryin' out from inside, "would you touch my cheek and not shrink away?"

What do you want them to think when they see you?

Walkin' down the street . . .
That guy over there, will he turn his head?
Will that grrrl in the pickup truck smile out the window at me?
Kids, kids everywhere . . . will they laugh?

I have this collection of a few moments in my head,
like porn films.
Here's my fave:

It was one of those hot nights in New York, August.

Me in tight jeans and tank top, no bra, and the fridge is broken where I'm staying at my friend Linda's, and I hafta go to the store for something cold to drink, and the guys are spilling outta the bar onto the sidewalk in front of me, and they go all quiet when I walk through them. One guy stumbles his way directly in front of me. "You're the girl of my dreams," he says to me, "Oh god," he slurs, "I've been waiting for you all my life." And I smile and keep walking, trying to feel the sidewalk through my cowboy boots. "She's the one," he's telling his friends as I'm almost out of earshot. "Isn't she the one for me?"

I play that one in my mind on the days I'm paralyzed in front of the television set, watching *Headline News* over and over and over again. The theme song from that show won't leave my brain alone.

How would you like to be heard in the world?

I've been smoking too much and my already smoky voice is turning into a croak.

"Hello," I say into the phone on a bad day. "This is Kate Bornstein."

"Hi, Ken," says the voice on the other end. "How can I help you?"

My friend Riki Wilchins writes relentlessly . . .

So here it is again: not that it's any of my business, but what is it that makes you so sad, Kate?? What is "sad and frightening" all the time? Ever since I've known you, you wear sadness like a chemise under whatever garb is on top.

And I write back to hir, reckless in the face of hir perception . . .

Riki, I feel like a fucking alien here. Feel like Ishmael. Or maybe the captain of the Flying Dutchman. And then I curse myself for being hackneyed! Ya gotta laugh.

What is it that makes you feel like you're the only one?

I know I'm not the only one who feels like that, but that doesn't help me. Not when I'm in the middle of feeling like that. Best I can do on a bad body day is gothic standup.

So this angel walks into a bar.

And she walks up to the first cowboy and she says, Hey . . . how do you people tell each other apart? You all look so much alike. And this cowboy turns to her real slow, and he says, "What makes you think we can tell ourselves apart?"

No, no, no, that's not it.

This angel walks into a bar, and she asks the bartender, "Hey mister, how do you people tell each other apart? You all look so much alike." And the bartender turns to her real slow, and he says, "Well, ma'am, it matters to us who we're talkin' to . . . so we pay attention."

No, no, no. That's not it.

This angel walks into a bar and she asks the guy in the three-piece suit with the martini in his hand, she asks him "Hey mister, how do you people tell each other apart? You all look so much alike?" And the guy in the suit turns to her real slow and he pulls out a .45 and he blows this angel away. Don't ask those questions around here, he says to her, we don't like those questions around here. Whacky guy.

I keep writing to Riki . . .

```
    I think it's the combined sorrow of all those good-byes, that's
the essence of the sorrow.
    As to fear. ::rolling my eyes:: Fuck, hon. . . . I haven't got clue
one. It's little kid fears that're always there. Monsters in the
attic, mom won't be there when I get home, nobody loves me, someone's
gonna hurt me, no one's gonna rescue me, I'm gonna be all alone and
lonely to the bone.
    ::shaking my head to clear the fog . . . fog won't clear::
```

And Riki writes me, ze says . . .

```
    I can't believe how many transpeople are "lonely to the bone," and
I can't believe how *little* we talk about it, even amongst each
other. I don't know. I've felt the same way. You just want to say
"fuck it" and check out. On the other hand, I think all that depres-
```

> sion is partly my anger turned inward on myself. And I remind myself
> the system is *designed* to make me self-destruct and self-destruc-
> tive. And that it's doing this to so many people I love. And then I
> get outraged, and decide someone's got to do whatever they can to
> change this fucking system so it doesn't keep doing this to the next
> generation.

Outrage. Oh man, I've been doing my best to manage or focus all the anger I've had all my life because when I was a guy I never knew how to express it without hurting someone. I don't wanna hurt anyone anymore, I just don't.

And whaddaya do when you're hurting?

My rage comes in part, I'm thinking, from having been told "You're not our kind" so many times in so many places by so many people. It's why I want to see "transgender" mean "transgressively gendered." That way, we all can belong to the same team if we want to.

And where do you hang out to get away from it all?

There's a new clubhouse on the block, it stretches as far as the eye can see. It's for people like me who want to belong somewhere, but every time I get close to signing on the dotted line, people take one look at my back and they see these wings of mine and they say,
"Hey, Angel, have a seat . . . got time for me?"
They say,
"Hey, Angel . . . can I touch your wings?"
They say,
"Hey, Angel, would you put in a word for me with the Big Fellah?"
They get all chummy like that, and that's when I stretch these wings of mine out past the walls of the room we're in. Those walls come tumbling down, and I smile and I say,
"Look . . . these are *my* wings, this is how *I* fly."
And that's when they decide they want all my feathers.
What a whacky world, huh?
All I can do is talk about this stuff with my friends.
When I can't sleep,
When I've watched the headlines on *Headline News* so many times that I can lip-synch to the president of some corporation whose stuff I could never afford anyway.
I write email, I write this stuff, and Riki's voice comes back to me in

ASCII. Ze's talking about the rage and the shame and the fear and the loneliness and the sadness.

> It is one of the great, unbroken silences of this community. While we're being amusing, or passing, or telling our life's stories in hope of acceptance, or just responding to all the charges made against and about us, most of the transpeople I know are depressed, terribly lonely and profoundly tired. The personal is political, and [in my opinion] these are the effects of a systemic oppression.

Yeah, yeah, yeah. Systemic fucking oppression. And I'm thinking to myself, who the fuck *isn't* oppressed for some reason or other? Who in the culture who's seen as Other isn't sad sad sad or angry angry angry about all this? But the *triggers* are unique to gender outlaws, and are perhaps more pervasive in the culture, simply because gender itself is so damned pervasive. And that means that anywhere I turn, there's something in the culture that shames me for fucking with gender to the degree that I have and continue to do. There's something in the culture that pegs me, pretty much everywhere I go. Not easy. Not pretty.

So I pick up the phone to call my friend Alice in Philadelphia, and I dial her number, and this strange woman answers the phone and she says,

"Hello, is this Kate?"

And I say, "Yah, it's Kate, but you're not Alice . . . who are you?"

And this woman on the other end of the line, she chuckles and she says,

"Oh you know me well enough. How've you been?"

"Fine," I say, 'cause I'm always a sucker for the How've-you-been question. "Fine," I say, "who are you?"

"I'm an angel," says this voice at the other end of the phone.

"OK, Angel," I say. "Whatsup?"

"Well, I had some questions," she says.

"Shoot," I say.

"OK," she says, "I wanna know how you tell yourselves apart."

So I hang up the phone, and look out the window.

There's a madness that comes . . .

There's a madness that comes with not being one or the other.

This madness is the crazy feeling that there's room enough in my mind to be anything. It's the crazy feeling that I could go for a walk deep inside my heart and never come back.

And it doesn't matter that I live in rain-drenched Seattle, cuz I change cities about as frequently as I change genders; what I see lookin' out this window is San Francisco in the drought. And I think maybe we don't get enough rain because our tears are enough. I think maybe that fog rolling in over the hills isn't a fog after all, maybe it's a curtain drawing itself across all the lives we used to be. And I think to myself, maybe we've got all these hills so we've got some way to climb up and talk with the angels.

The sadness that comes from being a freak is compounded by the fact that as gender outlaws, we step forward into our freakdom. At some point we make the decision to say fuck it, this is how I'm going to live my life. We leave one identity behind, and take up another. And if we change identities over and over again, searching for "the one that's going to work," or "the real me," well, we've got a lot more good-byes to say, no? For nearly fifty years, I've been acquiring identities and abandoning them, and I finally realized that as long as it was a specific identity I was abandoning, I'd only acquire and get stuck in yet another one. I think it's identity itself I want to quit now.

But Let's Throw Caution to the Wind

Right, so we've got some tools with which we can reduce our gender to nothing. We can take on another gender or genders. Of course, there's a big difference between doing this stuff in a workbook, indoors alone, or with supportive friends, and taking this kind of gender play into the big bad world out there. Take another look at Diane's maze on pages 191–192.

The question becomes: Assuming it's not going to hurt anyone else, how can I do what I want to do, express myself the way I want to in the world, when I'm well aware of the dangers and pitfalls that await me?

The tremendous sorrow, grief, rage, shame, and loneliness is going to be there. There's no way out of it for anyone who's Other in a culture. It's how we *deal* with it that makes a difference. Leslie Feinberg recently coined the term *transgender warriors* in hir book by the same name. I think we can learn a great deal from a warrior ethic. I think that's how we can turn the fear into strength, sadness into laughter. Our rage and loneliness can be eased, I think, by mindful political action in all areas of our life. So . . . let's learn to be warriors.

And that, my darling, brings us to politics and revolution.

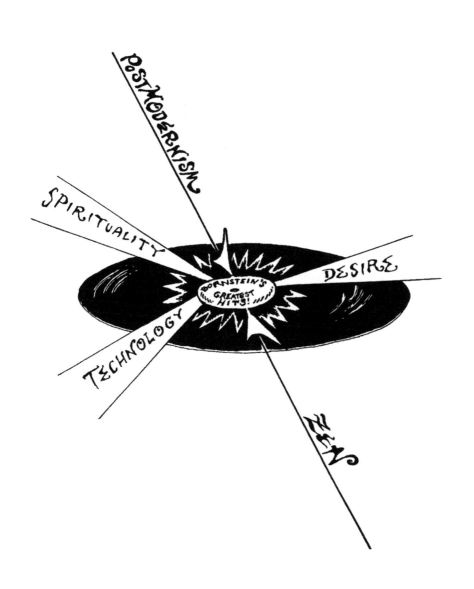

This Quiet Revolution

It's one thing to play around with gender in the privacy of our own homes, or within the safe confines of "playgrounds," surrounded by others like us. As soon as we step outside the door, however, we run smack into social and legal restrictions, exclusion, and oppression.

What most of us don't run into are the children thrown into the streets by their families by reason of the child's transgender nature. Most of us don't run into savage beatings, rape, and murder at the hands of outraged people, not to mention the same or similar treatment at the hands of the very police whose job it is to protect us. Some of us run into job discrimination; but we forget that most of us never had jobs to begin with. We'll cry about losing our lovers and our community, but we don't get a chance to look into the eyes of a bone-lonely homeless transgendered person. We need to know these obscenities exist, and we need to dedicate some part of our lives to being of service to the less-privileged members of our tribe.

Over the couple of years since the publication of *Gender Outlaw,* I've had the opportunity to talk and write with quite a few folks, sharing our experiences outside the world of gender binaryism. What I found was that most folks agree that political action on behalf of gender transgressors is necessary, but not too many people know exactly what kind of political action to take.

I think of personal politics as the sum total of skills necessary to navigate a situation in which my values, standards, or boundaries are in conflict with another's or others'. When the others in question have more power, and there's no relief to the conflict in sight, (assuming our own motives to be harmless and inclusive) that's when a revolution is necessary. That's when I need to look beyond my own personal politics and assume a position within a political movement, part of which is lending a hand to the rest of us at every moment of the day. So it's a dance . . . moving back and forth between taking care of myself and taking care of my family. There are quite a few transgender activist groups out there these days. Some are dedicated to social reform; some to community building;

some focus on legislative representation; others make education their priority. It's a political smorgasbord out there, a place for virtually every kind of activism you can think of. And if you can't find an existing group that would serve your political aims, start one up yourself and you'll have members within a month's time.

The point of this section is not to tell you what to do. That's no one's call but your own. The point of this section is to provide some more universal guidelines for whatever it is you *do* choose to do.

The way you do anything is the way you do everything. That's a good concept to keep in mind when it comes to politics and political activism. It resonates with the concept of integrity.

---

⑥ First There Is a Gender, Then There Is No Gender, Then There Is

> Every day I go to work in Miami and all the kids under 8 think I am a man. As they get older they ask are you a man or are you a lady. I say you figure it out. If they tell me I'm a man, I tell them to look more closely.
>
> —Jacky Jack

I've been saying for some years now that I don't have a gender; that gender is a trap, a chimera. And it's all well and good to say there's no such thing as gender. I think it's even all well and good to believe that. The sad fact is that despite all our wonderful spiritual or philosophical takes on identity and the nature of gender, gender is here in the world and people are oppressing other people for no other reason than gender itself. The "first there is a gender . . ." reference above is from a koan used to illustrate a student's progress of through Zen:

A beginning student exclaims to the elder, "Look, what a beautiful mountain!" The elder smiles and replies, "Mountain? There's no mountain there." The student, baffled, goes off to study and contemplate the elder's words. Ten years later, the student returns, a broad smile on hir face, saying "Elder! I understand! There is no mountain! We are all one! I am everywhere and everything, as are we all. What I saw before was only an illusion, created by my need to be separate!" To which, the elder responds, "Oh really? Well, all I can say is you're missing a splendid view of this mountain I'm looking at."

Gender *is*. Oppression *is*. We need to forge a politic that deals effectively and finally with gender oppression as it impacts each one of us, gender transgressors and gender defenders alike.

◎ Cohesiveness and Community

I'm still up in the air about this idea of a "transgendered community." I think defining any community by the identity of its members is ultimately a dead-end, because despite their more or less common identities, the values of its members are inevitably going to be in conflict. For example, look at the Log Cabin Republicans or the North American Man/Boy Love Association and their relationships to the larger gay and lesbian community.

I think that if we're going to put some kind of community together (one that I'd like to be a member of anyway) it's going to have to be based less on some notion of a transgender identity, and more on the idea of a transgender value. What that agreed-upon "transgender value" might be is a matter to be hashed out by all of us. Who's "all of us?" The community that I'd want to belong to would include anyone who wants to overcome gender oppression in any shape or form. That would be a meaning or mission I could get behind.

It would include the young woman who stands up to her male boss and says "No."

It would include every lesbian, gay man, or bisexual person.

It would include sex workers and S/M players.

It would include the housewife who refuses to be barefoot and pregnant in her husband's kitchen.

The transgender community I'd like to see would also include transsexuals, transvestites, crossdressers, drag kings, drag queens, he-shes, she-males, and male and female impersonators.

It would include hermaphrodites, intersexed people, and anyone whose physiology casts them as "not men" or "not women."

I have labeled myself "female-to-femme transgender" first and foremost as a sign of my solidarity to a group of feared, harshly misunderstood people who don't have enough allies. Because I am a white, decent-looking woman who wears skirts, it would be very easy for me to shut up and go along. But I don't.

I was born female, and raised as expected/accepted. I cooperated, unquestioning, until I came out as a feminist in high school and looked hard at the way I had been presenting myself. Trans people cross rigid sex/gender lines, allowing themselves to project an individual expression that feels comfortable. Usually, though, the change occurs from one gender to another. See, I can't even pass for androgynous. I tentatively approached that line between masculine/feminine and came running back. I do enjoy being a girlie. This doesn't make me less queer—it only makes me less visible.

I have realized that this—being skirted and lipsticked—is how I'm most comfortable. And that I can acknowledge my socialization and still be me. I crossed from one gender to an *acceptance* of that gender expression. I am not simply female; my self-awareness has made me femme.

—Hanna Bordas

This larger community would include men and women of races other than "white" who are constantly seen by many whites as "not really men and women" by reason of their race.

It would include working-class and homeless men and women who are seen by many of those in the middle class as "not really men and women" by reason of their class.

All seniors and children would be included in this community, because they're so commonly perceived as either "beyond their manhood and womanhood" or "not yet having attained it."

Membership in this community would be dependent not only on the common struggle to dismantle an oppressive system, but also every member's willingness to acknowledge each other's unique gender oppression. Until that's reached, I don't think there's much hope for a community that's anything more than a temporary bulwark against the system that would eventually wipe us all out.

The focus for each of us needs, I think, to be on our own spirit of inclusiveness. We need to get over the idea of "We're the only ones who are oppressed by the gender system." If we get over *that,* we'll have the basis for a community that thrives and supports not only its members, but its valued allies and friends. So here're some interesting questions for you:

EXERCISE: Do you choose your friends solely on the basis of their identities?

_____ yes _____ no _____ somewhat

Which is *more* important to you:

_____ your identity
_____ your principles?

Exactly how have you determined the principles of those around you? What criteria do you use?

What qualities or values do you look for in a friend?

Now measure your political affiliations by the same standards you choose your friends. Note the similarities and the differences.

The cohesiveness of any successful transgender movement will depend on basing the movement in values rather than identity.

⑥ Where Do We Look for Direction?

I bristle at the term "equal rights" when it comes to gender. I prefer the term "universal rights." It's not that I disagree with the concept of equal rights, it's just that by stating the concept of universal rights in terms of equality, we're setting up and keeping in place some us-and-them situation, if only by using the word *equal*, which is usually taken in gendered circles as implying equality *between men and women*. That doesn't work for a movement that has the potential for universal inclusivity of many genders.

I think we need, each of us, to hammer out our own goals and purposes. We need to name what's blocking us from achieving those goals and purposes. Then we can phrase for ourselves the specific rights we need to overcome whatever's blocking us, taking into account the goals, purposes, and rights of others who are in search of freedom of gender expression.

EXERCISE: Okay, let's suppose it's a long way off in the future, and you've come to the end of your life. You're lying there on your deathbed, and you're content with the life you've lived. You're happy with your life, and you're ready to move on to whatever might lie beyond your death. Looking back on your life:

1. What did you achieve that's making you content?
2. What specific rights did you personally need in order to achieve that?
3. When you got those rights for yourself, and achieved what you achieved, what did that make you?
4. If you had a wish you could utter at this moment of your death and it would come true for future generations, what would you wish for?
5. Bonus Question: Suppose there were some wonderful afterlife. It's as good as you'd want it to be. And suppose you were given the option of staying there after you die, or returning to this earthly existence for yet another life so that you could help make your dying wish for future generations come true. What would you do?

For a true gender revolution to occur, each individual needs to name hir own needs, rights, and only then to set about achieving those needs and rights in harmony with others who have done the same work.

⊚ Where's Our Motivation?

Quite often, we're motivated to political action by either the idea or the reality of an enemy: someone who's doing us in or who we think has nefarious plans for us. A great deal can be accomplished by pointing fingers at an oppressor. That oppressor can indeed be toppled. There's a drawback to this tactic, however, when it comes to a transgender movement: Who's the oppressor?

We can't say it's "the patriarchy." We can't say it's "all traditionally gendered people." As the transgender movement includes anyone who is transgressing gender, we're opening the door to every single human being on the face of the planet to be a member of this movement; that means everyone is a potential ally and member of the group. So, whose face do we use for the enemy?

While it might be politically expedient in the short run to paint a face on our oppression, say the face of Senator Jesse Helms from North Carolina, that wouldn't help us if we were to learn that the good senator wears his wife's underwear when she's away at her bridge club meeting. All of a sudden, Jesse would be family!

Besides, if we think that gender oppression is only going to come from the distinguished senator and his ilk, we'll be caught unaware when some form of that oppression spills from the mouths of our next-door neighbor, our friends, family, lovers, or children. And that's where it's going to come from. Our gender oppression can come from anyone who's more highly placed, or even, differently placed, on the gender/identity/power pyramid than ourselves. So I don't think we can afford to under- or overestimate our oppression by naming it as an identity, any more than we can afford to shorthand our movement by naming it as an identity. Gender oppression is like a particularly nasty computer virus that spreads throughout an entire system, leaving bits and pieces of itself everywhere on our hard drive. We need to name the acts of oppression and exclusion. We need to name the values that precede those acts, because our politics *can* hope to change values.

EXERCISE:

1. Name three incidents in which you were, or believe you might have been, oppressed or excluded by reason of your gender expression.

2. Now climb inside the head of the person or persons oppressing you for those three incidents, and name the *value* (e.g., greed, prestige, laziness, etc.) you suppose might have preceded that oppressive or exclusive act.

Those *values* are the enemy, and they can and do show up in anyone, including ourselves. If we're going to truly crusade against oppression, we need to start right here at home. So-o-o-o . . .

3. Name three incidents in which you may have oppressed or excluded someone else by reason of hir gender expression.

4. Now climb inside your head, and name the *value* (e.g. greed, prestige, laziness, etc.) you suppose might have preceded your oppressive or exclusive act.

The enemy to true freedom of gender expression is nameless.
The enemy to true freedom of gender expression is a value system, the expression of which needs to be dealt with on a person-to-person basis.

---

⑨ **What Kind Of Political Attention Do We Want?**

Movements need to attract attention to themselves. Well, gender outlaws get attention. Period. We're strange, we're attractive, and we're dangerous. That gets us plenty of attention. I've had to tell more than one squeamish publicist to use my freak status to promote my theater work. Why not? But what about the *unwanted* attention we garner? For example, when a gender outlaw uses a public (gendered) bathroom, that's often an act that not only gets us unwanted attention, it calls for political ingenuity and/or action. What action can we take, when it seems that every move we make in this culture not only attracts attention, but also flies into the teeth of some law or social convention? I don't know. I don't know what action to take. I just know that we're entitled to live a rich life free from harm or harming others. In that context, and keeping in mind the principle that the way you do anything is the way you do everything, I think we can come up with some political guidelines that draw on the strengths we've developed as gender outlaws.

The master's tools will never dismantle the master's house.
—Audre Lorde

_____

How about putting the book down just now and contemplating the implications of Ms. Lorde's statement in light of what you've been studying here.

_____

◎ If Not the Master's Tools, Which Tools <u>Can</u> We Use?

Here are some of the tools I've become familiar with over the course of my own gender journey, tools that are available to most gender outlaws for use in any of our political actions.

Compassion

I've spoken a great deal about compassion in this book so far. Compassion is the foundation of a transgender politic, beginning with compassion for ourselves and extending outward to compassion toward other outlaws, friends, allies, family, and ultimately compassion even for those who recoil from us in horror.

Patient Persistence

At this writing, the appearance of gender outlaws on the streets of the wide wide world is a startling one. We need to keep on appearing on the streets, in the workplace, at the bars, in the clubs, and on the very doorsteps of those who would brand us freaks. We need to do this despite the initial pain, shame, and humiliation it might bring us. We need to appear over and over again in public, and we need to do it with honor.

One strength we possess as gender outlaws is our ability to take baby steps on any journey, persistently moving forward no matter the opposition. We never wanted to be pushed, rushed, or beaten into questioning gender. Those of us who've transitioned from one gender to another never wanted to be browbeaten into doing it. We wanted to be treated kindly with understanding, and we wanted to proceed at whatever speed was comfortable for us at the time, which for many of us meant that our transitions took a little longer than we would have liked. Most of us learned patience and all of us learned persistence.

So one principle of a transgender politic might be to use the smallest, most compassionate means possible to bring about a reconciliation of conflicting ideas and values that keep all parties concerned from living a rich life free from harm or harming others, and to patiently yet persistently up the volume or intensity of our actions until we reach that reconciliation.

When I experience an instance of exclusion or oppression now, I try to identify with the person excluding or oppressing me. Their hatred or fear of me is no greater than the hatred or fear I had for myself back before I came to a point of self-acceptance. How can I rage at them when they're only expressing to me what I'd expressed to myself for nearly all my life? Sure, there are going to be times to write Congress. There will be times to march in the streets. There are going to be times when we're oppressed by something so insidiously institutional that in order to even get the attention of those we need to negotiate with, we need to make some noise. But I don't think this needs to be the *first* action we take. The first action might be simply taking a fellow student aside and explaining to them why, when they've known us to be a woman, we've suddenly grown a mustache.

EXERCISE: Write down some instance of exclusion or oppression you've either experienced or might experience as a result of your messing around with gender.

What is the gentlest, most compassionate action you can take in response to that?

And if that doesn't work, what's the next most gentle, compassionate action you can take?

And if that doesn't work, what's the next most gentle, compassionate action you can take?

> And if that doesn't work, what's the next most gentle, compassionate action you can take?
>
>
> And if that doesn't work, what's the next most gentle, compassionate action you can take?

I think that's the way we need to proceed. Of course, there are going to be rough decisions to make. Faced with a knife at our throats, or to the throats of our loved ones, we need to act swiftly to prevent harmfulness. We need to become adept at assessing what kind of oppression calls for what kind of political response.

As to persistence, I have this Woodrow Wilson quote hanging on the wall in my house. It was given to me nearly thirty years ago by my friend, Gail Harris, who found it excerpted in an ad for McDonald's hamburgers:

Press On!
Nothing in the world can take the place of persistence. Talent will not; nothing is more common than unsuccessful men with talent. Genius will not; unrewarded genius is almost a proverb. Education alone will not; the world is full of educated derelicts. Persistence and determination alone are omnipotent.

Well, I don't believe that persistence and determination *alone* are omnipotent, but I do believe they're necessary components to a successful politic.

Flexibility and Fluidity

Gaining recognition and acknowledgment from those who would defend the gender binary isn't going to be easy. The very act of questioning gender has the potential to change the face of the gender system forever. And the fun news is that there's no defense against our honest questioning, because an honest question is never an attack. What's more, there is no methodology by which a person can prove the gender binary is either basic or essential to humanity. Wary self-proclaimed opponents to this idea of shattering the binary have not come up with a single effective defense against non-linear reasoning, save brute force. And I think that on some level they know that. These gender defenders have their own code of honor; they have their own faces to save. Yes, we're in the right by saying we simply want to live our harmless lives free from harm. However, there's an old old principle at work here, one it would be well to keep in mind while making allies from within the ranks of those higher up on the pyramid:

When surrounding an enemy, make sure you leave them a way to escape.
—*Sun Tzu*

When we confront a gender defender with our genderfree selves, we're backing them up against a wall, because a gender defender really believes in binaries and, well, we tend to *break* binaries. We color our identities outside the lines, and we're great at doing it. It's who we are, it's our value to this culture. But we're not going to get anywhere by backing a snarling, powerful opponent into some corner without a way for that person to save face.

We know how to be flexible. Given the exercises in this book, we've got the skills we need to adapt our identities to whatever situation we're dealing with. We're fluid in that we can use that flexibility to shift our identities as rapidly or as often as we please. In short, the nature of our gender journeys depends not one bit on *any* binary, linear construct. If we're living our lives like that, then maybe it's against our nature to use a linear, binary politic.

Maybe it's *important* that our revolution not rely on binary, linear methods, lest by relying upon them in one area of our lives, we fall back into relying upon binaries in all or many things that we do. Again, please remember the principle, the way you do anything is the way you do everything.

For me, gender has always been a social thing, not so much a biological thing or even a psychological thing. When I'm by myself my gender goes away, especially if I'm immersed in something like work or a book or household chores. But put us together, be you the closest of friends or the most anonymous and silent of passing strangers, and my gender engulfs me. It's Who I Am in the world, it's an expectant look in your eyes and all your assumptions, it's my need to satisfy those expectations.

—Sharon Minsuk

EXERCISE: Let's put your flexibility and fluidity to a little test. Here are some common binaries at work in our culture. Cross out the ones you honestly don't subscribe to, and circle the ones that still are operating in your life.

Male/Female	Deserving/Undeserving	Right/Wrong
Man/Woman	Civilized/Uncivilized	Good/Bad
Young/Old	Nice/Not Nice	Beautiful/Ugly
Rich/Poor	Good/Evil	Active/Passive

Normal/Weird	Legal/Illegal	Win/Lose
White/Colored	Faith/Fear	Humans/Other Life Forms
Dying/Living	Male-to-Female/Female-to-Male	Popular/Academic
Acceptable/Embarrassing		Mind/Body
Bravery/Cowardice	Transgendered/Gendered	Pain/Pleasure
God(dess)/The Devil	Birth/Death	In/Out
Kinky Sex/Vanilla Sex	Plants/Animals	Workers/Bosses
Fat/Thin	Peaceful/Violent	Angels/Demons
Me/You	Patriarchal/Feminist	Sameness/Difference
Able-bodied/Disabled	Enough/Too Much	Public/Private
Student/Teacher	Fight/Flee	Consensual/Non-consensual
Silence/Confrontation	Everything/Nothing	War/Peace
Up/Down	Sad/Happy	Acceptance/Denial
Manic/Depressive	On/Off	Material/Spiritual
Capitalism/Socialism	Homosexual/Heterosexual	Penis/Vagina
Female/Male	Diseased/Healthy	Exclusion/Inclusion
Sadist/Masochist	Them/Us	Healthy/Dysfunctional
Closeted/Out	Open/Closed	Full/Empty
Masculine/Feminine	Girl/Boy	Work/Play
Light/Dark	Lucky/Unlucky	Goddess/Slut
Powerful/Powerless	Radical/Assimilationist	Macho/Wimp

Are there any other binaries that you either subscribe to or *don't* follow? List them here and circle the ones you subscribe to:

> EXERCISE: Take a sheet of paper for each binary your circled, and divide the page in half vertically. For each binary, use the right-hand side of the page to list out all the ways the binary is true. On the left-hand side, list out all the ways it's not true.
>
> Now look at the page as a whole, without using the true/not-true binary.
>
> Now write down your thoughts about that binary.

If we're truly going to develop a politic that's going to dismantle the gender binary, we need to rid ourselves of binary thinking as our sole way of thinking and our own binary methodology as our sole way of doing things.

A Note on Exclusivity

Bernice Johnson Reagon has made what I think is the simplest statement about the foolishness of exclusivity:

> We've pretty much come to the end of a time when you can have a space that is "yours only"—just for the people you want to be there. Even when we have our "women-only" festivals, there is no such thing. The fault is not necessarily with the organizers of the gathering. To a large extent it's because we have just finished with that kind of isolating. There is no hiding place. There is nowhere you can go and only be with people who are like you. It's over. Give it up.
> —West Coast Women's Music Festival, 1981
> Yosemite National Forest, California

Any outlaw, any Other, knows the pain associated with being excluded, locked out, or forbidden some form of freedom of expression. Most outlaws, gender or otherwise, are also familiar with the phenomenon of one oppressed or excluded group oppressing or excluding others. *Some* group, *someone*, has to stop the self-devouring hierarchy of under-represented groups that prey on less-strong under-represented groups. It's our turn to try to stop that miserable buck.

⊚ Do you belong to some group that wants to exclude others by reason of their identity?
⊚ Are there some gender outlaws whom you would see as not really transgressing gender?
⊚ Do you believe that the way you're transgressing gender is better than the way someone else is?

☺ Do you believe that the way someone else is transgressing gender is better than the way you are transgressing gender?

EXERCISE: Here's a list of some identities. Let's say you were going to hold a meeting to discuss the politics of gender. All the following people arrive at the meeting. Be real honest now (this isn't a test to see how politically correct you can be), and circle the identities of people you would rather *not* attend the meeting.

Pre-operative male-to-female transsexuals

Post-operative male-to-female transsexuals

Non-operative male-to-female transsexuals

Mormons

Drag queens

Jews

Drag kings

Drag queen prostitutes

Born-again Christians

Heterosexual male-to-female transvestites

Homosexual male-to-female transvestites

Bisexual male-to-female transvestites

Muslims

People who don't speak English well

Transsexual lesbians

Cross-dressers

Republicans

Transsexual gay men

Transsexual young urban professionals

Pre-operative female-to-male transsexuals

Democrats

Post-operative female-to-male transsexuals

Pre-teens

Men who wear their wives' underwear

Non-operative female-to-male transsexuals

Libertarians

African Americans

Heterosexual female-to-male transvestites

Homosexual female-to-male transvestites

Men who wear draw string pants

Bisexual female-to-male transvestites

Anorexics or Bulemics

Beautiful men and women

Straight white fraternity guys

Sadists

White people

Masochists

Lesbians

Police officers

Gay men

Heterosexual men

Witches

Homeless people

Heterosexual women

Butches

Femmes

Women who wear Birkenstocks

Ugly men and women

Are there any other kinds of people you would not want at the meeting? List them here.

Now, get some extra sheets of paper, one for each type of person you circled above. On each page, write the name of one type of person. Divide the sheet in half vertically, and on the left-hand side write down the reasons this person should be excluded. On the right-hand side, write down the benefits of including this person.

> Now, look at the page as a whole. Could you find it within yourself to include that person? Under what conditions?

The buck has to stop somewhere, and since we gender outlaws are new at this politics game, I'm hoping we refuse to build exclusion into the way we deal with others. I'm hoping we can include even those who would exclude us. One way of doing that is to keep in mind the metaphor of the "perfect identity" at the top of that pyramid: is there really anyone who isn't an outcast of some sort or another? It still gets back down to compassion, no?

ⓖ Gender Anarchy

Anarchy is natural to most of us. We're all anarchists in one or more areas of our lives. In my life, I refuse to obey the rules of gender. In your life, it may be the rules of the workplace, or the rules of sexuality. All of us disobey something, and disobedience requires a great deal of responsibility. We look at some rule, whether it be "Men don't wear dresses," or "You're not allowed to pirate cable television," or "It's against the law now to provide social services for illegal immigrants in the United States," and we ask ourselves, which of these can I responsibly obey and still maintain my integrity? Which laws have I been dealt which I must responsibly *disobey* in order to maintain my integrity?

This is one of the paradoxes of the democratic movement—that it loves a crowd and fears the individuals who compose it.
—*Walter Lippmann*

I'm gender-indifferent in a bunch of ways, but one I have the most fun with is probably my purse. It's been called a bag, a pack, a pouch, a . . . er, wallet-thing; it's none of these: it's a cute little Fiorelli purse, just big enough for my keys, my identification, and some money. For some liberal urban areas, I suppose it wouldn't be such a big deal, but for the conservative haven of mid-Michigan, a male of my size and appearance carrying a purse usually affords a second glance. Never a jeer, though, and never a stare: are *you* going to tell a six-foot 215-pound man with three earrings and two tattoos that he can't carry a purse?

—Brighn

The laws of the land in which I'm living now are derived democratically. That means they're made by other people who are supposed to have my best interests at heart. Well, the fact is that I cannot marry a woman in this country. The fact is that a transgendered child on the street is not going to be cared for by the social machinery created by the people who are supposed to have hir best interests at heart. Exactly why that's the way things are is beyond the scope of this book, but it boils down to this: democracy and outlaws of any stripe don't mix it up very well together.

Democracy, in fact most *any* centralized government or politics, doesn't include me for the simple reason that I keep trying to change who and what I am every day of my life, and Democracy seeks to govern by the representation of some clearly (to them) defined "average identity." Both Democracy and twentieth-century capitalism need people with fixed identities whom they can govern and sell to. I don't have a fixed identity, and I don't want one. The demographic surveys that try, with all good intentions I'm sure, to pinpoint me as a consumer are valid the day I answer them, but not necessarily that evening. I don't *want* to be a legal, recognized entity within a system that would expect me to remain statically identified for longer than, say, twenty-four hours.

I used to think I was politically apathetic. Now I'm seeing that I hadn't located a politic out there that actively embraces and encourages my individual growth, change, fluidity, and whimsy. The closest thing I can find is anarchy. I'm not talking about the cartoon version of the Russian anarchist holding up some home-made bomb. I'm not talking about bombs at all. I'm talking about measured, personal anarchy: something we can live.

Gender outlaws are outlaws because we live outside the laws of gender. We broke the rules, we found some personal freedom, a way to fully express ourselves. ::softly:: Why stop there?

I'm a lipstick lesbian with fat hair and spike heels . . . but does power tools and work boots. So there.

—Carole Taylor

No, I don't know exactly *what* it looks like. I only know what it *doesn't* look like. It doesn't look like rules, regulations, laws, by-laws, constitutions, or being silenced for being out of order. The political organization or activist group I want to support doesn't use fear tactics, intimidation, peer pressure, categories, or the expectation that I sacrifice my integrity or honor for "the good of the many." All those tactics are what the gender system used to keep me being a man or a woman. None of those methods got me this far, and I don't suspect they would get me any further; and further is exactly where I want to go.

> EXERCISE:
> What social taboos, if any, have you broken without harming anyone?
>
> What company or organizational rules or regulations, if any, have you broken without harming anyone?

> What spoken or unspoken codes of your family, tribe, or community, if any, have you broken without harming anyone?
>
> What laws, if any, have you broken without harming anyone?
>
> Did breaking any of those rules end up being beneficial to both you and others? If so, how?

Anarchy As Responsible Power Play

I'm a sadomasochist. I play with power, and the more I do, the less I find that power is able to play with me. I'm more and more aware when people try to either exert power over me, or conversely, when people manipulate me into exerting power over them. As a top in an S/M relationship, I choose to honor and respect the gift my bottom gives me: the gift of hir relinquished power. As a bottom, I'm very picky about who I choose to give my power to.

That's how I look at the gender system. I don't choose to give my power to it, not in the least. I'm going to disobey its laws, written or assumed. Why would I want to support a political system or even an activist group that would employ the same kind of abuse of power? I've said no to gender, and I'm going to keep saying no to systems that would reign me in, classify me, pin me down, or keep me in my place. Nope. Not gonna play that game any more. What's the worse thing that could happen to me? People are gonna call me names? I'm embracing most names that people call me these days anyway . . . it's a hoot.

Moderation in All Things, Including Moderation

I'm not saying we all need to embrace anarchy. I'm not saying you shouldn't pay your taxes, or obey the speed limits. I'll probably go to my grave

I am a transsexual in Bavaria. Yes, I am. For the moment I'm working very hard on my permission to become transgendered, from female to male. Please excuse my English, but I'll try to answer your questions as good as possible.

To live without gender is impossible without breaking gender conventions. Therefore you'd better learn to be good on the subject. For me, it became a sport. It's by the way the only sport never disturbed by your tits!

Of course I break rules. Doing this is easy: just ignoring. My favorite broken conventions concern clothing. The way I speak and behave is only unusual for female standards, of course. But people always identify me as a man, even without hormones yet, though I have no problems with it. The problem is practicing sexuality. I am a gay man with no own body to have fun with. The much I love and need physical contact, the much I fear it to be touched. For the moment I live as a kind of asexual, but I'm not born for this state of being. My way to overcome all those shit is, to work on my transgendering procedure. I think, the worst is behind me. To look forward helps.

—Chris Summer

having paid most of my taxes and having obeyed most of the speed limits. The point is, I've been learning to disobey some pretty heavy cultural rules by going through my various gender transitions, and I've been finding a great deal of integrity and satisfaction on the other side of those rules.

What I'm recommending is that we as gender outlaws continue to break the rules and laws that are necessary to break in order to achieve personal integrity and the personal integrity of those whom we love and care for. And this is not some new idea. It's the old "Render unto Caesar…" thang.

Enough lofty political talk of anarchy and power. Please take out some sheets of paper, and let's bring this down to something tangible.

EXERCISE: On your own gender journey *thus far*:

⊚ What rules have you followed?
⊚ What laws have you obeyed?
⊚ What conventions have you conformed with?
⊚ What sanctions have you accepted?

EXERCISE: To get to the point at which you'd like to arrive in your gender journey

⊚ What rules do you think you might need to ignore?
⊚ What laws might you have to disobey?
⊚ With what conventions would you need to break?
⊚ Which sanctions might you need to refuse to accept?

Gettin' angry? Oh, good!

⊚ Anger

I was angry with my friend:
I told my wrath, my wrath did end.
I was angry with my foe:
I told it not, my wrath did grow.
—William Blake

Anger is real. It's not going to go away. So, how can we use it? Well, we can start by naming the source of our anger, and I think the source of our transgendered orneriness isn't so much gender *per se,* but the heretofore inaccessibility to freedom of identity apart from socially mandated acceptable roles.

Roles provide the averagely gendered person on the street with an "off the rack" monogendered identity allowing them to spend their time thinking about the things that interest them. Gender outlaws don't have that luxury; we've got no place to conveniently hang our identities while we get on with the business of living life. Unless we claim membership in one of the two socially-sanctioned genders, we spend most of our time wondering how to navigate a gendered world.

Returning to the pyramid metaphor: no matter what face of the pyramid most concerns us, be it gender, race, age, class, or whatever, we're still attempting to overcome oppression in the name of what's become a "perfect identity" perched at the top of each of our struggles. We're each to some degree oppressed, held in check, violated, silenced, or shamed by one or more aspects of that perfect identity, and that's enough to make anyone angry. When that oppression is nearly universal, as in the case of gender oppression, race oppression, or class oppression, then our anger in the face of overwhelming opposition can become an underlying rage that impacts both our perception and our consequent response to the world around us.

- ⊚ What about another's self-expression has made you angry?
- ⊚ Can you think of a time when you were angry at someone for a good reason, and you got them to see why? If so, how did you do that?
- ⊚ What about your self-expression gets others angry at you?
- ⊚ Can you think of a time when someone was angry at you for a good reason, and they got you to see why? If so, how did they do that?
- ⊚ What's your response to a verbal threat?
- ⊚ What's your response to some symbol of a threat?

———
Anger feeds the strength of our passion, which in turn is guided by our reason and our honor, and the result is moderated by our compassion: that's anger's place in our new politic.
———

⊚ Nonviolence

The way I define violence is the nonconsensual constraint of, intrusion into, occupation of, or damage to another or others' body, bodies, possessions, or space. Violence can also be the nonconsensual exclusion of a person from a public space, or the barring of access to basic human rights.

A "Gender" Liberation Front could campaign for an end to sex designation not just on TS birth certificates, but on Marriage—enabling lesbian marriages etc—we can move the focus away from places like Rape Crisis Centres to places like Smedley Hydro—the Birth Registry—We can set a profoundly radical pluralist agenda for this group—what sort of actions would be most effective—why they shouldn't bomb buildings with people in—those sorts of ideas. Can you imagine the costs of providing security for every registry office in the UK!?

—posted on the Internet

One of my favourite near-daily occurrences is the ol' triple-take. That's when someone will see me somewhere in matter-life (doesn't matter where ::grin::) and do a double take at the happy "babe" with the long curly hair to try to catch which gender I am. (Like there are only two!) And then, they'll look again, (third take) sometimes staring right at me, peering to try to figure out if I'm male or female. I've even had people get right in my face, look me up and down and still not know if I am boy or girl. ::lol:: I like to flash them my best sexy grin and dance away, leaving them wondering.

::happy boy/grrl doing the Snoopy dance::

—Jos

There are all kinds of degrees of violence. Violence can be as ostensibly harmless as taking up to much room on public transportation. Violence can manifest as wholesale genocide. It's a form of violence to force people against their will to be something they don't feel they are. That's what's done to us by the gender/identity/power system, and while we're in the process of throwing off those constraints, none of us can afford to forward the practice of constraining others, intruding into or occupying their personal space, or wreaking any damage. In the ages-old "Battle of the Sexes," we must be the conscientious objectors.

⑥ Any Politics Has Gotta Be Fun, and the Laugh's Gotta Be on Us

Gender outlaws go to a lot of trouble to remake ourselves into the objects and/or subjects of our desire. Desire and the fulfillment of our desire comprise a substantial and valid reason for our gender transgressions. Let's face it: we're cute. We're more than cute, we're damned good-looking and sexy to boot. People have lots of fantasies about gender outlaws like us. We're the forbidden fruit: sweet or tart, juicy or firm, enticing or scary-looking, the fact is we rev up peoples' libidos.

Well, it's time to cash in on that. We can be as visible with our gender-blended sexuality as any traditionally gendered person is with hirs. Hey . . . drag kings and drag queens have been doing it for hundreds of years!

Emma Goldman is credited with having said, "If I can't dance, I don't want to be part of your revolution." Well, if I can't flirt, I don't want to be part of your revolution.

This Is Foolishness

In *Gender Outlaw,* I wrote briefly that the role of transgendered people in the culture might in effect be the role of the trickster or the fool: that we by our very presence hold up a mirror to the culture so that it might better see its own foolishness when it comes to its blind obedience on the subject of gender. And I still think that's the deal. That's how we're going to do it. We're seen for the most part as a joke; well, it's not that far a leap from joke to jokester, and jokester has an honorable tradition.

I break gender rules all the time by alternating between my femme persona and my butch persona. It gives me twice the wardrobe . . . and it is so much fun to confuse everyone!

—Puppylove

"Congratulate me!' shouted Nazrudin to a neighbour. "I am a father."
"Congratulations! Is it a boy or a girl?"
"Yes! But how did you know?"
—Idres Shah

Whether ze's referred to as Coyote, Nazrudin, Tortoise, Lucifer, Legba, Trickster, Shaman, Wounded God, or simply as fool . . . that's the position open to each of us who teeters along any border set by the culture. We hold up to each side of that border the foolishness of *both* sides; and we're not gonna be loved or revered by the folks who live comfortably on either side. We do what we do with a sense of humor, sure, but is there anyone who as a child saw some circus clown and wasn't frightened?

We frighten you because we walk through walls,
Like ghosts, like saints, contagion;
Everywhere is borderless to us,
There are no borders to our nation.
You cannot raise an army to defend,
You cannot make a mirror that repels,
You may expect that we will pay a toll,
But do not waste your intake breath with spells.
The only way for sure to kill the fear
That we may walk right through the walls of you
Is to knock them down,
And then the fear is gone.
—Dragon Xcalibur, Ferryman

We scare people, plain and simple. For lots of reasons, we scare them. Well, that can be sexy too under the right circumstances, but in terms of political action we need to soften that fear with a sense of humor.

As part of a movement, we can educate, reform, succor, lobby, and protest. But who's got the energy to be part of a movement twenty-four hours a day, seven days a week, for all their lives? And when we're not being "politically active" as part of some group, it's gonna come down to one-on-one politics. In *that* arena, we as fools can only shock into aware-ness, or seduce and recruit. As members of a political movement, yeah, we need to address gender. As individual fools, I don't think we should be shackled to any identity . . . not even transgender.

Sometimes I feel like a stranger.
Sometimes I tell lies.
Sometimes I act like a monkey.
Here comes the night.
—*Laurie Anderson*

⊚ Why Have You Been Studying and Practicing All This

So, now you're near the end of this book. You know what gender can mean. You know how gender can connect with desire, fear, identity, power, and even spirituality. You have some tools to work with this stuff when you want to or need to. You have some tools to help form an integral politic around gender freedom. Are you done with gender? Is it something where you can put this book down with a sigh and say, "Wow, I got through it!"? I don't think so.

Unfortunately or fortunately, depending on your point of view, the only way out of this gender trap seems to lie directly through the thick of it. We won't, I think, be able to fully abandon this system until a vast majority of people (starting with me and you) first choose to push its borders, experi-ence its possibilities, and take responsibility for its impact on the condition of humanity. We may accomplish this and scare people as in the poem by Dragon Xcalibur excerpted above. Or we may choose another route: delight.

Here's a fun exercise for you: Take another read of M. Xcalibur's poem, only this time replace the word frighten *in the first line with the word* delight. *The piece works both ways.*

We *do* naturally frighten people. I think we need to take responsibility for that entirely predictable phenomenon. We need to consciously disarm and delight, and *delight* transcends politics. Delight is what we get, and get to give others as a result of putting all this work together and living it, if only a little bit every day.

It takes a great deal of courage to be delightful in this world. Whole religious systems have risen up, joined by governments, to outlaw delightful people. But who, more than delightful people, do we like to hang out with? I think our job now is to find out for ourselves exactly how we can best express our delight in this world, and how to best acknowledge others that are doing that. And that brings us to the last chapter of this book. Ready? Okay—turn the page.

Okay, Now What?

To have attained to the human form is a source of joy.
But in the infinite evolution, there are myriads of other forms
that are equally good. What an incomparable bliss it is
to undergo these countless transitions!
—*Chuang Tzu*

Are we real men or real women? It seemed like such an easy question. It might still be easy for many of us to answer. But here's a somewhat deeper question for all of us: Who among us has an unshakable, immutable identity? Who among us is a real *anything?* Who among us is "real" or "perfect" at any socially defined identity? Goodness knows we're all pressured, to some degree, to become the unattainable "real man" or the unbearable "real woman" that the dominant culture would like us to be. Each of us tries to be real at some identity, but *do* any of us, in fact, have the exact same identity we had, say ten minutes ago? Or have our identities been continually and subtly altered, the course of our lives almost imperceptibly shifting, to the point where we're no longer quite so sure of the purity of our own identities? If so, then what is it exactly that's being altered? What is it within us that reaches a point of satisfaction once we've found an identity we're comfortable with? And what inside us fiercely struggles against change? I think these are some healthy questions to be asking. They're not within the scope of this book, but hey . . . it's the end of the book, and how could I finish without asking some questions that might be leading to the *next* book?

No Tidy Strings on This Package

Existence does this switching trick,
giving you hope from one source,
then satisfaction from another.
—*Rumi*

Okay, this may or may not be easy to hear, especially if you've done some or a great deal of work in this workbook so far, but here it is: I'm thinking it's not gender. I'm thinking gender isn't *the big deal,* the ultimate mountain to climb. In fact, in the scheme of history, gender is quite insignificant. Sure, it's been given a great deal of importance by the culture, but who says the culture's right? And what's more important: If gender isn't the big deal, what is?

I don't know, but I want to find out. My gnawing on gender has only led me to see that gender is one of many stumbling blocks to self-growth and self-realization. Age, race, class, body type, that whole laundry list of factors—they're just symptoms. Having delved as deeply as I have thus far with gender, I want to look beyond it; and now that you've done all or some of this workbook, so might you.

Remember the basic premise of this workbook?

The way you live without gender is you look for where gender is, and then you go someplace else.

Well, that's what I've been trying to do, and that's what I want to do more of. I want to go someplace else.

Someplace Else

I give up my fisted touch,
my thoughts strung like fences
My totem-pole stature body chipped to the bone.
I'm nobody's saviour, and nobody's mine either
I hear the desert wind whisper,
"But neither are we alone."
—Ferron

I think that a transgender identity and, indeed, a transgender movement both have a built-in obsolescence. If in fact we're setting about to dismantle the binary of gender, the system against which we're transgressing; and if in fact transgressing gender is a worthwhile thing to do for a while and if in fact everyone is transgendered according to the pyramid metaphor, then there's going to come a time when more people admit it than don't. When that time comes, when most of us are saying, "Yeah, I transgress gender," then gender will be relegated to the status it deserves: a plaything. When that happens, there won't be any value to the term "transgender," and a new challenge will have risen up, new political identities will raise their heads, and the transgender movement will be shown to its proper place as some historical oddity, back in the days when people thought there were only two genders.

But for now, something really interesting is happening. We're the new game in town. We're chic. We're something to be studied. We're a new flag to rally around. More and more people are coming to see gender as something they transgress anyway, and they're claiming transgender as a value, and this movement is taking off. And while all this is going on, I have to tell you that something's happening to me that I don't like: I'm becoming known as an expert.

In *Gender Outlaw,* I wrote a small section about the role of fools in a culture: how fools point out doorways, how they trick people into laughing about whatever's been most important to them. I like that role, it's very satisfying to me. It makes me feel quite light, and I find it fulfilling. I also wrote about what happens to fools when they become allied with a movement or an identity: they cease being fools. I've found out that being a fool is important to me, and I want to play around with lots of ways of being that. "Expert," gender or otherwise, doesn't seem like a fun way to play for me.

What I most want
is to spring out of this personality,
then to sit apart from that leaping.
I've lived too long where I can be reached.
—*Rumi*

I just want the opportunity to explore all of my life, in much the same way I've been encouraging *you* to do in this workbook. I'm nearly fifty years old and I want to look at the *fun* part of this bad grrrl I've been becoming. ::wide grin:: There are parts of my life, like my current fascination with serial killers, that simply are not polite dinner conversation, let alone appropriate to discuss from some podium at a political rally.

I'm not really as bad as they say I am.
I'm actually a very nice person. Hahahahahahaha.
—*Juliette Lewis as Mallory Knox,* Natural Born Killers

I want to act. At this writing, I'm packing up here in Seattle and getting ready to move to New York City to see what I can do.

And of course I'm going to continue writing about gender. It's only been the major influence in my life! I want to write some good gender-questioning scripts for television . . . maybe even *Star Trek!* I've got a fictionalized autobiographical novel I want to do. I want to explore this leukemia I've got. I was diagnosed with it just as I started to write this book, so I haven't had much time to get into all the implications, experiences, and revelations of the dying thing.

———

The kind of leukemia I have is the wayyyyyyy slow kind. It probably won't kill me. But it does slow me down from time to time—that's why this book took so long to complete—and I'm finding that fascinating.

———

In short, I have to go do what I've been urging you to do all through this workbook. I have to go explore myself, and I have no idea where that's going to lead me. I just know I have to leave this gender theorizing behind right now. Everything I know or believe about gender is in this book, *Gender Outlaw,* or *Nearly Roadkill.* I need to move forward in my life, and while it scares the hell out of me, I'm drawn like a moth to a flame. Or better, like a butterfly that needs to escape hir cocoon.

⊚ This Is Only the Beginning

No way [do I live without gender], although it's an ideal. I suspect I'll always long to be something I am not. Although I do what I need to do to make the longing less and to find as much satisfaction as I can, I think I'd be more at peace if I could figure out a way to be genderless. It would be wonderful if the gap between what I am and what I want to be was no longer a gulf, but instead I encompassed what is important to me. I have no idea how I could do this, although I continually try to find out.

—Ulrike Dann

You've had the opportunity to look at gender now from more angles than most people. These aren't *all* the angles, to be sure, but judging by the written information on the subject available in the world today, the work you've had the chance to do here has made it possible for you to examine gender in a uniquely well-rounded way. It's conceivable that we're the first folks to have looked at gender like this for the past few thousand years. Assuming that might be true, then this book is bound to be deeply flawed. It's a baby step in this field, and like anyone learning to walk for the first time, I'm likely to have fallen down more than once in the attempt.

I've tried to make this overview of gender as comprehensive as possible, but as a broad public discourse on this subject does not exist, my blind-spots are going to be painfully apparent to some people, perhaps many, whose viewpoints desperately need to be represented in this discussion.

⑨ Argue This Book—Please!

Even if you never question your own gender, ever in your life. If you never attend a protest rally, or if you move to some neighborhood where you never have to see another gender outlaw for the rest of your days, please argue the concepts in this book. If nothing else, people will think you're deep for talking about this. Who knows . . . it could get you a date or two.

I've shown early drafts of this book to several close friends, and while they were for the most part delighted, I managed to offend each one of them in some way. I'm sorry if anything I've said offended you or made you feel left out in any way. If that was the case, please accept my apology. It was not intentional, it was my blindness. It just means that your voice needs to be raised in this discussion, and the odds are I'm not the person to speak on your behalf.

Look, gender is everywhere present in this world today, and the form it has taken has the possibility to lead us further and further away from free self-expression, happiness, security, even survival itself. Your questions need to be raised. Please ask them. Ask your friends. Ask the person sitting next to you on the bus. Who knows what you might learn? Ask members of your community. Maybe this is interesting to them too, and no one's raised the question before.

> I don't live without gender. Every day I'm forced to make a conscious choice about what part of myself to reveal on that specific day. How vulnerable am I willing to be? How strong do I feel? Somedays it's great fun and sometimes it's a real drag. It's never not an issue, but it makes me who I am.
>
> —Justin Bond

Your disagreements with anything I've written here are valid. Please examine them as deeply as you can. Read more books on the subject. Get yourself online and raise these questions in discussion groups on the Internet. You're disagreeing with what I've said because you have a valid point of view based on some experience I've not had. Sure, I wrote a book. So what? That doesn't make me an expert. It only makes me a person who was in the right series of places at the right series of times. It only means I've made some choices in my life that are different than yours, and I ended up with a passion to write about this stuff. That's all it means. Your disagreement might be exactly what this notion of transgender needs in order to ground itself as a valid movement in the world. Or you might topple it entirely because you're the one who's found the fatal flaw in all my meanderings. It's important that you speak your disagreements and make your point of view known.

Your voice needs to be heard. Please speak up. Join a neighborhood planning committee, or a tenants' rights organization. Make yourself as visible as you can while maintaining the safety and security you need to go on living in the world. I'm not exhorting you to "come out." You know I'm a big fan of personal safety. I'm not going to try to manipulate you passive-aggressively by saying you need to come out "for everyone else's benefit." That's not why *I* came out initially. I came out because all these thoughts were boiling in my head, and I was going mad without the opportunity to talk about them. Every time I make myself talk about these fearful ideas, I end up feeling better. Who knows why, I just do. Maybe you will too. Maybe not. But please, *try* talking about these issues on some scale. If anything in this book made you think, tell someone.

⑥ Why Go to All That Trouble? And It Is Trouble.

I have an idea that the human race has a shot at nobility. All of us. I'm under no delusion that this nobility can be achieved in my lifetime, or that it can be achieved over the next few hundred years to the degree I believe possible. But I do believe it's worth planting the seeds now. That itself seems to me an act of nobility. It makes me feel good. It gives my life some meaning. I try to live my life with the notion that the human race has some potential for a truly honorable shared value system. I'm realistic enough to look at all of us with the understanding that we've got a long long long way to go.

Putting honor and nobility aside for a moment, there's very little chance that the apparency of the bi-polar gender system is going to change dramatically over the next few generations of our species. And that's only *one* of various interlinked systems of oppression that are keeping us all down. There is however a great chance now for more and more people to find their own personal freedom from gender constraints, but that's only going to happen if we speak up, tell our deep true stories, and ask our most terrifying questions. Those questions of ours are terrifying for a reason! Our troubling questions are trouble for more than just you and me. Our questions are trouble for everyone who has come to depend for their own survival on the bipolar apparency of gender to keep hidden its connection to identity and power. To some degree that's most if not all the people on this planet, including you and me. When we speak about this, we are troublemakers headed for trouble. Culturally speaking, Bart Simpson has nothing on us.

Please don't take my word for it. Just look at how the dominant culture has responded to the earlier gender movements like the women's movement, the gay and lesbian movements, the bisexual movement and the sex workers' movement. Look at how the dominant culture has treated the struggle by races other than white to simply be human. Look at the systemic oppression by class, age, body type, religion, and spirituality. How has the USA-based dominant culture responded to any struggles against that sort of identity-based oppression?

We have a shot here of making a difference. At first, we'll be viewed as the latest crackpot minority. Then, maybe, we'll be pitied for our disability. Inevitably, however, we're going to be attacked big time. That's just the way it goes. And it's still worth doing. It's worth telling our stories and asking our questions because if just one more person can become aware of the intricate system of gendered chains and gendered punishment in this world, we've made some headway.

The media isn't going to do it for us, not as long as it has to earn its daily buck. We can't count on existing civil rights organizations to champion us, no matter how much they take our issues into their agendas. God knows they're overloaded as it is. Even transgender activist groups, however impassioned, are bound to miss a point or two that might be the exact points you or I need dealt with in order to get on with our lives. No, it needs to start with you as an individual.

Maybe one day, people will look back on our day and age and wonder to themselves at our barbarism. I fervently hope that will come to pass. If there's any *chance* of that happening even on a small level, say within the circles you travel, it's going to start with you. You need to talk, argue, listen, reason, negotiate, puzzle, challenge, and question.

One word of advice: Honey, when you're doing all that? Be fabulous!

◎ Okay, I Love You. Buh-Bye.

I want to thank you very much for taking the time to go through this book. I know it couldn't have been all that easy on you, but I'm hoping it was gentle. I have just a few last things to say.

If you've gotten this far, and you're still not in any mood or head space to question your gender, I wish for you the compassion to allow others the right to question their own genders. I hope those of us who do question our genders can count on you as a friend and ally.

If, on the other hand, you're questioning gender on a personal basis, I wish for you the strength it's going to take to make this journey. I wish for you every comfort you deserve. And I wish for you the compassion you'll need to deal with others you'll meet along the way.

Whatever your gender identity, it's now time for you to walk in the world embodying the questions you've been working on in this book. You've got some armor if you need it. You've also got a sense of humor, don't you? Me, I intend to have myself a delightful life, and that's precisely what I wish for you: a delightful life.

Okay, I love you. Buh-bye.

Where I Found the Words in this Book that Aren't Mine (and what to do if some of those words are yours)

The older I get, the more people there are to thank and the more filled my heart becomes with gratitude for those who've helped me. I've done my best to both credit and acknowledge the contributions of others throughout this book.

⊚ All the Great Outlaw Words

It was several years ago that I began to collect many of the words included in the boxed quotes, and indeed much of the "101 Outlaws" section came to me by email in 1995. I was pretty sick for some time, and when I recovered and attempted to contact the contributors, many of their addresses, email addresses, and phone numbers had changed.

Here's the deal. I only added correct names to the quotes for which I was able to obtain written or emailed permission. Some contributors wished to remain anonymous, so the names were changed. And I changed the names for all the pieces whose authors I was unable to contact. So, if you spotted your words in this book, but you weren't properly credited, please let me know by writing in care of the publisher. In the event this book goes into additional printings, I'll make sure your name is added if that's what you'd like. I'm very grateful to all the wonderful people who took time to write for this project, and I sincerely apologize for any hurt feelings my inability to contact you might have caused.

101 Gender Outlaws Answer the Question "Who Am I?"

The following folks contributed to 101 Gender Outlaws. (pages 81–89).

3. Shannon Coulter
4. Theresa Marie Hart
6. John Snead
8. Diana Riggs
10. Paul/a
13. Jordy Jones

14. Ian Fried
15. Kirsten Kjell Rybczynski
16. Nancy Nangeroni
17. Diane DiMassa
18. Jami Kae
19. Reid Vanderburgh
21. Kelli
22. Jodi A. O'Brien
23. Sylvanwulf
25. Jake Fawcett
27. Kim Russo
28. Liz and Al Pierce
29. Jennifer DiMarco
30. Del Grace
33. Dragon Xcalibur
34. Mona Barnhart
36. Spike Katz
40. Dianne Hackborn

41. Gwen Smith
43. Spencer Bergstedt
44. Greta Schwerdtfeger
45. Sandra Lee Golvin
47. Bear Thunderfire
49. Catherine M. Gross (aka NOTNILLA)
52. Susan Benner
53. Sharrin Spector
54. Ilya
56. Michael Hernandez
58. Tammy Campbell
60. Cherry Smythe
62. Rebecca Kaplan
63. Jake Hale
66. Tamar Kay
69. Marna Deitch
77. Jordynne Olivia Lobo

79. Jamie Ray Walker
90. Barbara Scott Winkler
91. Kate More
92. Angela MacLeod
93. Karin Luner
94. Amy Hunter
97. Susan Stryker
98. Stacey Montgomery
99. Destiny Densley
100. Amy Millward
101. Karen X. Tulchinsky
102. Angela Brightfeather Sheedy
104. Jordan Jaeger
106. JJF2M
107. Jerry Kellen McCracken

◎ Nifty Words from Other Books

pg. x: words from Diane Arbus, Amelia Earhart, Sylvia Plath, and Patti Smith all come from *Glibquips: Funny Words by Funny Women*, by Roz Warren, 1994 Crossing Press, Freedom CA; and *Untamed Tongues: Wild Words from Wild Women*, by Autumn Stephens, 1993, Conari Press, Berkeley CA.

pg. 24—"You can't imagine how I've looked . . ." (Rumi). This, and the other quotes by Rumi all come from *Delicious Laughter: Rambunctious Teaching Stories from the Mathnawi of Jelaluddin Rumi*, versions by Coleman Barks, 1990, Maypop Books, Athens GA; or from *The Essential Rumi*, translations by Coleman Barks with John Moyne, 1995, HarperSanFrancisco, San Francisco.

pg. 26—"She has sex, but no particular gender . . ." (Marlene Deitrich on Greta Garbo) from *Loving Garbo: The Story of Greta Garbo, Cecil Beaton, and Mercedes de Acosta*, by Hugo Vickers, 1994, Random House, New York.

pg. 38—USFDA Food Group Triangle courtesty of the United States Food and Drug Administration.

pg. 68—"Insecurity, commonly regarded as a weakness in . . ." (Miranda Richardson) comes from the Microsoft Bookshelf 1996–1997 Edition CD-ROM.

pg. 121—"Men mistakenly expect women to think . . ." comes from *Men are from Mars, Women are from Venus*, by John Gray, 1992, HarperCollins, New York.

pg. 123—"Keeping people divided . . ." comes from *Transgender Warriors* by Leslie Feinberg, 1996, Beacon Press, Boston.

pg. 123—"It is helpful to remember that sex reassignment . . ." comes from *Information for the Female to Male Cross Dresser and Transsexual* by Lou Sullivan, 1990, Ingersoll Press, Seattle.

pg. 124—"The following [are the first two points . . ." comes from *Trans-sexuals: Candid Answers to Private Questions* by Gerald Ramsey, 1996, The Crossing Press, Freedom, CA.

pg. 124—"By the time people reach adulthood . . ." comes from *The Lenses of Gender* by Sandra Lipsitz Bem, 1993, Yale University Press, New Haven and London.

pg. 124—"Nonsexist counseling is another direction . . ." comes from *The Transsexual Empire* by Janice G. Raymond, 1979, Beacon Press, Boston.

pg. 125—"The struggle has been the right to self-naming . . ." comes from *Lesbians Talk Transgender* by Zachary I Nataf, 1996, Scarlet Press, London.

pg. 129—"An empty mirror and your worst destructive habits . . ." (Rumi, op cit).

pg. 133—"They've been writing the script and directing the action . . ." comes from *Clit Notes (A Sapphic Sampler)* by Holly Hughes, 1996, Grove Press, New York.

pg. 142—"Parental gender stereotypes . . ." comes from *Gender Bending: Confronting the Limits of Duality*, by Holly Devor, 1989, Indiana University Press, Bloomington and Indiana.

pg. 144—"Anything that challenges the definition . . ." comes from *Gender Shock: Exploding the Myths of Male & Female* by Phyllis Burke, 1996, Anchor Books, New York.

pg. 167—"Bridle the mind, for it is like a wild horse . . ." comes from *I Ching: The Book of Changes and the Unchanging Truth* by Hua-Ching Ni, 1990, Shrine of the Eternal Breath of Tao, Santa Monica.

pg. 168—"What is Matter? . . ." and all the other quotes in this section come from *Zen to Go*, compiled and edited by Jon Winokur, 1990, Plume, New York.

pg. 168—"Mu: Literally "no" or "not . . ." is by Jon Winokur (op cit).

pg. 175—"Do you think I know what I'm doing?" (Rumi, op cit).

pg. 184—"How do I know that loving life is not a delusion . . ." comes from *Death: An Anthology of Ancient Texts, Songs, Prayers, and Stories* edited by David Meltzer, 1984, North Point Press, San Francisco.

pg. 185—"Denial and Isolation . . ." is from *On Death and Dying* by Elisabeth Kubler-Ross, 1969, Collier Books, New York and Toronto.

pg. 205—"In my sex fantasy . . ." (see page vii above).

pg. 238—"You're just jealous because I'm a real freak . . ." Danny DeVito from the movie, *Batman Returns*, directed by Tim Burton.

pg. 245—"Life is a glorious cycle of song . . ." (see page x above).

pg. 262—"The master's tools . . ." (Audre Lorde) comes from *Her Heritage: A Biographical Encyclopedia of Famous American Women*, a CD-ROM edited by Robert McHenry, produced by Rhonda Richards, 1994, Pilgrim New Media, Cambridge.

pg. 265—"When surrounding an enemy . . ." comes from *The Art of War* by Sun Tzu.

pg. 269—"This is one of the paradoxes . . ." (see pg. 68 above)

pg. 272—"I was angry with my friend . . ." (see pg. 68 above) pg. 275–"Congratulate me . . ." comes from *The Exploits of the Incomparable Mulla Nasrudin* by Idries Shah, 1983, The Octagon Press, London.

pg. 276–"Sometimes I feel like a stranger . . ." comes from *Stories from the Nerve Bible* by Laurie Anderson, 1994, HarperCollins, New York.

pg. 279–"To have attained to the human form is a source of joy . . ." comes from *The Way of Chuang Tzu*, by Thomas Merton, 1965, New Directions, New York.

pg. 279–"Existence does this switching trick . . ." (Rumi, op cit).

pg. 280–"I give up my fisted touch . . ." is from the song PROUD CROWD/PRIDE CRIED by Ferron, from her album *Shadows on a Dime*.

pg. 281–"What I most want . . ." (Rumi, op cit).

pg. 281–"I'm not really as bad as they say I am . . ." from the movie *Natural Born Killers*, directed by Oliver Stone.

◎ Roll Credits

I'm so grateful to my mother, Mildred Vandam Bornstein, who passed on to me her love for life, her strength in the face of adversity, and her high femme sensibility. My mother died a few years ago now, but it's a lot of her spirit you read in this book. Thanks to Ava Apple who managed the early collection and filing of all the information for this book. Ava is Mary to my Rhoda, Thelma to my Louise, Sally Bowles to my Holly Golightly, and Earth to my Water. Thanks to my guy, David Harrison, for the love and support that never went away. Thanks also to Caitlin Sullivan who, when this book's deadlines overlapped with deadlines for *Nearly Roadkill*, graciously and generously took on the lion's share of editorial and administrative work on our novel and Website, www.nearlyroadkill.com. Thanks to Linda Donald, Stewart Wilson, Kaylynn Raschke, Rose Pascarell, Holly Hughes, Diane DiMassa and Jessica Patten for giving me safe haven, tears, and laughter. And Gwydyn and I both thank Goalie, Chippy, Charlie, and Petunia for the generous spirit they share with their housemates.

Thanks to Gail Leondar-Wright who's been publicizing my work for the past four years. Thanks to my agent Malaga Baldi for riding herd on where my words get published. Thank you Craig Dean and Susan West for booking my stage work, lectures, and workshops around the country. Thanks to Riki Wilchins for continuing to hold up a mirror to me. Thanks to Jodi O'Brien for teaching me the concept of mindful construction; and to Rachel Gold for suggesting Captain Kirk as the perfect gender.

Thanks to the editors and writers of, and contributors to the "Lesbians Talk . . ." series from Scarlet Press in the United Kingdom. Each book in the series contains the voices of many lesbians, and this approach gave me the idea for the inclusion of the gender outlaw voices in this book.

Love and gratitude to Barbara Carrellas who came into my life so fully during the final edits. Barbara works with sex the way I work with gender. Oh, yum!

I wrote a lot of this book at The Easy, Four Angels Cafe, the SpeakEasy, and The Wildrose, four great places to meet outlaws in Seattle. Thanks to the grrrls and boyz who made it so nice to write and eat there. I wrote this book on my Apple Macintosh PowerBook, and desktop Performa. I used *Microsoft Word*, *Inspiration*, and *Dyno Notepad*. I kept track of all my notes in *InfoGenie*. For reference, I used Microsoft's *Bookshelf* and *Encarta* CD-ROMs. For research, I used my AccessOne internet account; and for e-mail and live chats I used my America OnLine accounts. Thanks to Bill, Alex, Ron, Lynette, Allie, David, Nick, Deborah, and all the folks at Routledge who contributed to making this a real live book. The writing was alone-work, but the production of this thing . . . ::shaking my head:: . . . that took a lot of people!

The rest of my friends and family who were any combination of supporting, challenging, entertaining, being sweet and patient (or not so sweet and patient, but certainly forbearing), inspiring, and comforting for me while I was researching and writing this book: Elsa, Ilya, Jackal, Paul/a, Robin, Mariette Pathy Allen, Nikki Appino, Gwen Bartleman, Lauren Batten, Christine Beatty, Francis Berkowitz, Dana Blumrosen, Justin Bond, Becky Boone, Alan Bornstein, Andrew Bornstein, Stacey Bornstein, Jordan Buck, Loren Cameron, Tammy Campbell, Sue-Ellen Case, Wendy Chapkis, Kris Clarke, Robert Coffman, Shannon Coulter, Ivan E. Coyote, Marna Deitch, Dominique Dibell, Bear Dyson, John, Uli, and Eric Emigh, Leslie Feinberg, Susan Finque, Stacey Foiles, Rachel Gold, Del Grace, Jamison Green, Karen Green, Spike Harris, Sophie B. Hawkins, Jenny Hubbard, Jamie Kae, Roz Kaveney, Kristin Knapick, Iris Landsberg, Karin Luner, Dona Ann McAdams, Melanie Moody, Nancy Nangeroni, Glovina Nichols, Jules Odendahl, Dini Petti, Rachel Pollack, Minnie Bruce Pratt, Isabella Radsna, Red Reddick, Susi Rosenthal, Martine Rothblatt, Howard and Mary Rower, Liz Rudd, Alaine Ruse, Mark Russell, Isabel Samaras, Eleanor Savage, Nadja Schefzig, Amy Scholder, Marina Schoup, Lori E. Seid, Sarah Sidman, Pamela Sneed, Sharrin Spector, Bonnie Strickland, Tristan Taormino, Jayne Thomas, Bear Thunderfire, Lamar Van Dyke, Roz Warren, Lois Weaver, Ingrid Wilhite, Stacey Woods, Dragon Xcalibur, and Alice Zander.

I wrote this book during a particularly hard few years of my life, and I owe a great deal to a great number of people. I'm sorry I don't have the space here to thank each and every one of you by name. Travelling around the country these past few years, I've made friends with students, faculty, and administration members of many educational institutions that welcomed my presence and my words. I've met some wonderful artists, critics, journalists, media people, and interviewers with whom I've had some great thought-provoking conversations. I've met some wonderful audience members who have come up to me after performances and expressed their thanks and appreciation. And I still get great email from readers of *Gender Outlaw*, although my ability to keep up with answering all that email has dropped off considerably. To all these folks, thank you so much for embracing me in your life during the time that you did. And finally, to my sweet Gwydyn, friend and fellow traveller for over twelve years now: I promise I'll get you your dinner as soon as I'm done with this sentence, okay?